THE GOLD OF EL DORADO

THE GOLD OF EL DORADO

Presented by Benson & Hedges
in association with Times Newspapers Limited
and The Royal Academy of Arts

The Royal Academy Piccadilly London
21 November 1978 – 18 March 1979

Catalogue written and compiled by Warwick Bray

First published 1978

Text © Warwick Bray 1978

Published by Times Newspapers Limited
on behalf of The Gold of El Dorado
Exhibition
All rights reserved

Designed and produced by
George Rainbird Limited
36 Park Street
London W1Y 4DE

Designer: Patrick Yapp

Production Controller: Clare Merryfield

Cartographer: Tom Stalker Miller

Filmset by Oliver Burridge Filmsetting
Limited, Crawley, Sussex
Colour plates originated by Gilchrist
Bros. Limited, Leeds, West Yorkshire
Printed and bound by Jarrold & Sons
Limited, Norwich, Norfolk

Printed in England

ISBN 0 7230 0226 6

Notes on the Catalogue

The source of each exhibit, and its
museum number, are given at the end of
each caption. Abbreviations as follows:

AMNH	American Museum of Natural History, New York
BL	The British Library, London
BM	The British Museum, London
BM/CM	British Museum, Department of Coins and Medals
BM/MLA	British Museum, Department of Mediaeval and Later Antiquities
BP	Museo Arqueológico del Banco Popular, Bogotá
CMAA	Cambridge University Museum of Archaeology and Anthropology
MAM	Museo de América, Madrid
MM	Museum of Mankind (Department of Ethnography, British Museum), London
MN	Museo Nacional, Bogotá
MO	Museo del Oro, Bogotá
TL	H.M. Tower of London
UMP	University Museum, University of Pennsylvania, Philadelphia
V & A	Victoria and Albert Museum, London

Where information on the provenance of
an exhibit is not included in the caption,
this indicates that the find spot is
unknown.

Exhibition organisation: Carlton Cleeve
Limited
Exhibition design: Alan Irvine, Buzas &
Irvine, Architects

Photographic Acknowledgements

With the exceptions listed below,
photographs of exhibits were kindly
supplied by, and copyright remains the
property of, the museums and collections
lending the exhibits.

Fig. 20: Photo Museo de América, Madrid
Fig. 34 and no. 319a: Photo Joaquín Parra
Rojas
no. 5a: Crown copyright reserved,
reproduced by permission of the
Director, Royal Scottish Museum,
Edinburgh
no. 235: Colour photograph Christian
Poite, Geneva
Exhibits from the Museum of Mankind
(Department of Ethnography, British
Museum), London, and no. 2: Photos
Mike Burgess © Times Newspapers
Limited
Exhibits from Museo Nacional, Bogotá,
Museo Arqueológico del Banco Popular,
Bogotá, and Colombian private
collections: Photos Rudolf, Bogotá
© Times Newspapers Limited. British
private collections: Photos Roz Jupe and
Warwick Bray
Exhibits from Museo del Oro, Bogotá:
Photos Museo del Oro; Wolfgang Sievers
and Brian Hart, Melbourne, courtesy the
Australian Art Exhibitions Corporation;
Rudolf, Bogotá; Luis Fernando Barriga,
Bogotá; Landscapes and archaeological
photographs in the Introduction by
Robert M. Gerstmann, Tecnifoto,
Wolfgang Sievers and Brian Hart

Frontispiece
Muisca mummy with coca bag and lime
gourd, found in a cave at Pisba, Boyacá.
(Museo del Oro, Bogotá)

Contents

Committees		*page*	*6*
Foreword by Sir Hugh Casson, President of The Royal Academy			7
Acknowledgements			8
Author's Note			9
Introduction			10
1	Spain and the First Contacts		11
2	Expeditions to the Muiscas		15
3	Lake Guatavita and the Legend of El Dorado		18
4	Attempts to drain Lake Guatavita		20
5	Miners and Goldsmiths		24
6	Technology		27
7	Styles and Dates		39
8	Sinú Region		41
9	Tairona Region		45
10	Muisca Region		47
11	Quimbaya Region		49
12	Tolima Region		53
13	Popayán, San Agustín and Tierradentro Regions		55
14	Nariño Region		59
15	Tumaco and Lowland Nariño Region		61
16	Calima Region		63
Colour Plates			65
Catalogue of Exhibits			97
Room 1	Spain and the First Voyages	*exhibits* 1–10	98
Room 2	Lake Guatavita and the Legend of El Dorado	11–32	107
Room 3	Technology and Uses of Gold	33–155	117
Room 4	Muisca Life	156–196	138
Room 5	El Dorado Gold		146
	Sinú Region	197–252	146
	Darien Pectorals	253–260	160
	Tairona Region	261–328	162
	Muisca Region	329–357	179
	Quimbaya Region	358–428	186
	Tolima Region	429–451	203
	San Agustín Region	452–454	208
	Popayán Region	455–457	209
	Tierradentro Region	458–465	210
	Nariño Region	466–500	212
	Tumaco Region	501–524	220
	Calima Region	525–554	224
Room 6	Death and the Afterlife	555–582	231
Bibliography			

Committees

Committee of Honour

H.E. Jaime García Parra	formerly Colombian Ambassador to London
H.E. Kenneth J. Uffen, C.M.G.	H.M. Ambassador at Bogotá
Sr Germán Botero de los Ríos	Gerente General, Banco de la República, Bogotá
Sir Hugh Casson, K.C.V.O., P.R.A.	President of The Royal Academy
Dr Luis Duque Gómez	Director of the Museo del Oro, Bogotá
Mr J.A.L. Morgan	Head of Cultural Relations Department, Foreign and Commonwealth Office
Sra Gloria Zea de Uribe	Director of the Instituto Colombiano de Cultura, Bogotá

Policy Committee

Sir Hugh Casson, K.C.V.O., P.R.A.	President of the Royal Academy
Sir Denis Hamilton, D.S.O.	Chairman, Times Newspapers Limited
Mr Hume Stewart-Moore	Chairman, Gallaher Limited
Dr Warwick Bray	Academic Adviser, Gold of El Dorado Exhibition
Mr Roger de Grey, R.A.	Treasurer of the Royal Academy
Mr Sidney C. Hutchison, C.V.O.	Secretary of the Royal Academy
Mr Derek Jewell	Times Newspapers Limited
Mr Leonard Owen	Benson & Hedges
Mr Peter Saabor	Organiser, Gold of El Dorado Exhibition
Mr Peter Wilson	Benson & Hedges

Executive Committee

Dr Warwick Bray	Academic Adviser
Mrs Margaret Green	Benson & Hedges
Miss Griselda Hamilton-Baillie	The Royal Academy
Mrs Candida Hunt	Times Newspapers Limited
Mr Sidney C. Hutchison	The Royal Academy
Mr Alan Irvine	Buzas and Irvine
Mr Derek Jewell	Times Newspapers Limited
Miss Pauline Kennedy	Exhibition Manager
Mr Leonard Owen	Benson & Hedges
Mr Ian Pearson	W. Wingate & Johnston (South) Limited
Mr Norman Rosenthal	The Royal Academy
Mr Peter Saabor	Carlton Cleeve Limited
Mr Peter Stiles	CDP/Aspect Limited
Mr Kenneth J. Tanner	The Royal Academy
Miss Kate Trevelyan	Carlton Cleeve Limited

Foreword

For four hundred years or more the Gold of El Dorado has been a legend. A legend, for most of us perhaps, it has remained. I suspect that many people would have to admit, as I do, that they still have little knowledge of the life-style of ancient Colombia or of the extraordinary achievements of its craftsmen in gold.

Now, thanks to the imagination, scholarship, energy and generosity of many helpers in many lands, building on the suggestion of Mr George Rainbird and with the active interest of Sir Denis Hamilton, The Royal Academy – in partnership with Benson & Hedges and Times Newspapers Limited – is able to mount this spectacular exhibition of treasures from Colombia's early cultures. The objects on show are not confined to those of ritual ceremony: they include simple weapons, needles and cooking utensils, everyday domestic pieces to which everyone can immediately respond. Some of them are shown in re-created versions of their original settings – all of them beautifully designed and wrought.

The Royal Academy is delighted to be in partnership with Benson & Hedges and Times Newspapers in this enterprise, and wishes to record its sincere appreciation of their full co-operation; and also for the invaluable support of His Excellency Jaime García Parra, lately Colombian Ambassador in London (and now Minister of Finance), and his Minister Counsellor, Miss Niñón Millán, as well as that of our own Ambassador at Bogotá, His Excellency Kenneth J. Uffen, of Mr John Morgan, Head of Cultural Relations at the Foreign and Commonwealth Office, and Viscount Montgomery of Alamein.

The preparations for an exhibition of this scale and quality have taken years and have involved many people and organisations – scholars and experts, designers and administrators, government institutions and private individuals. To all of them The Royal Academy is as grateful as surely you will be when you have seen for yourself the splendours that lie spread before you.

Hugh Casson

Acknowledgements

This Exhibition is presented by Benson & Hedges in association with Times Newspapers Limited and The Royal Academy of Arts, and was organised on their behalf by Carlton Cleeve Limited. We are most grateful to the President and Council of The Royal Academy for allowing this splendid Exhibition to be shown in their galleries. Many of the staff of The Academy, and of the sponsoring companies, gave of their valuable time to bring many months of planning to a fruitful conclusion. The Exhibition would not have been possible without their active support.

A special vote of thanks must go to Dr Luis Duque Gómez, Director of the Museo del Oro, Banco de la República, in Bogotá, and to his colleagues, Clemencia Plazas de Nieto and Alec Bright. The Museo del Oro provided the great majority of the exhibits, and we are privileged that they agreed to loan such an unprecedented number of items so that the Exhibition could truly represent the most comprehensive display of prehispanic Colombian gold outside South America. In this context, we are also specially indebted to Señor Germán Botero de Los Ríos, Gerente General, Banco de la República. We are also most grateful to Señora Gloria Zea de Uribe, Director of the Instituto Colombiano de Cultura, and to the Instituto Colombiano de Antropología (Director, Dr Alvaro Soto Holguín), in respect of loans from the Museo Nacional in Bogotá; and to the Junta del Fondo de Promoción de la Cultura del Banco Popular and Señor Pedro Restrepo Pelaez, Director of their Museo Arqueológico, for the loan of many of the ceramics in the Exhibition. There are also important loans from private collections in Colombia, and we would like to thank Dr Hernán Borrero, Señor Guillermo Cano Mejia and Señor Jaime Errazuriz.

We are fortunate to have been loaned many significant exhibits by museums and private lenders in the United Kingdom, Europe and the United States. In this respect we would like to thank Her Majesty the Queen, the British Museum and the Museum of Mankind, the British Library, the Victoria and Albert Museum, the Tower of London, the Science Museum, the National Maritime Museum, Dundee Museums and Art Galleries, the University Museum of Archaeology and Anthropology, Cambridge, and Mr George Ortiz. Special mention should be made of the exhibits so kindly made available by the American Museum of Natural History in New York and the University of Pennsylvania Museum in Philadelphia, and particularly of the unique loan of five pieces from the 'Treasure of the Quimbayas' in the Museo de América in Madrid. In this regard we are most grateful to Señor D. Carlos Martinez Barbeito, the Director of the Museum, and Señor D. Evelio Verdera, Director General del Patrimonio Artistico, Archivos y Museos, Ministerio de Cultura.

Dr Warwick Bray is Academic Adviser to the Exhibition. His has been a vital contribution, as he has not only been involved in the selection of the exhibits but has also contributed invaluable advice on all aspects of planning and organisation.

The Exhibition has been designed by Alan Irvine of Buzas and Irvine, Architects. His visual interpretation of the storyline of the Exhibition provides a marvellous setting for the exhibits. The Exhibition contractors were F. W. Clifford Limited. Special work on the Conquistador figure was carried out by Mary Schoeser; the Muisca hut was made by Preview, of Westerham, Kent; the Golden Man figure was modelled for Preview by Deirdre Phillips; the tomb model is the work of Luis Barriga; and Lake Guatavita was photographed by Wolfgang Sievers.

The consultant on packing and transport was Ian Pearson of Wingate and Johnston (South) Limited, with the help of Inter-Continental Cargo Agencies in Bogotá. In this regard, we very much appreciate the generous assistance of AVIANCA, the Colombian national airline, who have been responsible for the transport of the exhibits from Bogotá. Exhibition security is handled by Consolidated Safeguards, with Trevor Williams, formerly security adviser to national museums in the United Kingdom.

The advertising agency was CDP/Aspect, and Peter Stiles was the Account Director. We are indebted to Jaeger, who have most generously clothed the sales staff.

The selection of publications and merchandise for the Exhibition has been in the hands of Times Books Limited and of Selective Marketplace Limited, both subsidiaries of Times Newspapers Limited. They were ably assisted by Pauline Kennedy, who is also Manager of the Exhibition; she brings a great deal of experience to this vital role.

Peter Saabor

Author's Note

During the preparation of this Exhibition and its Catalogue, I have tried the patience of many people and have learned a great deal in the process. Besides the committee members, museum directors and collectors already listed, thanks are due to Roberto Alvarez, Penny Bateman, Junius Bird, Claude Blair, Sylvia Broadbent, Guillermo Cano, Elizabeth Carmichael, Margaret Cooper, Peter Dorrell, Ian Eames, Victor W. von Hagen, John Hemming, Leslie Hunt, Lea Jones, Roz Jupe, J. P. C. Kent, Francis Maddison, Craig Morris, Brian Moser, Joaquín Parra Rojas, Kathleen Romoli de Avery, Lucía R. de Perdomo, Anthony Ray, Vidal Antonio Rozo, Juanita Sáenz, Mary Schoeser, Marianne and Rudolf Schrimpff, David Scott, Kate Trevelyan, Sarah Tyacke, María Victoria Uribe Alarcón, Helen Wallis, and G. M. Wilson. All these people were unfailingly generous with their time and knowledge. For their work on the production and design of the Catalogue, I would also like to thank Georgina Dowse, Candida Hunt, Patrick Yapp and Elizabeth Blair.

My greatest debt, since it has been accumulating for more years than we care to remember, is to three friends and colleagues from the Gold Museum, Bogotá. For their indispensable help with this Exhibition, and in recognition of all they have taught me over the years, my contribution to The Gold of El Dorado is dedicated to Alec Bright, Clemencia Plazas de Nieto and Ana María Falchetti de Sáenz.

Warwick Bray

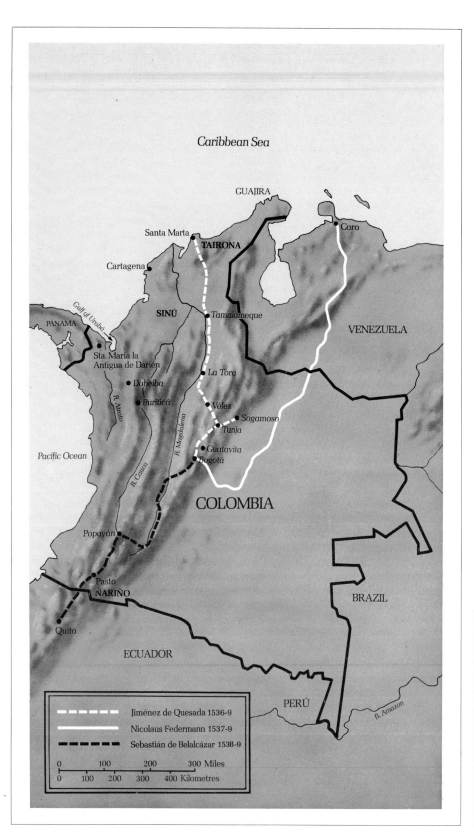

Caribbean Sea

GUAJIRA

Santa Marta
TAIRONA

Coro

Cartagena

SINÚ

Tamalameque

VENEZUELA

Gulf of Uraba

PANAMA

Sta. Maria la
Antigua de Darién

La Tora

• Dabeiba

R. Atrato

• Buriticá

Vélez

• Sogamoso

R. Magdalena

Tunja

• Guatavita

R. Cauca

Bogotá

Pacific Ocean

COLOMBIA

Popayán

Pasto
NARIÑO

BRAZIL

Quito

ECUADOR

R. Amazon

PERÚ

	Jiménez de Quesada 1536-9
	Nicolaus Federmann 1537-9
	Sebastián de Belalcázar 1538-9

0   100   200   300 Miles
0   100   200   300   400 Kilometres

Atlantic
Ocean

COLOMBIA

Pacific
Ocean

1 Spain and the First Contacts

Gold is the most exquisite of all things . . .
Whoever possesses gold can acquire all that he
desires in this world. Truly, for gold he can
gain entrance for his soul into paradise.
Columbus

The first European ships to touch at what is now Colombian territory visited the Guajira peninsula in 1499, but sailed no further west. Serious attempts to explore the coast of Caribbean Colombia did not begin until 1501–2, nine years after Columbus's first landfall in the New World. The partners in this enterprise were Rodrigo de Bastidas (a Seville merchant) and Juan de la Cosa, formerly a pilot with Columbus. During their voyage from the Guajira to the Isthmus of Panama, Bastidas and de la Cosa discovered and named the harbour of Cartagena (later to become one of Spain's principal Caribbean ports), traded with the chiefs of the Sinú region, and returned with a good quantity of gold from the Gulf of Urabá.

This visit passed off peacefully, with no attempt at colonization, but by 1503 the Spanish (under Ferdinand II and Isabella) were preparing to establish settlements along the mainland coast, and on 30 October of the same year Queen Isabella issued an order forbidding the Spaniards to harm any of the Indians, with the exception of 'a certain people called Cannibals':

> I give license and power to all and sundry persons who may go by my orders to the the Islands and Tierra Firme of the Ocean Sea . . . that if the said Cannibals continue to resist, and do not wish to admit and receive to their lands the Captains and men who may be on such voyages by my orders, nor to hear them in order to be taught our Sacred Catholic Faith and to be in my service and obedience, they may be captured and taken to these my Kingdoms and Domains and to other parts and places to be sold.
>
> Quoted in *Sauer*, 1966, p. 162

The Cartagena region was specified as 'Cannibal' territory in this document, and the Queen's ordinance in effect gave the Spaniards a *carte blanche* for the exploitation and maltreatment of the Indians that followed.

In 1508 Ferdinand authorized the first attempts at settlement of the mainland, concentrating in particular on the search for mines. The first permanent Spanish town was Santa María la Antigua de Darién, founded in 1510 on the western shore of the Gulf of Urabá. Soon afterwards, in 1526, Bastidas established a city and port at Santa Marta; and in 1533 Heredia founded Cartagena. These three Caribbean cities were the centres from which exploring and raiding parties opened up the interior of Colombia.

The search for Dabeiba

The first important expedition left Darién in 1512, under the leadership of Vasco Núñez de Balboa, with the objective of reaching the territory of a chieftain named Dabeida, who lived in the mountainous interior to the south. According to the Indians of the coast, it was this cacique who provided all the gold which reached the Gulf of Urabá. In two campaigns of reconnaissance, Balboa explored the Rio Atrato and its tributaries, approaching within sight of the cordillera only two days' journey away from the land of Dabeiba. At this point he turned back, having gathered enough information for a future campaign. The results were summarized in a letter to the King:

Fig. 1 Colombia in 1539, with the routes of the three expeditions to Muisca territory

Many Indians who have seen it tell me that this cacique Dabeiba has certain baskets of gold, and that it requires the whole strength of a man to lift one of these onto his shoulders. This cacique gets the gold from some distance away, in the mountains, and the manner by which he gets it is thus: two days' journey away, there is a beautiful land where the people are very Carib and bad. They eat as many humans as they can get. . . . They are the owners of these mines, which, according to the news I have heard, are the richest in the world. . . . There are two methods of collecting the gold, without any effort. One is to wait until the streams have risen in the ravines, and then, when the floods have passed and the river beds are dry again, the gold is exposed, having been washed out from the banks and carried from the mountains in very sizeable nuggets . . . Another way of collecting gold is to await the time when the vegetation has dried in the mountains, and then to set it on fire. After the burning, they go and look in the heights and in the most likely places, and they collect it in great quantity and in fine nuggets. The Indians who collect this gold, bring it in grains, just as they find it, in order to have it melted, and they trade it with this cacique Dabeiba.

In exchange he gives them boys and girls to eat, and women to serve them as wives, whom they do not eat. He also gives them peccaries, of which there are many in this land, and much fish, cotton cloth and salt, and also such objects of worked gold as they desire. These Indians trade only with the cacique Dabeiba, and nowhere else . . . This cacique Dabeiba has a great place for melting gold in his house, and he has a hundred men continuously working gold.

Vasco Núñez de Balboa, 20 January 1513

Even though based on hearsay evidence about an area the Spaniards had not yet seen, this letter is one of the most detailed surviving accounts of the organization of the metal trade in Colombia. It was fully confirmed in 1538, when Juan de Vadillo eventually reached the mining centre of Buriticá (*Trimborn,* 1943, 1944, 1949).

As a consequence of these early reports, in 1513–14 Ferdinand II ordered the old name of *Tierra Firme* (The Mainland) to be changed to *Castilla del Oro* (Golden Castille) for the new Caribbean governorship then being organized. Under this new name, it appears on the world map of 1529 (*see* no. 2).

Exploration of the Sinú

It was not from Darién but from Cartagena that the first successful expedition explored the lagoons and savannas of the Sinú, and in doing so initiated Colombia's first real gold rush. This expedition departed in 1534, and was led by Pedro de Heredia, governor of the Province of Cartagena, to whose jurisdiction 'Cenú' was assigned.

The looting of native burial mounds at once became the main occupation of the Spaniards in the Sinú, and the letters and documents of the period capture the atmosphere of gold-fever and mutual distrust which go with *guaquería* (robbing of ancient sites) up to the present day.

Some of the tombs proved to be enormously rich. Heredia's men 'looted more than two hundred thousand pesos [a peso is 4.18 grammes] for they opened rich graves, and it is certain that in the first one there was gold to the value of more than 20,000 pesos.' (*Martín de Guzmán,* 1535)

The profit which the royal treasury derived from the Sinú tombs was considerable:

Since the time when it was first settled and the office of Treasurer was created, that is from 15 January 1533 to 11 December 1534, this province has yielded about 110 lbs. of fine gold and 53 lbs. of base gold. From December 1534 to 13 July 1537, the sum is 545 lbs. of fine gold and more than 176 lbs. of low grade gold.

Juan de Vadillo, 1537

The very richness of the province soon created problems. Illegal exploitation of the graves, and conflicts between Spaniards, became rife. By 1536 the

Fig. 2 Coastal landscape, Tairona region.

Crown had begun to fear for its own share, and issued the first legislation to regulate these activities:

> Of all the treasures that might be found of gold, silver, stones, pearls, copper, lead, tin, clothes and other things, both in burials, sepulchres . . . houses or temples of the Indians and in other places in which they offered sacrifices to their idols . . . whether sought intentionally or found by chance, the fifth must be paid to us from the metals, pearls or stones, smelted or worked . . . And of the remainder, the half of everything will be turned over to our Royal Treasury without any discount of anything, leaving the other half for the person who has found and discovered it.
>
> Quoted in *Falchetti,* 1976, p. 25

Nevertheless, in 1537 the greed, treachery and squabbling had become so bad that the King sent special instructions to Vadillo, '. . . you shall not take gold from the sepulchres except in the presence of the Overseer, officials of His Majesty or their Lieutenants.' Already, however, after the first years of frantic activity, the importance of the Sinú had begun to decline as the gold started to run out. As early as 1535, the officials of Cartagena were informing the King that 'the sepulchres of Cenú become poor and they extract very little from them.' (*Friede,* 1956, IV: 94)

Santa Marta

In this area there was a long period of contact between Spanish and Indians, and it was not until about 1600 (after a series of native rebellions) that the last of the Tairona groups submitted to Spanish rule.

Despoilation of Tairona villages and graves began as soon as the settlement was secure. In a document of 1528, Pedro de Cifuentes, a merchant of Santo Domingo in Hispaniola, complained about the problems of melting down native jewellery. 'The hollow parts are filled with an earth which is very heavy', he grumbled, 'and there is little gold laid over it, so that almost a half of it consists of earth, especially in the animals and birds which they make.' (*Friede,* 1951, p. 200) But in April 1529 the Governor of Santa Marta was writing to describe a series of burials with 12,000 pesos of alloyed gold, and in the following month a letter from the City Treasurer informed the King that an expedition to certain Tairona villages had obtained 22,000 pesos of low grade gold (*Duque Gómez,* 1958, pp. 301, 303).

2 Expeditions to the Muiscas

All who knew about it considered it a great
marvel for men from three governorships – those
of Peru, Venezuela and Santa Marta – to join
up in a place so far from the sea, as remote
from the South [Pacific] Sea as from the
North [Caribbean].

Juan de San Martín and *Antonio de Lebrija,*
in a letter to the King, 20 September 1539

Gonzalo Jiménez de Quesada, 1536–9

News of the riches of Inca Peru began to reach the Caribbean ports during
the 1530s, and caused the Spanish colonists to wonder if there might be a
land route southwards to the Pacific. In 1536, Gonzalo Jiménez de Quesada,
second in command to the Governor of Santa Marta, proposed an expedition
to search for the sources of the River Magdalena, which, it was believed,
might lead to Peru. Quesada may also have been prompted by the knowledge
that in this general direction lay the emerald mines which supplied the
Taironas and the coastal tribes.

Quesada's plan was to send one party upstream by boat, carrying stores
and provisions, while the main group would strike out overland to the river.
With Quesada's land party were a large number of Indian porters, with
some six hundred soldiers, eighty-five horses, a little group of priests, and royal
notaries to count the spoils. In the forests and swamps the expedition became
bogged down and made slow progress, contending with flooded rivers,
constant hunger, fever, insect pests, jaguars, snakes, and 'alligators, which . . .
are fish some 10, 12, 15, 20 and more feet long, lizard-shaped, and as ferocious
as man-eating beasts or wild Cannibals.' (*Aguado*, 1916, I: 186)

Eventually the Spaniards reached the river at the native trading centre of
Tamalaméque, sacked only five years before by a German-led expedition
from Venezuela. Quesada's situation was critical. The Indians were hostile;
the provision fleet was late; men were dying and deserting, and the soldiers
were so desperate with hunger that Quesada threatened death to anyone who
killed a horse for food.

When, after many delays, the fleet joined up with Quesada's land party, the
combined group pushed upstream to La Tora. Here, Quesada began to realize
that he was indeed midway along a trade route linking the highlands with the
coast.

As we gradually ascended the Río Magdalene we noticed that all the salt which the
Indians ate reached them by means of trade, and that it came to them from the sea and
from the coasts of Santa Marta. It was bartered in granular form for more than 70
leagues from the mouth of the river. By the time it had reached this point, so little
remained that it was very dear, and only the rich could afford to eat it. Poor people
made their salt from human urine and from the powdered ashes of plants. After
passing La Tora, we came across another salt, not in grains like the other, but in solid
loaves, and as we journeyed upstream this salt became cheaper and cheaper among
the Indians. For this reason, and because of the difference between the two kinds of
salt, we concluded that the granular salt was traded upstream, and that the salt loaves
came from the opposite direction, and were traded downstream.

Gonzalo Jiménez de Quesada, March 1537

Fig. 3 Valley of the River
Magdalena, Tolima.

These salt loaves, the local Indians informed him, were brought (with emeralds and painted cotton mantles) by traders from the high mountains to the east, the homeland of a rich and powerful people.

Quesada was now within striking distance of the Muisca kingdoms, and he left the main river to follow the salt trail up the Rio Opón and into the highlands. This was a well-travelled route, and Quesada's troup emerged at Vélez, a market centre at the northwest corner of Muisca territory.

Once on the high Muisca tableland, the Spaniards began to reap their rewards. They visited the emerald mines at Somondoco, and the salt-producing towns of Nemocón and Zipaquirá; they sacked the royal capital at Tunja and carried away 150,000 pesos of gold and two hundred and thirty emeralds; at Sogamoso they burned down the temple after stealing its golden ornaments. They must also have heard, for the first time, about the Gilded Man and the ceremonies which took place at the sacred lagoon of Guatavita.

But before he could turn his attention to the lake, Quesada heard disquieting news; another expedition, led by the German, Nicolaus Federmann, had reached Muisca territory by a quite different route.

Nicolaus Federmann, 1537–9

Federmann's presence in the New World is explained in his own words:

> On the second day of October in the year 1529, I, Nicolaus Federmann the younger, of Ulm . . . left in a ship given to me by Messer Ulrich Ehinger, belonging to Messers Bartholomew Welser and Company, of which I was appointed captain, and also commander of 123 Spanish soldiers and of 24 German miners. My job was to take them to the country of Venezuela, situated in the Great Ocean Sea, whose government and dominion were conceded to the said Welsers, my masters, by His Majesty the Roman Emperor.
> *Nicolaus Federmann, 1557*

The terms granted by Charles V in 1527 to the German mining and banking house of Welser permitted the Company to 'discover, conquer and populate' the Venezuelan littoral, to enslave Indians and import up to four thousand Negroes, to erect forts and to found two Spanish cities, to bring in horses, send out gold, and to pay only minimal taxes (*Friede*, 1961, pp. 135–46).

From their base at Coro, Ambrosius Alfinger reached Tamalameque, on the Rio Magdalena, in 1531, and obtained 110 kilogrammes of gold ornaments. He also heard news of the salt and gold route which Quesada was later to follow. Between 1535 and 1538, Governor Georg Hohermuth (whose departure from Spain is illustrated in the Codex Köler; *see* no. 13) crossed the lowland plains and – following Indian reports that the gold ornaments were traded from the high, cold mountains to the west – got within 80 kilometres of the Muisca outpost at Sogamoso before he was forced to turn back (*Hagen*, 1974).

Federmann himself set off while Hohermuth was still away. Crossing the vast grasslands east of the Andes, he turned westwards up the Rio Ariari to discover a pass across the bleak and unpopulated páramo of Suma Paz. Within forty days he had climbed from near sea level to a height of over 3500 metres, and the cold was intense. Most of his Indians died, and several Europeans too: 'I lost many people and horses. Of the 300 with which I left, no more than 90 survived, and in the march there died 70 men.' But he succeeded in his objective. The survivors, tired out and dressed in skins, broke through into the Muisca domain – only to find Quesada already in possession.

Quesada, too, had his problems, for he already had news of the imminent arrival of yet another Spanish force, entering Muisca territory from the south, and led by Sebastián de Belalcázar.

Sebastián de Belalcázar 1538–9

Belalcázar had served with Pizarro during the conquest of Peru, and, after receiving his share of Atahuallpa's ransom, had moved north to attack the Inca general Rumiñavi and to found the city of Quito at the site of the Inca's northern capital. It was near Quito, according to Castellanos, that an Indian from Bogotá told Belalcázar about a land of gold still further north, where there lived 'a certain king who went naked aboard a raft, to make offerings ... smeared all over with resin and with powdered gold from head to foot, gleaming like a ray of the sun.'

If so, of the three captains Belalcázar was the only one who was consciously searching for a 'Gilded Man' rather than for a generalized source of riches somewhere in the interior.

It makes an attractive story, but has no factual basis (*Ramos Pérez, 1973; Hemming, 1978*). Castellanos was writing long after these events, at a time when the Guatavita ceremonies were a matter of common knowledge, and when El Dorado tales were circulating all over South America. His information seems to have come from Belalcázar's son (hardly an unbiased witness), and, in the confusion of claims and counterclaims among rival Conquistadors, Castellanos may have been deceived.

Documentary sources indicate that, during the campaign against Rumiñavi in 1534, Belalcázar's men did indeed capture a chief they called '*el indio dorado*', but his kingdom was somewhere in southern Colombia, only twelve days' march from Quito. Belalcázar himself seems never to have mentioned El Dorado until after 1541, when the legend was already well established in Quito. Nor does his subsequent conduct suggest that he had any other objective in view than to explore the lands north of Quito and to obtain them for himself.

Instead of rushing to Bogotá, he waited until 1538, and then moved slowly, taking with him dogs, cattle, horses and a great number of pigs – as well as five thousand Indians and a service of silver plate. His route followed the cordillera northwards to the headwaters of the Rio Cauca and the city of Popayán, which he had founded two years earlier. From here, with some two hundred Spaniards, he crossed the central range of the Andes to the Rio Magdalena, and followed this river to the southwestern edge of Muisca territory, where he met Quesada's envoys.

It was a difficult situation for all the participants. Confronting each other in the Muisca heartland were three quite independent forces, of roughly equal size, each one led by an ambitious man who was technically a mutineer, or – at very least – had exceeded his authority. Instead of fighting it out among themselves, as was the custom in Peru, the three leaders came to an agreement. 'These generals got on very well together; and though minor rifts soon began to appear, the gold converted them into laughter.' (*Juan Rodríguez Freyle*, 1636)

On 6 August 1539 there took place the formal ceremony of the foundation of Santa Fe del Nuevo Reino de Granada (Bogotá), and soon afterwards the three commanders departed together to argue their respective claims before the officials in Spain.

3   Lake Guatavita and the Legend of El Dorado

He went about all covered with powdered gold, as
casually as if it were powdered salt. For it seemed
to him that to wear any other finery was less
beautiful, and that to put on ornaments or arms
made of gold worked by hammering, stamping, or any
other means, was a vulgar and common thing.

Gonzalo Fernández de Oviedo, 1535–48

The Muisca towns and their treasures quickly fell to the Conquistadors.
Taking stock of their newly won territory, the Spaniards realized that – in
spite of the quantity of gold in the hands of the Indians – there were no golden
cities, nor even rich mines, since the Muiscas obtained all their gold from
outside. But at the same time, from captured Indians, they began to hear
stories of El Dorado (the phrase simply means 'The Gilded Man') and of the
rites which used to take place at the lagoon of Guatavita.

There were Indians still alive who had witnessed the last Guatavita ceremony, and the stories these Indians told were consistent. Every one of the
Spanish chroniclers refers to the Gilded Man, but probably the most authori-
tative account comes from Rodríguez Freyle, who learned it from his friend
Don Juan, nephew of the last independent lord of Guatavita.

The ceremony took place on the appointment of a new ruler. Before taking
office, he spent some time secluded in a cave, without women, forbidden to eat
salt and chilli pepper, or to go out during daylight. After this:

> The first journey he had to make was to go to the great lagoon of Guatavita, to make
> offerings and sacrifices to the demon which they worshipped as their god and lord.
> During the ceremony which took place at the lagoon, they made a raft of rushes,
> embellishing and decorating it with the most attractive things they had. They put on it
> four lighted braziers in which they burned much *moque*, which is the incense of these
> natives, and also resin and many other perfumes. The lagoon was large and deep,
> so that a ship with high sides could sail on it, all loaded with an infinity of men and
> women dressed in fine plumes, golden plaques and crowns ... As soon as those on the
> raft began to burn incense, they also lit braziers on the shore, so that the smoke hid
> the light of day.
>
> At this time they stripped the heir to his skin, and anointed him with a sticky
> earth on which they placed gold dust so that he was completely covered with this
> metal. They placed him on the raft, on which he remained motionless, and at his feet
> they placed a great heap of gold and emeralds for him to offer to his god. On the raft
> with him went four principal subject chiefs, decked in plumes, crowns, bracelets,
> pendants and ear rings all of gold. They, too, were naked, and each one carried his
> offering. As the raft left the shore the music began, with trumpets, flutes and other
> instruments, and with singing which shook the mountains and valleys, until, when
> the raft reached the centre of the lagoon, they raised a banner as a signal for silence.
>
> The gilded Indian then made his offering, throwing out all the pile of gold into the
> middle of the lake, and the chiefs who had accompanied him did the same on their
> own accounts. After this they lowered the flag, which had remained up during the
> whole time of offering, and, as the raft moved towards the shore, the shouting began
> again, with pipes, flutes, and large teams of singers and dancers. With this ceremony
> the new ruler was received, and was recognized as lord and king. From this ceremony
> came the celebrated name of El Dorado, which has cost so many lives.

Juan Rodríguez Freyle, 1636

Above Fig. 4 The first
published illustration of Lake
Guatavita, from Humboldt and
Bonpland's *Vue des
Cordillères,* 1810

Below Fig. 5 Lake Guatavita
today, showing Sepúlveda's
cut

This, then, is the reality behind the legend of El Dorado. But the imagination is never satisfied with realities, and El Dorado became a myth and a dream; city, personage or kingdom, it always lay beyond the next range of mountains, or deep in the unexplored forests. The search for this other, non-existent, El Dorado, in various parts of South America, was to occupy men's efforts for another two centuries. (*Friede, 1961, pp. 99–106; Hagen, 1974; Ramos Pérez, 1973; Hemming, 1978*)

4 Attempts to drain Lake Guatavita

It has come to our notice that in the lagoon
they call Guatabita . . . there is definite information
that the bed contains great riches in gold, and,
that although many different persons have
several times tried to drain the said lagoon,
none has succeeded. We, at our own expense
and risk, with our own persons, industry and
effort, wish to drain it.

From an application of 1625, Archivo Nacional, Bogotá

Reports of the Guatavita treasure continued to reach the Spaniards from all sides. The ruler of the town of Simijaca attested that, in the days of his predecessor, he had personally accompanied a caravan of forty Indians, loaded with gold which they threw into the lake. Other local chiefs had also sent offerings, and, in corroboration of these stories, the Spaniards themselves had found a few gold items in the shallows. Having robbed the living Indians of most of their gold, it was time to attack the richest treasure of all.

Lázaro Fonte and Hernán Pérez de Quesada
The first to take up the challenge was Quesada's lieutenant, Lázaro Fonte, but, for lack of money and resources, he achieved very little.

In 1545, or thereabouts, another attempt to drain the lake was made by Hernán Pérez de Quesada, brother of the Conquistador. During the dry season he formed a bucket chain of labourers with gourd jars, and in three months' work managed to lower the water level by about 3 metres – enough to expose the edges of the lake bed, though not its centre. According to contemporary accounts, he obtained between 3000 and 4000 pesos of gold.

Antonio de Sepúlveda
Many unknown Spaniards tried their luck with Guatavita, some of them with success (*Posada,* 1912, p. 238). The most serious of the recorded attempts was made by Antonio de Sepúlveda, a rich merchant of Santa Fe de Bogotá. In the 1580s he began operations on a large scale, building houses on the lake shore and taking soundings from a boat. Using eight thousand Indian workmen, he cut a great notch in the rim of the lake, through which some of the water ran out, lowering the level by 20 metres before the cut collapsed, killing many of the labourers and causing the abandonment of the scheme.

A report in the Archive of the Indies, dated 1586, notes that, after deducting what belonged to him under the terms of the contract, Sepúlveda sent the royal share of the gold to King Philip II in Madrid, and also an emerald weighing 2 *onzas* (nearly 60 grammes) and valued at 500 pesos by the experts in Bogotá. Pedro Simón describes Sepúlveda's finds as 'breastplates or pectoral discs, serpents, eagles', a staff covered with gold plaques and hung with little golden tubes, and an emerald the size of a hen's egg, 'making a total of five or six thousand ducats for the royal treasury'.

The best epitaph for Sepúlveda (apart from his cut, which is still a prominent feature of the landscape) comes from one of his old friends:

He said that, from the part of the lake margin that he managed to uncover, he obtained more than 12,000 pesos. Much later, the desire came over him to make another attempt at drainage, but he could not, and in the end he died poor and tired. I knew him well, and I helped to bury him in the church at Guatavita.

Juan Rodríguez Freyle, 1636

The attempt of 1625

With Sepúlveda dead, a new consortium of twelve partners petitioned the authorities in Bogotá for permission to drain the lake. The contract was drawn up in 1625, and the papers are preserved in the National Archive.

After examining the previous agreement with Sepúlveda, the authorities recommended acceptance on the same terms. The consortium was awarded exclusive rights to 'all the gold, silver, pearls, and other things of value' that it could extract. All finds had to be registered, and a quarter share (up to a value of 50,000 pesos) was reserved for the King, after which the royal share rose to fifty per cent – the division of the spoils to be carried out in the presence of the Crown's nominee. The partners were allowed to use Indian workmen (to be paid at the same rate as soldiers), and the authorities were empowered to halt the work if it damaged neighbouring properties. The results of this attempt appear to be unrecorded.

Alexander von Humboldt

Fig. 6 Alexander von Humboldt

In 1801, Alexander von Humboldt, the foremost natural scientist of his day, spent two months in Bogotá, during which he visited Guatavita, where he commented on Sepúlveda's cut and measured the heights of the mountains overlooking the lake.

Back home in Paris after his travels, Humboldt tried to calculate how much gold the lake might contain. Estimating that one thousand pilgrims might have visited Guatavita each year, over a period of one hundred years, and that each visitor threw in five objects, he arrived at the figure of about 500,000 offerings, worth (in 1807) some 300 million dollars. This was later recalculated, and raised to a higher total, by a French scholar, and had already entered the popular travel literature by 1825:

> According to a calculation, made from a basis laid down by Monsieur de la Kier, of the Royal Institute of Paris, who particularly examined every document relating to the lagoon, there ought to be gold and precious stones yet buried in it to the amount of one billion one hundred and twenty millions sterling.

The writer of this passage was Captain Charles Stuart Cochrane, son of Admiral Lord Cochrane who had commanded the Chilean fleet during the Wars of Independence.

José Ignacio Paris

Soon after Colombia achieved its independence from Spain, Don 'Pepe' Paris, a prominent citizen of Bogotá and a friend of Bolívar, formed a company to try to drain Guatavita. Public interest was intense, and the enterprise was a favourite subject of drawing-room conversation. Cochrane's journal catches the flavour of the period, but also gives practical details about the progress of the attempt during 1823.

In September of that year, Cochrane gave a breakfast party for the Vice-President and some seventy guests, at which he rigged up a siphon to demonstrate how the lake might be drained if existing methods failed. The demonstration was a huge success. 'Guatavita shares consequently greatly increased in value, and we had much good humour and laughing on the subject . . . there were many excellent speeches, and some good singing.'

October 3 Cochrane and Paris visited Guatavita. The work was already running into difficulties since the water was eroding and undermining the sides of the tunnel. Cochrane proposed shoring and planking but was unable to persuade his friend. The distance still requiring to be cut was about 40 yards.

October 16 '. . . found the work going on but slowly, in consequence of which I determined to stop and direct it . . .'

October 20 Cochrane opened 'a considerable number of sepulchres', on condition of paying a levy to the state of five per cent of any treasure. He found only pottery and bones.

October 25 'Having completed the canal, so that eight feet of water might be drawn from the lake in two or three days, I determined on opening an embouchure, sufficient to let two square feet of water keep running out during the night. This I did, and retired to rest . . .'

October 26 The level of the water had dropped a further six inches, but erosion of the canal sides was causing problems. Cutting 'some hundreds of planks from the neighbouring wood', Cochrane began to shore up the sides.

November 12–15 The planking was finished and the lake level reduced by ten feet, making it necessary to deepen the canal. At that point, having 'put everything in a fair train for speedily draining the lake', Cochrane handed over to a Señor Ramirez and rode back to the capital.

Nothing came of these prospects, as another traveller, Colonel J. P. Hamilton, reported in 1827:

> It is upwards of three years since he [Paris] commenced this great undertaking, much of which time was employed, at no small expense, in endeavouring to cut through a hill to let out the water of the lake, but as the opening had not sufficient slope, the rocks and earth fell in seven times. As his design had no chance of success this way, he was advised to dig a subterraneous tunnel, about thirty feet lower than the bed of the lake, in the same direction he had taken in making the first fissure, which at the time we were there he had nearly accomplished; but I afterwards learned that some unforeseen mishap had occurred.

Guatavita shares, which had once stood as high as 2000 dollars, 'diminished much in value'.

This is the first enterprise from which an archaeological specimen is preserved (*see* no. 20).

'The Company for the Exploitation of the Lagoon of Guatavita'

In 1898 a Colombian company was formed with the aim of draining the lake. The rights changed hands a number of times during that year. Little seems to have come of these efforts, and, by a complicated transaction, the concession passed to Contractors Ltd, a London joint stock company.

Contractors Ltd

The intermediary in this deal was a certain Hartley Knowles, a British resident in Colombia (*see* nos. 28, 29). On 16 September 1899 Eustacio de la Torre (general manager of the Colombian company) ceded to Knowles all rights to drain the lake, in return for 41 per cent of any treasure raised. Knowles accepted these conditions in a terse telegram: 'Guatavita, the offer is accepted. In consequence of revolution work will be commenced as soon as possible after War is over. Reply by Telegraph immediately requires signature Torre.'

Knowles got his signature, and promptly sold out to Contractors Ltd for £24,000, or rather for 96,000 five-shilling shares in the British company. Contractors promised to appoint Knowles as Managing Director for a period not exceeding five years 'with such powers and upon such terms as are usually and properly conferred on a Managing Director in a Foreign Country', at a salary of £25 per month, with a share of the profits.

The unfortunate history of Contractors Ltd is documented in the Public Records Office. The initial prospectus raised £6000 and attracted 966 shareholders, many of them small investors, like Ernest Clark, fish salesman of Eastcheap, with two five-shilling shares, or Augusta Taylor, widow, of Ascot, with only one.

The Company's aim was simple – to drain away the water through a tunnel that would come up in the centre of Guatavita, with sluices to regulate the outflow and mercury screens to catch any gold objects or emeralds. Miraculously, the scheme succeeded. The tunnel came up as planned, the water flowed out – and there is a photograph to prove it (Ramírez, 1972, p. 10).

But the triumph quickly turned sour. When the lake bed was first exposed, it was several feet deep in mud and slime, so soft that no one could walk on it. Next day, the sun had baked the mud to the consistency of cement, so hard that it could not be penetrated. By the time the Company had obtained drilling equipment, and returned to Guatavita after a lapse of several weeks, it was already too late; the baked mud had blocked the sluices, the tunnel was sealed, and the lagoon filled up again to its former level.

Although gold objects to the value of £500 had been sent to London by 1910, capital was running low, and more fund-raising brochures were necessary. One of these (see no. 21), dated 1911, and still quoting de la Kier's figure of more than £120 million as the value of the treasure remaining in the mud, gives the state of the project at that time:

> A depth of 30 feet has been obtained in the centre and along the ditch to the tunnel, through which all the mud is being washed ... Many beautiful gold ornaments have been found, particularly during the last 12 months, together with quite a collection of emeralds, strings and strings of beads, and a lot of quaint old pottery.

These items were sold by auction at Sotheby's in December 1911 (see nos. 22–27).

By the end of 1911 new investments brought the cumulative capital up to £15,000. The plan was now to 'acquire and erect a steam shovel in the centre, and sink down 40 or 50 feet in search of the bottom. There will be no doubt when it is reached, for gold dust and nuggets will certainly be found.'

But soon the new capital, too, was spent, and in 1913 it was announced that 'the company, by reason of its inabilities, cannot continue its business'. Even this bankruptcy was not the end. A new company was promptly registered, with the same name, same directors, and same purpose. The usual prospectuses were issued, investors provided almost £9000 of new funds, but by 1914 the Company was in trouble again, with assets of precisely £241.1s.10d. At this point, work was suspended, though Contractors Ltd did not finally die until 1929.

From 1914 to the present
Several more expeditions have tried to conquer the lake, with every kind of equipment, from drills to mechanical drags and airlifts (Roden, 1963, p. 50). Although the central zone remains untouched, many of these teams had partial success and picked up a few more gold items to add to the spoils, until in 1965 the Colombian Government brought Guatavita under legal protection as part of the nation's historical and cultural heritage.

5 Miners and Goldsmiths

Gold is what gave them breath;
For gold they lived, and for gold they died.

Juan de Castellanos, 1589, on the miners of Buriticá

Most of the gold used by the Indians was obtained from placer mines in the rivers of the western and central cordilleras, employing only the simplest equipment: fire-hardened digging sticks to break up the earth, and shallow wooden trays (*bateas*) in which to carry and wash it.

> They take the earth, little by little, from the mine to the washing place, and there they clean it with water to see if there is gold in the bateas . . . And to wash this earth, and work the mine, they do thus: they put certain Indians inside the mine to dig out the earth . . . and with this excavated earth they fill up bateas, which other Indians carry to the water, in which are those who do the panning, both men and women. The carriers empty their bateas into other, larger ones which those who are washing have in their hands. And the porters return for more earth while the washers pan what has already been brought . . . It is worth noting that each pair of Indians who wash must be served by two persons to bring the earth, and two more who excavate it and break it up to fill the carrying trays.
>
> *Gonzalo Fernández de Oviedo*, 1535–48

Oviedo also notes that streams were sometimes diverted to expose the gold-bearing gravels of their beds. Using similar methods in the last century, it took only six to eight minutes to process a 20-lb load of gravel (*Nisser*, 1834).

Archaeological evidence for placer mining is scanty, though Luis Arango (in his reminiscences of treasure-hunting in the eighteenth and early nineteenth centuries) describes occasional chance discoveries of miners crushed by falling rocks:

> . . . these unfortunate men carried with them . . . clay jars in which they deposited the grains of gold which they collected, and these have been found beside their corpses. Close to one of these skeletons lay a gourd containing gold worth 12 castellanos [about 57 grammes] . . . When they found very fine gold dust . . . they used soft clay to pick it up, and at a convenient moment they broke up the clay and extracted the gold. Clay balls of this kind have been found in several tombs, and by applying this procedure the gold was removed.
>
> *Luis Arango Cano*, 1924

Spanish chronicles also note that the Indians dug shafts to reach the gold-bearing quartz veins of the cordilleran regions of Caldas and Antioquia. The mines of Marmato (Caldas) are mentioned in sixteenth-century documents, and tools made of tumbaga (see p. 27) were found in one of the shafts (*Pérez de Barradas*, 1954, I: 8). During the nineteenth century, the British engineer Robert White visited Los Remedios in Antioquia (once the richest town of its size in the Indies), and discovered an extensive area of mine shafts, spaced some 3.5 to 4.5 metres apart, each shaft no more than one metre wide. White estimated that thousands of men could have been employed there. The deepest shafts had steps cut in the sides, and went down as much as 24 metres. The sloping shafts (inclined at about 30°) were up to 36 metres in depth, and so narrow that a man could not turn round in them. Each shaft was a simple tunnel, with no side galleries and no attempt at shoring or ventilation. From these mines White collected a series of polished stone axes or chisels, some chipped stone flakes, and part of a Spanish jar (*White*, 1884).

Fig. 7 Indians panning gold in the early Colonial period. Woodcut from *La Historia General y Natural de las Indias* by Gonzalo Fernández de Oviedo y Valdés, 1535–48.

Buriticá

In prehispanic times, as at present, small-scale mining may have been a part-time occupation, carried out during the dry season when stream beds were exposed. Some localities, however, supported specialist communities of full-time miners and smiths. The most renowned site of this kind was Buriticá, in the mountains of northern Antioquia, mentioned in Balboa's letter (*see* p. 12) and later visited by the expeditions of Juan de Vadillo (1538) and Jorge Robledo (1541).

Buriticá was a true industrial centre, exploiting both alluvial and vein gold, and exchanging the surplus for food and other necessities. It was a town of 'big houses, set close together' on a fortified hilltop, and it seems to have been the capital of an area containing several other mining and metal-processing communities. Cieza de León, who was there with Vadillo, noted that all the houses belonged to miners. Oviedo, basing his account on a letter by Vadillo, wrote:

> They found the mines, each of which was reserved for a particular Indian, and in them they saw seams or veins of gold . . . And some mines were 3 estados [about 5 metres] deep. The Indians said that in a day each man could collect 80 or 90 pesos . . . The Licenciate Vadillo had some of the earth taken out and, from a quantity sufficient to fill an ordinary shield, he got grains weighing a ducat [3.5 grammes] . . . A soldier found a stone, about the size of two human heads, all of which was shot through with gold.
>
> *Gonzalo Fernández de Oviedo, 1535–48*

Spanish accounts indicate that much of the labour was carried out by slaves, and Pedro Simón adds the further grisly detail that the local chiefs killed slaves to provide fat for the lamps, and then sold off the flesh for food.

At Buriticá itself, and in the surrounding villages, the Conquistadors found workshops for melting down the metal, with crucibles, braziers and balances to weigh out the gold. The chronicles do not distinguish between the melting of bulk metal, and the melting of gold as a preliminary to making trinkets and jewellery, but the general impression is that Buriticá exported both finished items and raw metal to be worked up elsewhere.

Some gold and jewellery was exported to the Quimbaya and Muisca peoples, but most of it was traded northwards to Dabeiba, where a community of specialist goldsmiths grew up on the basis of imported raw material. From Dabeiba, a trade route led to the Sinú and supplied the entire coastal region from Urabá to Cartagena. At places along the route were market centres where professional merchants exchanged coastal products (fish, salt, cotton cloth) for Sinú jewellery and ingots of raw metal from Antioquia. Vadillo, who had first-hand knowledge of both areas, commented that Dabeiba goldsmiths made objects in a style which he already knew from the Sinú.

Goldsmiths

Mining and jewellery manufacture are two quite distinct technical skills, each with its own economic pattern. The existence of Dabeiba, a jewellery centre with no gold sources of its own, illustrates the physical separation of the two halves of the metal business, but Spanish chronicles say very little about the men who worked there. Our only documentation about the status of metalsmiths refers to the town of Guatavita.

> For the greater part, the Guatavitas were craftsmen who worked gold, and among other Indians had the reputation of being the most subtle in these trades. Thus, many of them travelled through the neighbouring provinces, far from Guatavita, earning their living by their skills, without fulfilling the obligations due to their Ruler according to his laws. He, realizing that he was losing both people and revenue in this way, commanded with great rigour that all those goldsmiths should declare themselves his subjects, and that any other Ruler who employed one of these men in his country should send two of his own vassals to reside in Guatavita while the goldsmith was away.
>
> *Juan de Castellanos,* 1589

In this way, says Castellanos, Guatavita rapidly filled up with two thousand idlers and 'good-for-nothings', implying about a thousand travelling goldsmiths, if the figure can be taken seriously. In the end, this policy resulted in the ruler's downfall, for the foreigners rose in revolt, massacred the chief, and delivered Guatavita to the rival kingdom of Bogotá. If the story is not pure invention, it gives an indication of both the number and the high prestige of goldsmiths among the Muiscas.

Workshops

Not a single workshop site has been excavated by trained archaeologists; our scanty information comes entirely from Spanish chronicles and the reminiscences of nineteenth-century treasure-hunters and travellers. The following account of one of these lost sites comes from the memoirs of Luis Arango Cano, one of the great figures in the history of *guaquería* (tomb-robbing) in Quimbaya territory:

> At 15 km from Amalfi was an Indian site measuring about 20,000 square varas. The earth of this site was washed and panned in 1851. It is said that it yielded not less than 20 arrobas [230 kilogrammes] of gold in the form of trimmings, scraps, drops of melted gold etc. There were also remains of what seemed to be an ancient foundry. The principal finds included five perfectly round balls of fine gold, four smaller ones a little under the size of a hen's egg, and another as big as a billiard ball . . . Among the slag and debris were pieces of wood charcoal, many fragments of pottery, and various broken crucibles made of clay.
>
> *Luis Arango Cano,* 1924

6 Technology

They are accustomed to find [in tombs] chisels,
awls and burnishers of metal, and hammers and anvils made
of quartz, still showing traces of crushed gold.
They also find little clay vessels which seem to be
crucibles, and some moulds.
Andrés Posada Arango, 1871

The principal metals exploited in prehispanic times were gold and copper. Of these, gold was readily available, but the distribution of copper and its ores was more restricted. Two other metals, platinum and silver, were of regional importance, though their use was limited. Platinum, from the rivers of Pacific Colombia and Ecuador, was employed by jewellers in the Tumaco region. Silver, which is found in most archaeological specimens in proportions of up to 25%, was not deliberately added, but was present naturally in the gold. Only in Nariño, which has strong technological links with Ecuador and Peru, did the Indians take a serious interest in silver as a metal in its own right.

Since Colombia lacks tin, it was unable to develop a native tradition of bronzeworking. Instead, the favourite material was *tumbaga* (a gold-copper alloy with some accidental silver) which, under the names *guanín gold* or *caricoli*, was in use all round the Spanish Main at the time of the first European visits. As Oviedo remarked, 'they work this gold, and have the custom of mixing it with copper and silver, and they adulterate it as much as they wish, and so it is of various purities and values.'

Sir Walter Ralegh described (*see* nos. 18, 19) the technology of the tribes of interior Guiana:

Fig. 8 'How the Guianians are accustomed to cast their golden images'. Engraving by Theodor de Bry, 1599 (no. 19)

... [who] put to it [the gold] a part of copper, otherwise they coulde not worke it, and ... they vsed a great earthen potte with holes round about it, and when they had mingled the gold and copper together, they fastned canes to the holes, and so with the breath of men they increased the fire till the mettell ran, and they cast it into moulds of stone and clay, and so make those plates and Images.

Sir Walter Ralegh, 1596

Ralegh's basic information was accurate, for tumbaga offers several technical advantages. It is easier to cast than any of its constituent metals alone, and it reproduces fine decorative detail more accurately. The exact melting point depends on the composition, but the alloy of 20% copper and 80% gold melts at 911°C. compared with 1064°C. for pure gold and 1084°C. for copper. This alloy is harder than its individual constituents, and metallographic examination has shown that chisels, axes and awls of tumbaga were cold-hammered until the working edges were almost as tough as those of bronze tools (*Nordenskiöld*, 1931; *Hultgren*, 1931).

Melting

In the Archive of the Indies, in Seville, is a document, dated 1555, which describes how the Indians of Tamalameque, in lowland Colombia, melted their gold:

And then the said chief and Indians burned a little charcoal on some baked clay with three cane blowpipes, and placed a crucible on this with a piece of caricoli ... along with small quantities of low grade gold ... After it had melted, they took the crucible and poured a little water over it.

Tamalameque, 1555, Archive of the Indies

Clay crucibles are mentioned by several nineteenth-century treasure-hunters, and two archaeological crucibles (both of them larger than average) were collected from the Cauca Valley (*see* fig. 9). The goldsmiths of La Tolita, just over the Ecuadorian frontier, dispensed with crucibles altogether, and melted their metal with the aid of a blowpipe in a hollow scraped in a charcoal slab. From incompletely fused specimens, it is clear that they also collected scrap metal for remelting (*Bergsøe, 1937*).

The nearest thing to Ralegh's 'earthen potte' is a portable terracotta furnace or brazier from a tomb near Manizales, in the Quimbaya zone (*see* fig. 10, and *Bruhns, 1970*). Since the Indians had no bellows, the blowpipes were essential to raise the heat of a charcoal fire to the temperature required to melt pure gold or copper. The cane blowpipes described for Guyana and Tamalameque have

Above Fig. 9 Clay crucible (no. 39)

Fig. 10 Metalworker's brazier. Height 29 cm

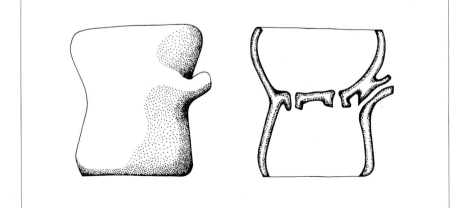

not been preserved, but from Pasca (in Muisca territory) have come a number of terracotta tubes that may well be the mouthpieces from such implements (see fig. 11, and *Bright*, 1972).

The result of the melting process is a *tejuelo*, a little button of metal with one face flattish and the other rounded, where it follows the contour of the bottom of the crucible (see fig. 12).

Hammering

Hammering was used to stretch and planish the flat parts of certain cast pieces, to make simple discs, plaques or nose ornaments, and as a technique for producing sheet metal.

The belief that hammering of sheet metal is a 'primitive' technique, and therefore must be more ancient than casting, is a long-standing one (*Root*, 1964), but is not supported by the evidence from Colombia, where the two techniques seem to have been introduced simultaneously. Since gold normally occurs as specks or as small nuggets, the first stage in making any large sheet item is to prepare an ingot of *cast* metal by the process already described. Analysis shows that most Colombian sheet metal objects are of man-made alloys that have passed through a melting process. In addition, every one of the regional gold styles of Colombia includes both cast and hammered items. It is therefore impossible to recognize a stage of development represented exclusively by the hammering of unmelted gold nuggets.

Spanish chronicles describe the use of hammers and cylindrical anvils made of hard, fine-grained stone (see fig. 14 and no. 43). As Benzoni's drawing shows (see fig. 13), these hammerstones were not hafted, but were held in the hand, and the metal was worked by alternate hammering and annealing (see below) into sheet whose thinness and evenness compare well with today's industrial product.

Annealing

Annealing was an essential part of the process. Pure gold is soft and fairly easy to beat, but under continual hammering many of the alloys become 'strain-hardened'; the microstructure of the metal changes so that the sheet first becomes springy and difficult to work, then finally turns brittle and starts to crack. Malleability can be restored by annealing – replacing the object in the furnace until the metal glows red, followed by quenching in water (*McDonald and Sistare*, 1978). After this, the metal can be hammered once more.

Above Fig. 11 Mouthpiece of blowpipe (no. 40)

Below Fig. 12 Two ingots (*tejuelos*) of cast metal and a lump of melted gold (nos. 42 and 41)

Above left Fig. 13 Indian metalsmith using a stone hammer. From *Historia del Mondo Nuovo* by Girolamo Benzoni, 1565

Below left Fig. 14 Stone hammers and anvils from Nariño (Errazuriz Collection, Bogotá)

Right Fig. 15 'How the Indians poured melted gold down the throats of the Spaniards'. Woodcut of Panamanian Indians, from Benzoni, 1565. Note the use of cane blowpipes.

... and in this way, placing it in the fire, taking it out and putting it in water and hammering it on an anvil with the stones described, they worked it until they had increased its size many times.

Tamalameque, 1555, *Archive of the Indies*

Successful annealing requires skilled judgment and experience. With only the colour of the metal as a guide to temperature, the smith has to remove the object from the furnace at just the right moment. Too much heating, and the metal will begin to run; too little, and the process is ineffective.

Repoussé work

The techniques used to manufacture the objects themselves were relatively simple. An outline drawing was scribed on the sheet (sometimes with the aid of a template), and tool marks show that a narrow-bladed chisel was used to cut out the shape. For decorative effect, but also to give strength and rigidity to large objects of flimsy sheet, the metalsmiths pressed out repoussé designs, working from the back, with the object resting on a bed of some yielding material: pitch in the West Indies, but more probably thick leather or a bag of sand in Colombia.

These repoussé designs were improved by working on the front of the piece, using a chasing tool to deepen the designs and to sharpen their edges, and additional freehand patterns were sometimes traced directly onto the metal.

Raised designs were made by pressing and hammering the sheet metal over carved patterns, and the same technique was used to mass-produce sets of identical pieces, such as necklace pendants (see no. 51). Throughout all these processes, continued annealing was necessary.

Bowls, cups and helmets were made by 'raising'. Starting from the base, a flat disc of metal was hammered, with constant turning, over a horizontal stake or a series of anvils, so that the metal was simultaneously thinned and forced upwards and outwards.

Joining

Multi-piece ornaments, hollow figurines, lime-flasks, etc., were made by joining several previously shaped pieces of metal by hammer-welding, soldering, brazing, or by mechanical methods such as pinning (*see* fig. 17 and no. 459),

Left Fig. 16 Detail of traced zigzag decoration on a nose ornament (no. 396)

Centre Fig. 17 Pin holes below the chin of sheet gold mask (no. 458)

Right Fig. 18 Tairona pectoral: detail of reverse to show how the bird heads were attached to the base plate by folding over and crimping (no. 309)

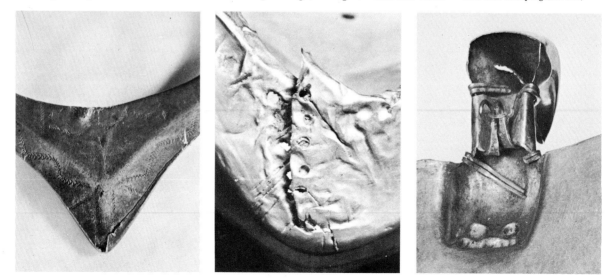

Fig. 19 Small beads made by granulation (no. 77)

stapling, lacing with thin and pliable metal strip, or 'clinching' (in which the edges to be joined are overlapped, folded over, and then hammered down) (see fig. 18). Using similar methods, gold foil was laid over non-metallic objects such as wooden staffs, trumpets and conch shells.

Granulation, or diffusion bonding

Ordinary soldering becomes impracticable for very fine work, when a great number of joins have to be made over a small area. This problem arises when many tiny elements, little balls or fine wires, are to be joined to each other or to a backplate (see fig. 19). The method used in Colombia and Ecuador is the one employed in the ancient civilizations of the Old World, and described by Pliny – though not re-discovered in Europe until some fifty years ago (*Roberts*, 1973). A copper compound, such as copper hydroxide or acetate, is mixed with an organic glue, and the mixture is used to stick the delicate gold elements into place. Once assembled, the object is heated in the reducing (oxygen-free) atmosphere of a charcoal fire until the glue burns away and a natural gold-copper brazing alloy forms, resulting in metallic bonding at the point of contact. Because the resultant join is hardly perceptible, it is often difficult to distinguish between an item made by granulation and one produced by lost-wax casting.

Casting in moulds

This was never common, though Ralegh mentions 'moulds of stone and clay' in Guiana, and there are several nineteenth-century references to the discovery of 'plaster' moulds in Colombian tombs. The type of mould is never specified, and no actual specimen has been preserved.

Simple, open moulds of stone or terracotta would suffice to cast chisels and axes – though all the extant Colombian examples seem to have been hammered and forged, rather than cast. For more complex shapes, closed moulds of two or more segments would have been required. The one Colombian item which shows evidence of this technique is the incense burner from the Treasure of the Quimbayas (see fig. 20 and no. 362). It has a distinct seam, inside and out, dividing the vessel vertically into two halves, and showing where a little metal ran into the join between the two segments of the mould. On the chin and forehead the seam shows only as a faint mark, but the join is clearly visible on the underside of the base, where the item was less carefully finished.

Fig. 20 Underside of no. 362, showing the seam left by casting in a multi-piece mould.

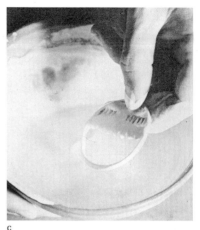

a

b

c

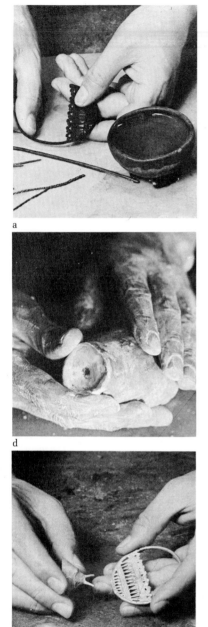

d

e

f

g

Fig. 21 Lost-wax casting of a Sinú ear ornament (cf. no. 57):

(a) Threads, braids and sheets were made in beeswax and then assembled to form a model of the ornament.

(b) When the wax model was ready, a funnel and channels (also of wax) were added to it.

(c) The model was then covered with successive layers of semi-liquid clay which filled any open spaces within the wax model.

(d) The object was enveloped in a clay and charcoal casing, and was left to dry for several days before being placed on a fire.

(e) On heating, the wax melted and was poured out, leaving an empty interior space to be filled by the molten metal.

(f) When the mould had cooled it was broken open to take out the casting, which was then cleaned to remove any remaining fragments of clay.

(g) Finally the funnel and conduits were removed, and the piece was retouched and finished.

Right Fig. 22
Muisca tunjo.
The surplus
metal which
filled the pouring
channels during
the casting
process has not
been removed
(no. 60)

Below Fig. 23
Four lost-wax
casting moulds
(no. 56)

Lost-wax casting

Complicated shapes, both hollow and solid, were normally made by the lost-wax (or *cire-perdue*) method, in which the goldsmith modelled the object in wax and then encased it in clay, leaving a channel to the exterior. On heating, the melted wax was poured out, and molten metal was poured in to replace it, leaving an exact metal copy of the wax original (*see* fig. 21).

Two unbroken clay casings were found in a tomb at Pueblo Tapado, Montenegro, in the Quimbaya zone (*Bruhns, 1972b*) and another set comes from Aguamona, in the Calima region (*see* fig. 23, and *Plazas and Falchetti, 1978*). Further technical details can be seen on the metal objects themselves, especially from the Muisca zone, where some of the *tunjos* (flat figurines) are virtually untouched, just as they came from the casing. Many of them still have black fragments of the clay and charcoal casing adhering to their surfaces. They were cast head downwards, and on some examples the smith did not trouble to remove the excess metal which filled the pouring channels and the cup-shaped reservoir at the top of the mould (*see* no. 59, and fig. 22).

Fig. 24 Muisca copper figurine, showing internal core (no. 63)

Hollow casting by the lost-wax method

The manufacture of hollow pieces required an interior core. The craftsman prepared this from clay mixed with powdered charcoal (see fig. 24), carved it to the shape of the finished product, and left it to dry in the sun for two days. This prolonged drying was necessary to remove all the moisture and reduce the chances of an explosion during the casting stage. The goldsmith next took molten beeswax, strained and purified it, and then rolled it out into a thin sheet. This wax sheet was laid over the core and pressed against it, to follow the shape exactly. At this stage, any final appliqué or incised designs were added to the wax model (see figs. 25, 26), and the pouring channel and air vents were added in the form of wax rods.

To give additional sharpness to the casting, the wax was brushed with a suspension of finely powdered charcoal in water or liquid clay, and, after drying, the whole thing was enveloped in a thick casing of clay mixed with coarsely ground charcoal – porous enough to allow air and gases to escape during casting.

The internal core was fixed in position by peg-like supports (chaplets) of green wood, which passed through the wax, leaving holes in the final metal casting. A single complicated piece might require between three and thirty-six of these supports (*Plazas and Falchetti*, 1978, p. 35). The small, circular holes were afterwards plugged with fresh metal, but their position can usually be recognized (see fig. 26).

The object thus assembled was now heated, in order to melt out the wax and to leave a space between the interior core and outer casing. While the mould was still hot (so that the metal would not set before flowing to all parts of the cast), molten gold was poured in to take the place of the wax. After cooling, the outer casing was broken open to extract the metal casting, and the interior core material was removed. Because the outer casing has to be broken each time, every lost-wax casting is a unique creation.

Fig. 25 Stages in making a hollow bell containing a clapper (no. 64):

(a) The clapper is made first, and then the internal core is built around it.

(b) The core is covered with wax sheet, and the spiral design is engraved on the wax.

(c) The pouring channel is added in the form of a wax rod.

(d) The whole thing is enveloped in the outer casing.

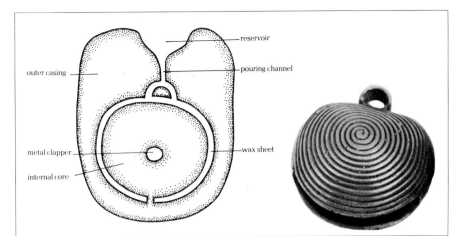

Right Fig. 26a–b Quimbaya lime-flask (no. 377), with a plugged chaplet hole at the shoulder (a), and open holes at the buttocks (b)

Below Fig. 27 Lost-wax casting of a hollow flask

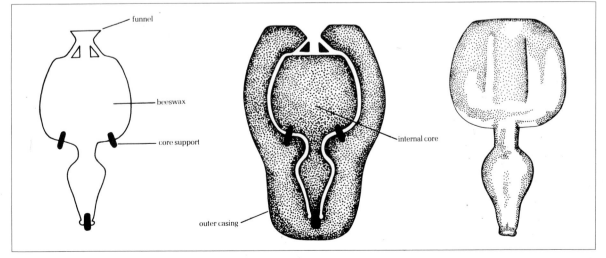

False filigree

At first sight, the Sinú ear ornaments and certain Muisca tunjos appear to have been made by the filigree technique, in which pieces of coiled and twisted wire are soldered to each other or to a backplate. Analyses show that most of these specimens are 'false filigree', not soldered at all, but cast. The model was built up from wire-like threads of wax, and the whole piece cast in a single operation by the lost-wax method. In a similar manner, hollow objects (bells, and models of animals, birds or shells) were formed by coiling wax thread around a pre-shaped core (see fig. 28).

Stone matrices

Muisca goldsmiths had perfected a method for mass-producing sets of identical cast elements for necklaces and figurine parts, with the aid of carved stone matrices (*Schuler-Schömig*, 1974). These stone blocks have raised reliefs on all six faces, and are virtually 'pattern books' of the most common Muisca designs: frogs, fish, long-beaked birds, human figures and faces, insect shapes and abstract geometric patterns (see fig. 29 and no. 68). Using these matrices, the jeweller could produce any number of wax models, all exactly alike. These were either cast individually by the usual *cire-perdue* method, or else were combined with other elements to form composite figures and ornaments which could be cast in a single operation (see fig. 30).

Platinum metallurgy

Platinum occurs as little grey flakes or grains in the gold-bearing gravels of the rivers draining to the Pacific coast of Ecuador and Colombia. Since the platinum is found as specks of pure metal, and does not in nature alloy with the gold, the two metals can be separated mechanically, by hand-washing and sorting.

About a dozen hammered platinum nose rings have been found in Colombian territory, but the Ecuadorian sites have yielded a wider range of nose ornaments, plaques, ingots and needles. Their platinum content varies considerably. A few items are apparently of almost pure platinum; others are nearly pure gold, with an admixture of 1% or 2% platinum – almost certainly an accidental impurity, resulting from poor sorting rather than from deliberate mixing. In these examples, the grains of platinum can often be seen with the naked eye.

Fig. 28 Tumbaga shell model, made by winding wax thread round a core (no. 76)

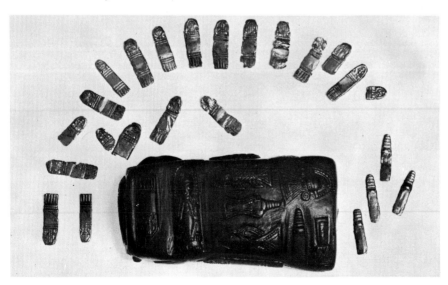

Fig. 29 Muisca stone matrix and matching necklace pendants (nos. 65, 66)

In the middle of the range come those objects containing platinum as a deliberate additive in proportions of between 26% and 72%. Because of its high melting point (1775°C.), the casting of pure platinum was impossible with the equipment available to the Indians. The native jewellers sidestepped the difficulty by mixing the platinum with a little gold dust, and heating the mixture until the gold melted and flowed, binding the platinum granules together. In addition, even though the platinum never approaches melting point, a little of each metal dissolves in the other. This gold-with-platinum was alternately hammered and heated until it formed a compact mass which could be forged or cast like any normal alloy (*Bergsøe*, 1937; *Rivet*, 1943).

The addition of platinum to gold has the effect of both hardening and whitening the mixture. In small concentrations the colour change is noticeable, and at higher percentages the mixture becomes a greenish yellow. This property allowed the jewellers of Tumaco and Esmeraldas to make composite objects of contrasting colours, perhaps using local platinum as a substitute for imported silver. There are also objects with a thin layer of 'platinum' over a gold or alloy base (*see* no. 38).

Gilding

Simple forms, like nose rings, were occasionally covered with gold foil, but more often the metalsmith employed some kind of 'depletion gilding' to produce a gold finish on a tumbaga item. The alloy was treated chemically with a substance which removed the base metals at the surface, but left the gold untouched. The result was a superficial layer of relatively pure gold, completely concealing the tumbaga core. Unlike gold plating, which involves the addition of extra metal, in 'depletion gilding' all the gold is already present as an original constituent of the alloy. The saving of gold is therefore minimal, since most of it remains 'unused' in the alloy core, and the main purpose of gilding may rather have been to protect the item against discolouration through rapid oxidation of the copper content at the surface (*Plazas and Falchetti*, 1978, p. 37).

Two gilding techniques were employed in ancient America, but only one of these (the *mise-en-couleur* process) is mentioned in those Spanish accounts that refer to Colombia. On heating in air, a layer of copper oxide forms on the surface of a tumbaga object, and this oxide can be removed with an acid solution made from the juice of certain plants.

Fig. 30 Detail of Muisca pectoral (no. 329). The face was made separately in wax sheet, using a stone matrix. The join is clearly visible.

... the herb they brought to give it colour was crushed on a stone and, once crushed in this way, they placed it in a small pot which they brought in, and added water and ground white salt, and stirred all together.

Tamalameque, 1555, *Archive of the Indies*

After polishing, heating, and quenching it in the solution several times, 'it attained the colour and finish it should have'. The same technique is reported from the Tairona zone in the sixteenth century (*Enciso*, 1974, p. 264).

In the words of another chronicler:

... they know very well how to gild the objects and items they make from copper and low grade gold. And they have such ability and excellence in this, and give such a high lustre to what they gild, that it looks like good gold of 23 carats or more .... They do this with a certain herb, and it is such a great secret that any goldsmith in Europe, or in any other part of Christendom, would soon become a rich man from this manner of gilding ... I have seen the herb, and Indians have taught me about it, but I was never able, by flattery or in any other way, to get the secret from them.

Gonzalo Fernández de Oviedo, 1535–48

The active substance may well have been oxalic acid, for present-day Indian goldsmiths in Ecuador still clean jewellery by heating the items in a copper pot containing a mixture of common salt, water, and macerated plants of the Oxalis family (*Zevallos Menéndez*, 1965–6, pp. 72–3).

For ternary alloys (containing gold, copper and silver) with less than 20% of gold, better results are obtained by 'superficial parting' or 'cementation', using a corrosive mineral substance rather than plant juice. In sixteenth-century Mexico, Bernardino de Sahagún described the use of a 'gold medicine' that looked like yellow earth mixed with salt, and modern laboratory experiments have reproduced the techniques used by ancient Peruvian jewellers to gild their silver-rich alloys (*Lechtman*, 1971, 1973). In the experiments, alloy sheet was coated with a paste of alum, common salt and potassium nitrate (or some other corrosive mineral). After heating, this paste was washed off, and the black scale left on the surface was removed with a hot, strong salt solution. This would also be the most satisfactory way of treating Colombian Nariño ornaments containing more than 50% silver (*Scott*, 1978, and *see* no. 37).

Using one or other of these methods, and treating only a part of the tumbaga surface, it is possible to produce designs of contrasting gold and coppery finishes (*see* nos. 79, 80).

Burnishing

Finally, the surfaces were cleaned and polished, not only to give a shiny finish, but also to consolidate and strengthen the superficial layer of gold on an object made of gilt tumbaga.

Various cleaning and polishing agents were employed. Oviedo found the Indians of Natá, Panama, using dried alligator dung, while in Tamalameque 'they cleaned ... with small quantities of fine sand that they brought in a maize husk, with their hands and water'. Polishing tools were made of metal, bamboo, antler or stone, the latter sometimes with 'streaks of gold still adhering to them.' (*White*, 1884, p. 248)

7 Styles and Dates

All creation of visual art is a conceptualization
and therefore reflects a corresponding intelligible
ideology.
Herbert Read, 1955

Within the Americas, the knowledge of metal technology spread from south
to north. The first use of beaten gold is dated around 2000 BC at the site of
Waywaka in the Andes of southern Peru (*Grossman*, 1972, 1975), after which
there was a long period of purely local Peruvian development, with new
techniques introduced into the repertoire from time to time. By contrast, metallurgy did not reach Mexico until some time between AD 700 and 900, and it
arrived fully developed, without any preceding stage of experimentation.

In space, and also in time, the metal industries of Colombia and the Isthmian
countries fall midway between those of Peru and Mexico, with complex
metallurgy (including casting) present in southern Colombia by the time
of Christ, and in Panama no later than the fifth century AD.

Colombia, Panama and Costa Rica can be regarded as a single metallurgical
province, characterized by a preference for gold-copper alloys, lost-wax
casting, depletion gilding and false filigree. Within this province, gold objects
were traded in both directions. Tairona, Sinú and Quimbaya pieces have been
found in tombs as far north as Panama and Costa Rica (*Aguilar,* 1972) and
were imitated locally; Colombian emeralds were incorporated in Panamanian
gold jewellery at Coclé (*Lothrop,* 1937), and Panamanian frog pendants have
been found as far south as Armenia in the Quimbaya region of Colombia.

Problems of dating and classification in Colombia

In spite of the vast number of specimens (more than 26,000 in the Gold
Museum alone), the classification and dating of Colombian goldwork still
offers problems. Few of these objects were excavated by trained archaeologists, and most of the museum pieces were obtained from collectors or treasure-
hunters who had little interest in the context of their finds. Except in rare
instances, they did not record which items were found together in the same
tomb, did not bother to save the pottery (which is often our best guide for dating), and did not collect such 'valueless' materials as charcoal, which, since the
1950s, has been used to provide radiocarbon dates for archaeological sites.

Other problems derive from the nature of the gold objects themselves. Being
small, portable and valuable, they were traded over long distances, and, in
addition, the goldsmiths themselves were mobile, working in areas away from
their homelands. As a consequence, provenance alone is not a reliable basis for
classification. Pieces made in one part of Colombia turned up in another, were
copied by local goldsmiths, and provided the stimulus for new, hybrid versions
of the local forms. When this happens, and a single gold object shows design
features drawn from two distinct regional styles, we can conclude that the
contributing styles were wholly or partly contemporary.

In some areas of Colombia, goldworking had been practised for more than
a thousand years before the European Conquest. During that long period,

tastes and fashions changed, so that the objects found in a single region may be of several different styles and dates. It cannot be taken for granted (as it was in some of the earlier studies) that all the gold items found in a particular geographical region were actually made there, still less that they are all of the same age, or were made by the tribe which inhabited that area at the time of the Conquest.

Regional Styles in Colombian Goldwork

In spite of these difficulties, several regional styles of goldworking can be recognized (fig. 32) and we can construct a tentative outline for the development of Colombian metallurgy.

Four groups of material (Tairona, Sinú, Muisca and Nariño) are well defined and fairly well dated. Within each region, most of the items share quite specific features of form or design, which are rarely found anywhere else. The presence of European trade goods (for example, iron tools and glass beads) in the same tombs as the gold is proof that these styles were current when the Spaniards arrived. For convenience, we can place these styles within a 'Late Period'. Since we are dealing with known tribes and peoples described by the first Europeans, the historical sources provide a wealth of background information.

Some metalwork is clearly older, and there are reasons for believing that the finest Quimbaya pieces belong to a 'Middle Period' of development, dated around the fifth to ninth centuries AD (see p. 51).

Metalwork of the 'Early Period', around the time of Christ, is represented by objects in the 'Early Calima style' and by the oldest pieces from San Agustín and Tierradentro, though in each of these regions there are items of much later date.

A good deal of Colombian goldwork cannot be fitted into this scheme at all, and exists in an archaeological limbo. Fig. 31 is therefore highly speculative.

Fig. 31 Chronology of Colombian goldworking areas

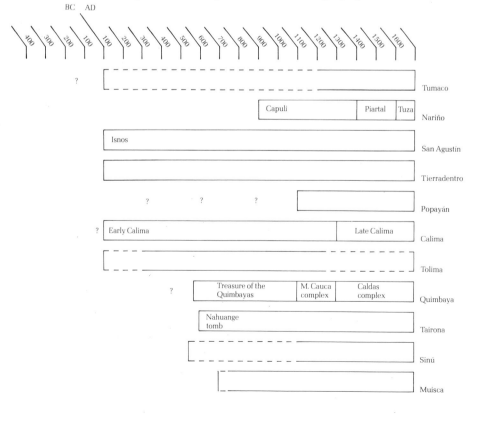

8 Sinú Region

The Indians were buried with as much wealth as possible,
and so they strove with the utmost diligence throughout their lives
to acquire and amass all the gold they could, which they took
from their own land and were buried with it, believing that the more
of the metal they carried away with them the more esteemed
they would be in the places and regions to which they imagined
their souls would go.

Pedro de Cieza de León, 1554

In the sixteenth century the Sinú was one of the richest and most populous
areas of Colombia. When Pedro de Heredia visited its principal town (probably located near the lagoon of Betancí) in 1534, he found very large, communal
or multi-family houses, each of which was surrounded by smaller buildings
for servants and stores. In a corner of the main square was a temple big
enough to hold more than a thousand people, and containing twenty-four
wooden idols covered with sheet gold. These images were arranged in pairs,
each pair supporting a hammock filled with golden offerings. Around the
temple were the burial mounds of chiefs, each mound topped by a tree whose
branches were hung with golden bells.

Juan de Castellanos (1589) noted that the Sinú goldsmiths made 'figurines
of various kinds, aquatic creatures, land animals and birds, down to the most
lowly and unimportant; also javelins with hoops of gold of various sizes, or
covered with gold leaf, and large drums, flutes, vessels of divers kinds, and
models of flies, spiders and other unpleasant insects.'

Most of the raw material came from further inland, from Buriticá and
Dabeiba. The Spaniards noted that Sinú gold was of fine quality, containing
some silver but little copper.

The Indians say that they bring it from certain mountains, from which comes the Rio
Cenú . . . They collect it in the gullies and valleys; and when it rains they stretch nets
across the streams, and as the water rises it carries down nuggets as big as eggs . . .
And what they collect, they bring to the place called Cenú.

Martín Fernández de Enciso, 1519

As the Europeans observed, Sinú goldwork was traded over a wide area.
Archaeologically, Sinú ornaments have been found inland along the Rio
Nechí, and also to the east in Tairona territory (*see* no. 73), and northwards as
far as Panama and Costa Rica (*Aguilar,* 1972).

The general accuracy of these early Spanish accounts has been amply
confirmed by archaeological evidence. In parts of the floodplain of the San
Jorge River, more than 100,000 hectares of land are covered with a corduroy
pattern of artificial ridges, providing well-drained fields for maize and root
crops (*Parsons and Bowen,* 1966). Along the Sinú and San Jorge rivers, and in
the lands between them, are settlements with house platforms and dome-
shaped burial mounds of the so-called *Betancí-Viloria phase* (*G. and A. Reichel-
Dolmatoff,* 1957). At Junguillo, near the lagoon of Betancí, the largest burial
tumulus was a huge mound with an oval ground plan measuring 60 x 40
metres. Surrounding the mound, and some distance from it, was a ring-bank

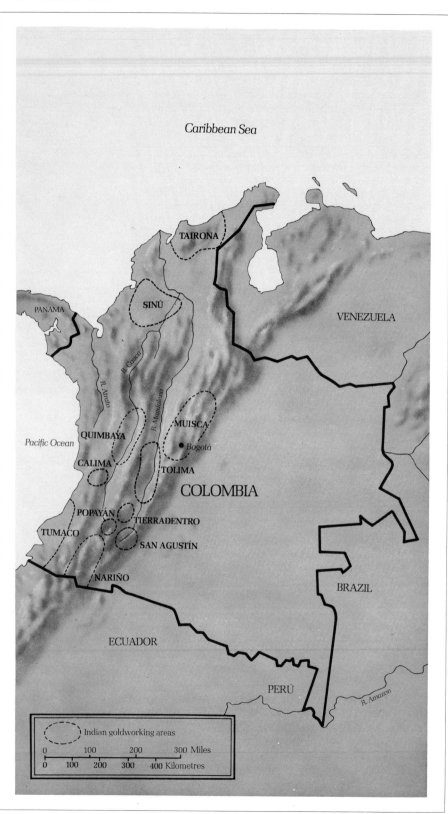

Caribbean Sea

TAIRONA

PANAMA

SINÚ

VENEZUELA

R. Atrato

R. Cauca

R. Magdalena

QUIMBAYA

Pacific Ocean

MUISCA

Bogotá

CALIMA

TOLIMA

COLOMBIA

POPAYÁN

TIERRADENTRO

TUMACO

SAN AGUSTÍN

NARIÑO

BRAZIL

ECUADOR

PERÚ

R. Amazon

Indian goldworking areas

0   100   200   300 Miles

0   100   200   300   400 Kilometres

Fig. 32 Gold styles and goldworking regions of Colombia

13 metres wide and 1 metre high. The common people were buried in smaller mounds, no more than 5 to 12 metres in diameter, each containing a single skeleton and a few offerings of pots, sea shells, spindle whorls, stone axes, and rare gold items.

Another circular mound at El Japón, on the east bank of the Rio San Jorge, covered two skeletons, each resting on a sloping stone slab. In the space below these slabs, and in little groups near the edge of the mound, offerings were deposited: a piece of cloth, a creature carved from shell, a double-spouted container made of stone, a mirror of black volcanic glass, several pots, flat and cylindrical terracotta stamps, and many gold pieces – breastplates, bracelets, a crown, beads, nose ornaments, bells, and ear ornaments of false filigree (*Falchetti*, 1976, pp. 204–9).

As a result of tomb-robbing, more than two thousand Sinú gold objects have reached museums (*Falchetti*, 1976). The most distinctive pieces are the 'staff heads', of unknown use, surmounted by figures of human beings, animals or big-beaked birds. Some of the finest Sinú goldwork is executed in the false filigree technique, seen at its best in delicate beads and in the matching sets of fan-shaped ear ornaments.

A few small, hammered objects may be older than the bulk of the Sinú goldwork (*Reichel-Dolmatoff*, 1958, p. 83), but most of it can be securely attributed to the Indians who lived in the area at the time of Spanish contact. Not only do the burial mounds and their contents match the chronicle descriptions, but there is also a radiocarbon date of AD 1505 $\pm$ eighty years for wood taken from one of the tombs at El Japón. From other graves at El Japón have come European glass beads, used in trade between Spanish and Indians (*see* no. 10c). The starting date for the Sinú style is less certain, and a very early radiocarbon date of AD 450 $\pm$ ninety years should perhaps be regarded with suspicion.

Fig. 33 Sinú landscape

9 Tairona Region

They wear a jewel made of gold in relief, in
the form of one man mounted upon another in
that diabolical and unspeakable act of Sodom. I
saw one of these jewels of the devil, twenty
gold pesos in weight, hollow, empty and well-
wrought, obtained at the port of Santa Marta,
on the coast of Tierra Firme, in the year 1514 . . .
I broke it up with a hammer, and smashed it with
my own hands on a silversmith's anvil at the
smelting house in the city of Darién.

Gonzalo Fernández de Oviedo, 1535–48

When the Spaniards arrived, the Tairona heartland in the Sierra Nevada de
Santa Marta was densely populated. Since 1973, more than two hundred
archaeological sites have been discovered, ranging from small settlements of
no more than thirty houses to large towns with a thousand or more dwellings
spread over an area of several hectares. The Taironas also constructed irriga-
tion canals and agricultural terraces for maize and a variety of other crops,
and their skill as engineers and architects is attested by the stone roads,
reservoirs, bridges and stairways which are widespread in former Tairona
territory.

The smaller villages owed allegiance to the largest towns, which served
as the capitals of mini-states, each with its own cacique or ruler, supported
by a class of noblemen and priests.

Of the many Tairona archaeological sites, only Pueblito has been extensively
explored and published (*Mason, 1931–9; Reichel-Dolmatoff, 1954; G. and A.
Reichel-Dolmatoff, 1955*). The town covers an area of about 16 square kilometres, and is spread over a series of ridges and valleys on the northern slope
of the Sierra Nevada. The wood-and-thatch houses have disappeared, but
their foundations are marked by rings of stone slabs, some 6 to 7 metres in
diameter, with two entrances. The hearth is usually placed off-centre, and
from the distribution of archaeological debris on the floor it seems that the
house was divided into separate areas for men and women. Clustering in one
part of the house are objects connected with women's work: cooking pots,
water jars, milling stones, and tools used for burnishing pottery. In the men's
zone are stone axes and chisels, weights for fishing nets, fine pottery, effigy
vessels containing quartz chips, and also a series of polished stone items used
in ceremonies and dances: forked staffs, hafted axes, and rectangular winged
objects (*see* nos. 319–324). Several of the houses also yielded trade items from
the Spanish settlement at Santa Marta, proving that Pueblito was inhabited
at the time of European contact.

The ceremonial houses were much larger than the ordinary dwellings, and
were sometimes provided with causeways, multiple entrances, stairways,
columns and stone tables or benches. One of the Pueblito ceremonial houses
contained caches of ritual stone objects buried in pots or underneath stone
slabs. Beneath the threshold slab was a terracotta whistle, beads of quartz,

Fig. 34 Indian of the Sierra
Nevada de Santa Marta, with
coca bag and lime-gourd (see
no. 137)

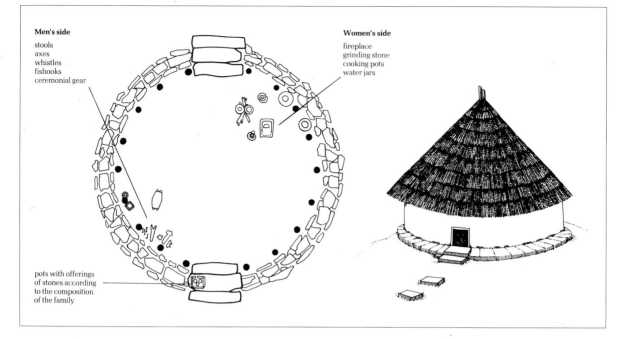

Men's side
stools
axes
whistles
fishooks
ceremonial gear

Women's side
fireplace
grinding stone
cooking pots
water jars

pots with offerings
of stones according
to the composition
of the family

forked 'sceptres' or staffs, and winged *placas sonajeras* of polished stone (*see* nos. 323, 324). Beside the entrance was a jaguar skull. Even today all the ceremonial houses of the Kogi Indians, descendants of the prehistoric Taironas, are dedicated to Cashindúcua, the jaguar god, and in former times the doors of these buildings used to be adorned with jaguar skulls (*Reichel-Dolmatoff*, 1953).

Spanish chronicles describe various methods for disposing of the dead (smoke-drying of corpses, burial in 'vaults', and collection of the bones after the flesh had been allowed to decay). These bones were then buried in urns (*see* no. 574).

There was a small-scale trade in gold objects between the Sierra Nevada and the Sinú, but the main commercial links were with the Muiscas to whom the Taironas sent gold nose ornaments, beads and sea shells in return for emeralds.

Tairona goldwork combines a technical mastery of casting with a love of fine detail. This shows itself in ornamental decoration (such as the delicate braided bands of cast wire, or the little balls at the centre of spiral appendages) and also in subject matter: the complex mythological creatures combining human, eagle and bat characteristics, or the human figures on which all the details of costume and jewellery are portrayed so clearly that there is no problem in identifying these miniature renderings with their full-size counterparts. Among the non-representational pieces are many forms unique to the Taironas (anchor-shaped pendants, lip-plugs shaped like round pillboxes, kidney-shaped nose ornaments, crescentic earrings with a border of wirework loops, etc.).

Most Tairona goldwork belongs to the final centuries before the Spanish Conquest, but an earlier stage of Tairona culture goes back to the sixth or seventh centuries AD and is represented by a burial mound at Nahuange on the coast, and by the fill of a terrace underlying a later house at Pueblito (*Mason, 1931–9; Bischof, 1969a, b*). Although the painted pottery from Nahuange is unlike the later Tairona wares, this tomb yielded gold objects and polished stone items which are the prototypes of those employed in the sixteenth century and among the Kogi up to the present day.

Fig. 35 Plan of an excavated Tairona house, and reconstruction of its probable appearance.

They have many woods and lagoons consecrated to
their false religion, where they are not allowed
to cut down a tree or to drink a drop of water
for all the gold in the world. In these groves
they also make their sacrifices, and bury gold
and emeralds there. They can be sure that nobody
will touch those things, for such a person will
soon fall down dead. The same is true of the
lagoons dedicated to their sacrifices, where
they throw in much gold and also precious stones,
which remain lost forever.

Antonio de Herrera, 1601–5

In Spanish chronicles the Muisca (or Chibcha) kingdoms of the high, temperate
plateaux of Cundinamarca and Boyacá are described in enthusiastic terms.
The land was fertile, with numerous towns of wood-and-thatch huts surrounded by palisades. The individual towns were organized into two loose
confederations. A chieftain with the title of Zipa controlled the southern
territory from his capital at Bogotá, modern Funza (*Broadbent, 1966*), while
another lord, called the Zaque, ruled the northern lands from Hunsa, present-
day Tunja (*Falchetti and Plazas, 1973*).

Religion centred on the cult of the sun, though offerings were made to a
multitude of other deities. At Sogamoso there was a large wooden temple,
but caves, hilltops, woods and lakes were also considered sacred places. The
five holy lakes (Guatavita, Guasca, Siecha, Teusacá and Ubaque) were
inhabited by snake gods, and became pilgrimage centres. At all these places,
idols were set up and offerings were made. Castellanos describes one form of
offering (see no. 162):

> ... the image of a person, completely hollow, made of pottery and ill-proportioned, open
> at the top, in which they put golden jewels, animals and figures. They closed the opening
> with a lid, also of clay ... And, when these were full, they buried them in a sacred
> place.

Juan de Castellanos, 1589

The dead were disposed of in various ways. Some corpses were interred,
stretched out or tied up in bundles, in cemeteries of pit graves, or buried with
a few poor offerings under stone tumuli or inside little semi-subterranean
chambers built of stone slabs. Other bodies were left until the flesh had
decayed, and the bones were then collected up and deposited in burial urns.
Caves and rock shelters served as burial places for mummy bundles (*see*
nos. 568, 569).

Since the Muiscas built in wood, the remains of their towns have long since
disappeared, and the visible traces of their culture are unspectacular: agricultural terraces, a few rock-paintings, and occasional stone statues or
enclosures made of stone columns (*Broadbent, 1963, 1964, 1965, 1970*).

Muisca metalwork divides into two categories: jewellery for the living, and
votive figurines (*tunjos*) to be offered to the gods. The tunjos are the most distinctive Muisca contribution to Colombian metallurgy, and were not intended
for everyday use. Unlike the jewellery and personal ornaments, these miniature

figures are rough and poorly finished. They are usually found buried in pots or thrown into lakes, and only rarely occur in graves or on house sites.

Like the 'ex votos' offered to Catholic saints today, their purpose may have been to thank the gods for past help, or to serve as gifts in anticipation of future services. And, as with present-day 'ex votos', the subject-matter was more important than the quality of the workmanship. Their makers were not concerned with realistic proportions. A typical tunjo consists of a simple plaque on which details are added in wax wire. The modelling is usually flat and one-dimensional, but, in a naive and conventional way, detail is faithfully rendered. The tunjos illustrate actual Muisca people, carrying children, holding shields, weapons, pots, lime-containers and everyday objects. There are a few composite genre scenes of people engaged in various activities, and, besides the human world, there are representations of creatures (snakes, birds and dragon-like animals) which played a part in Muisca mythology and religion (*Pérez de Barradas*, 1958; *Plazas*, 1975). No other Colombian art style tells us so much about the life of the common people.

In spite of its unsophisticated appearance, there is nothing inept about Muisca metallurgy. All the customary techniques were employed, with the addition of one (the use of stone matrices) which was a Muisca invention. Many hollow objects still contain their original cores, and from the charcoal content of these has been obtained a unique series of radiocarbon dates for the metal pieces themselves: AD 645 ± ninety-five years for a nose ornament from Guatavita, 840 ± sixty years for a copper shell from the lagoon of Chisacá, 960 ± ninety years for a nose ornament from Santo Domingo, and 1055 ± fifty-nine years for a copper figurine (*see* no. 63). If all these dates are correct – and the earlier ones need confirmation – the Muisca style of metalwork was almost nine hundred years old by the time the Spaniards reached Bogotá.

Above Fig. 36 Muisca clay vessel with votive figures (*tunjos*). (*Museo del Oro*)

Below Fig. 37 Landscape in the Muisca region, Sabana de Bogotá

11 Quimbaya Region

We went . . . one Antonio Pimentel and myself, to
examine the burial place of a chief name Yayo,
in which we found more than two hundred small
pieces of gold. . . . but as a horrible smell came from
the bodies we went away without getting all that
was there.

Pedro de Cieza de León, 1554

The term 'Quimbaya' has been misleadingly applied to all the goldwork and
pottery from heavily looted graves in the middle reaches of the Cauca valley.
In reality, the historical Quimbayas were merely one small tribe which lived
at the time of European contact in the area corresponding to the modern
municipios of Cartago and Pereira.

Cieza de León commented that the region from Antioquia to northern Valle
was the homeland of many different tribes, often speaking mutually unintel-
ligible languages. Although there were regional and local differences, all these
groups shared certain customs. The Indians were farmers who lived in villages
of wood-and-thatch houses, under the control of chiefs; they were rich in gold,
worshipped idols made of wood or wax, and had shamans who communicated
with the gods. They were also given to drinking bouts, and were warlike and
cannibalistic. After a series of elaborate rituals, the dead were buried in deep
shaft graves:

> When their chiefs die in a part of this province called Tauya, they place their bodies in
> hammocks and light fires all round. Holes are dug beneath, into which the melted fat
> drops, and when the body is half burned the relatives come and make great lamenta-
> tions, drinking their wine and reciting songs of praise to their gods according to their
> custom, and as they have been taught by their elders. This being done, they wrap the
> bodies in shrouds, and keep them for several years unburied. When they are thoroughly
> dried up, they put them into sepulchres which they make in their houses.

Pedro de Cieza de León, 1554

Guaquería (the location and excavation of ancient sites) has a long history
in the Quimbaya region and was a respected profession in the nineteenth
century. In the 1880s and 1890s, the search for rich graves was a major
stimulus for the colonization of unoccupied lands, leading to the foundation
of new towns (Armenia, Circasia, Calarcá, Montenegro) whose economies
were dominated by *guaquería* during the early years (*Parsons, 1968, p. 80*).
As a hobby for many, and a profession for some, this treasure-hunting continues to the present day (*Bruhns, 1972a*).

The early history of the region remains unknown, and the story does not
become clear until about AD 1000 (*Duque Gómez, 1970; Bruhns, 1976*).

Villages of the *Middle Cauca Complex* (AD 1000–1200) cover several hectares and are frequently close to areas of ridged fields like those of the Sinú.
Within these villages are cemeteries of shaft graves with side chambers
opening from the bottom of the shaft, the largest and richest tombs often
containing several bodies stretched out on the floor of the funerary
chamber – perhaps those of a chief and his retainers, as described by Cieza.
One of these shaft tombs gave radiocarbon dates of AD 1100 ± eighty, and
1400 ± seventy years.

Fig. 38 Landscape with bamboo
groves. Quimbaya region

Villages belonging to the *Caldas Complex* (AD 1200 to the Conquest) are smaller, and simple inhumation tends to be replaced by cremation or by urn burial. Many of the older pottery forms continue in use, but slab figurines make their first appearance (*see* nos. 418–428). During this terminal stage, contacts with the Calima valley were close.

Most of the Quimbaya gold comes from looted tombs, and exists in an archaeological vacuum. It is clearly not all of the same age, nor is it all the work of the historical Quimbaya tribe. A few categories can be linked with the Middle Cauca and Caldas complexes, but many of the simpler items (bells, frog pendants, discs and nose ornaments) are widespread in central Colombia and were shared by many tribes over a large area.

Within this mass of metalwork, one group stands out from the rest and defines the 'Quimbaya style' in its more restricted sense. At the heart of this collection is the Treasure of the Quimbayas, consisting of 121 items found in two graves at La Soledad, Filandia, in 1891, and later presented by the Colombian government to the Queen of Spain (*Pérez de Barradas*, 1966) (*see* nos. 358–362). Similar pieces have come from other tombs in the area, adding up to a considerable body of metalwork in a distinctive and homogeneous style. These specimens are often big and heavy, superbly finished, with a preference for large plane surfaces and restrained decoration. The essential unity of the style is shown by the treatment of the human figures used to embellish lime-flasks, trumpets, helmets and ornaments. Both men and women are represented, modelled in the round, with plump bodies and small hands and feet, naked except for their jewellery. The half-closed eyes, with their heavy lids, have a sleepy or drugged expression, and some of the figures carry lime-flasks and coca-chewing paraphernalia.

The precise age of this metalwork is unknown, for it has yet to be found in a datable archaeological context, but there are hints that it is older than AD 1000. Similar human figures are modelled on burial urns of the 'Brownware Incised style' (*see* no. 376), tentatively dated to the centuries before AD 800 (*Bruhns*, 1969–70). On the north coast, a hybrid gold figurine which combines Quimbaya and Tairona features was found at Nahuange in a burial mound of the sixth or seventh century (*Mason*, 1936, Pl. 148; *Bischof*, 1969a, b). Most of the Quimbaya export pieces found in Panama and Costa Rica are as lacking in archaeological background as those of Colombia, but there was little gold-work in the Isthmus before AD 400. The closest stylistic links seem to be with the metalwork of the early Coclé tombs in Panama, of the period AD 500–800 (*Cooke*, 1976). In the present state of knowledge, the 'Quimbaya style' in its restricted sense seems to belong somewhere between AD 400 and 1000.

12   Tolima Region

The gold lay so near the surface of the ground
that they collected it by the handful from between
the roots of the trees and grasses, and the
earth which was shaken off when they pulled these
out consisted more of gold than of soil . . . They
depopulated the country to provide labour for
the mines, until the yield began to fall and the
Pijao Indians . . . pursued the men who were excavating
this gold, which was the reason why the work
was abandoned.

Pedro Simón, 1625, on the early Colonial mines of Ibagué

In the sixteenth century the middle Magdalena Valley, in the modern department of Tolima, was the home of two distinct Indian groups. In the northern portion lived the Panches, a tribe of bellicose headhunters, of whom Friar Pedro Simón wrote: 'they were such ferocious people, and such great butchers of human flesh, that they did not know how to exist without continuous wars against their neighbours – not to expand their territory and kingdom, which is the usual reason for going to war, but to obtain human flesh to eat'. Their permanent enemies were the Muiscas, with whom they alternately fought and traded, exchanging the gold of Ibagué for the salt, emeralds and cotton mantles of the highlands.

Their neighbours in southern Tolima were the Pijao Indians, who had a similar reputation as warriors and cannibals, but were also skilled goldsmiths. One of their chiefs, the ruler of Amoyá, gave the Conquistador Francisco de Trejo what was described as 'a little present' of gold ornaments to the value of 1000 pesos, and after the Conquest the Pijaos still continued to pay tribute to the Spaniards in the form of alluvial gold from the Rio Saldaña (*Cubillos,* 1946).

Little systematic excavation has been done in Tolima, and it is still impossible to link any of the archaeological discoveries with the historical Panche or Pijao tribes. The evidence consists mainly of shaft tombs, elaborately painted or incised burial urns, and a whole range of pots with incised, stamped or appliqué ornament. Several different styles are represented, and are probably not all of the same age (*Cubillos,* 1954; *Reichel-Dolmatoff and Dussan de Reichel,* 1943; *Perdomo,* 1975; *Cardale,* 1976).

Most of the goldwork comes from looted cemeteries, and lacks background information. The most characteristic objects are flat, stylized human figures, terminating in crescent-shaped bases. Only once has Tolima gold been found by archaeologists in its original context – at Hacienda El Relator (Rioblanco) where typical gold ornaments were found, with several pots, in what seems to have been a ritual offering or cache, covered over by a layer of earth (*Cubillos,* 1945). Unfortunately, this site, too, is undated.

Tolima goldwork forms a stylistically homogeneous group, and may have been in use over a long period. The greatest concentration of finds is in the Pijao heartland along the Rio Saldaña, and this area was presumably the centre of manufacture. From there, a few items made their way south to Huila and San Agustín, and north into Panche territory, the Muisca zone and the middle Cauca valley. Some pieces were also traded across the cordillera into the Calima region.

Fig. 39 The Madalena Valley, Tolima

Even though we cannot yet fix a date for Tolima goldwork, it is clear that it overlapped in time with several of the other Colombian gold styles. The distinctive, square 'Tolima face' sometimes occurs on Popayán eagles (see no. 457). Near Rioblanco, Early Calima pins and breastplates are said to have been found by treasure-hunters in the same tombs as Tolima pieces (*Pérez de Barrados*, 1954, p. 224; 1958, p. 15). In the Guaca del Dragón (Quindío), it is reported that the finest and largest of all Tolima figures was found in a tomb that also contained Calima pins and a human face in 'Quimbaya style' (*Pérez de Barradas*, 1954, p. 217; 1958, pp. 40–1). If these *guaquero* stories can be believed – and they are not always reliable – then the 'Tolima style' must have begun several centuries before the Spanish Conquest, at a time when Quimbaya and Early Calima objects had not yet gone out of use. Whether it lasted up to the Conquest is still unknown. If it did not, there is an embarrassing lack of any other goldwork to set against Spanish accounts of the flourishing jewellery industries they observed in the sixteenth century.

Other clergy buried the dead,
but this vicar dug them up.
Alonso de Zurita, on the tomb-robbing activities
of the ecclesiastical vicar of Popayán in the 1550s

Although there are marked regional differences, the mountainous country around the headwaters of the Cauca and Magdalena rivers can be considered a single goldworking province. In it are two of Colombia's most famous archaeological sites: San Agustín and Tierradentro. Small-scale excavations near the city of Popayán have shown that this area, too, is potentially a rich one. The three sub-regions are linked by the presence of monumental architecture, a unique tradition of stone sculpture, and by the occurrence of certain categories of gold objects (notably 'Popayán eagles') throughout the entire province.

Popayán

The usual shaft tombs and house platforms are reported from this area, as well as a few isolated stone statues of nude male figures with hands folded over the stomach. The age of these statues is unknown (*Lehmann*, 1953; *Otero*, 1952). Metalwork from the tombs consists of copper and gold discs, and a series of pendants in which human features are combined with those of eagles or birds of prey (see nos. 456, 457). These 'Popayán eagles' are most numerous in the upper Cauca and upper Magdalena regions, but have been found also in other parts of Colombia (*Pérez de Barradas*, 1966).

San Agustín

San Agustín is not a single site, but a cluster of some forty smaller ones scattered over 500 square kilometres of rolling foothills near the headwaters of the Rio Magdalena. The entire landscape is man-made, with house platforms and rubbish dumps, trackways, ancient field boundaries and drainage ditches, cemeteries of shaft graves and stone cists, and a number of burial mounds containing stone-built funerary chambers.

By 500 BC, at the latest, the San Agustín area was dotted with small and widely scattered farming villages. A major change (perhaps due to the arrival of new people) took place in the first century AD, marking the start of the *Isnos period*. New pottery forms are introduced, including double-spouted vessels (cf. no. 463), and the technique of resist painting appears for the first time. Construction of large earthworks begins, and there is also the first evidence for goldworking at San Agustín in the form of crucible fragments, droplets of melted gold, and small pieces of wire or sheet metal (*Reichel-Dolmatoff*, 1975; *Duque Gómez*, 1964).

The oldest stone statues may also belong to the Isnos period, though the precise dating has still to be worked out, and some sculptures may be later. More than 320 statues are scattered over the archaeological zone, singly or in groups, on hilltops, slopes, and in underground burial constructions. These tombs are mounds of earth, some 25 metres in diameter, covering burial chambers made of large slabs. Inside are one or more statues. In certain cases, the statues and the walls of the chamber were once painted with geometric designs in red, black and yellow, as at Tierradentro.

The main theme of San Agustín sculpture is a human or semi-human personage, sometimes partly transformed into a jaguar with bared fangs, or else with a jaguar-monster crouching over his back and head. This concept of the *alter ego* or 'double' (a guardian spirit, simultaneously helper and protector) is widespread in Indian America today, where mythology and religion are also full of jaguar symbolism. With the aid of hallucinatory snuffs and drug-induced visions, the shamans communicate with the spirits, and can transform themselves into jaguars and other animals. Although details of costume, weapons etc. are realistically depicted, the sculpture of San Agustín belongs more to the spirit world than to the world of everyday life (*Reichel-Dolmatoff, 1972*).

A sequence of pottery styles continues the story of San Agustín up to the Spanish Conquest, but many of the stone monuments and looted tombs are not satisfactorily dated. The burial mounds (and, by implication, the kinds of statue they contain) are no earlier than AD 400, and went out of use several centuries before the arrival of the Europeans. Urn burial in shaft-and-chamber tombs appears to be a late custom in the area.

Surprisingly little gold has come from San Agustín. Some pieces show contacts with Tolima and the Calima valley; others are perhaps locally made, and can be matched by the jewellery carved on the stone figures. In one of the stone-lined cists was a skeleton wearing a diadem of gold wire, a round gold nose ornament and a necklace of stone beads with a gold eagle (*Duque Gómez, 1963, p. 46*). Goldwork of the Isnos period is illustrated by nos. 453, 454. At present, all one can say is that the gold objects from San Agustín span at least 1500 years and are of different ages and styles.

Fig. 40 San Agustín, stone sculpture at Alto de los Idolos

Tierradentro

The archaeological remains of the Tierradentro region consist principally of stone statues (less numerous and less elaborate than those of San Agustín), underground tombs, and scatters of pottery fragments marking the sites of ancient villages. The cemeteries, sometimes as many as eighty graves together, tend to be on ridges or other high places. The finest tombs consist of a spiral stairway leading to a roughly circular, subterranean chamber with niches round the sides, and a roof supported by columns of natural rock. Walls and roofs were sometimes painted in black, white, red and yellow, with geometric designs, stylized human faces, and lizard-like creatures (*Pérez de Barradas, 1937a; Silva Celis, 1943–4; Long et al., 1970–1*).

The largest burial vaults contain up to forty urns, each filled with the cremated bones of a single person, surrounded by offerings of pots which may once have held food and drink. Some vessels closely resemble those of San Agustín, and were perhaps imported from there; others are of purely local types. Comparison with the better-dated materials of San Agustín suggests that Tierradentro was occupied from the early centuries AD up to the Spanish Conquest.

Treasure-hunters have found some fine gold objects in the general Tierradentro area (*Pérez de Barradas, 1937b* and *see* nos. 458–462), but none has yet turned up in a scientific excavation.

Fig. 41 Tierradentro, interior of an underground tomb with painted walls and pillars

14 Nariño Region

When they die, they make the tombs very large
and very deep . . . And among them it is the custom,
as they informed me, that, if one of their lords
dies, each of the neighbours round about gives
the dead man two or three Indian men and women.
They take them to the place of burial and there
give these Indians much maize wine, so much that
they become drunk. And, seeing them without
feeling, they put these people into the tomb to
keep the dead man company.

Pedro de Cieza de León, 1554, on the Quillacingas

During the 1970s, objects in a previously unknown style of goldwork began to reach museums as a result of intensive treasure-hunting and tomb-robbing in highland Nariño. At the time of the Conquest this area was the homeland of the Pastos and Quillacingas, whose way of life is described in Spanish chronicles (*Groot et al.*, 1976).

Identical archaeological material is found also on the Ecuadorian side of the frontier and, in a cultural sense, the entire department of Nariño belonged more to the Central Andean than to the Colombian sphere in prehispanic times. Besides its tombs, the area has yielded a number of stone statues, and in several localities there are stone retaining walls supporting contour terraces, with scatters of pottery and domestic rubbish indicating the presence of ancient villages.

The early prehistory of the region is still unknown, and the picture does not come into focus until *c.* AD 800 (*Francisco*, 1969; *Perdomo et al.*, 1974; *Uribe*, 1977).

To the *Capilí period* (ninth to thirteenth centuries AD) belong the deepest tombs, with the funerary chamber entered from a narrow shaft as much as 40 metres deep. The most elaborate pottery of the period has black resist patterns over a red background (see no. 498), and the metallurgy of gold and tumbaga was already known. Many tombs contain shells traded from the Pacific coast. Another item of trade was coca. Pottery figures of coca-chewers are some of the most typical items of the Capulí repertoire (see nos. 150, 151), but the shrub does not thrive at high altitudes and the leaf must therefore have been imported from warmer regions. The most likely source is to the west, for at the time of European contact the tropical Pacific lowlands supplied the Pasto merchants with gold, cotton, shell beads and coca leaf (*Salomon*, 1978, pp. 295–307).

During the succeeding *Piartal period* (thirteenth to fourteenth centuries AD) the tombs were less deep but more elaborate, with red-painted walls and benches or false columns carved from the natural clay. Multiple burials, of up to fourteen corpses, were the rule. Some Piartal tombs, notably those at Miraflores (Pupiales), have produced large quantities of metalwork: nose ornaments, bracelets, discs, figurines, masks and musical instruments.

The final (Tuza) stage represents the culture of the Indians described by Cieza and the other historians, and there is a radiocarbon date of AD 1450 from a village of this period at Pilcuán. To this stage belong most of the surviving architectural remains: villages of up to sixty round huts (measuring 3 to 21 metres in diameter) with walls made of rammed earth, and roofs originally thatched with grass.

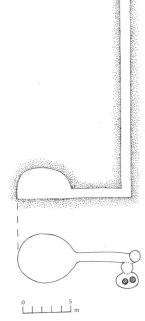

0   5
m

Above Fig. 43 Section and plan of a tomb at Las Cruces, Ipiales, Nariño, dated *c.* AD 1100 (see no. 497). The shaft is 22 m deep. From Uribe 1977.

Opposite Fig. 42 Nariño landscape

The goldwork of Nariño forms a distinctive body of material, whose stylistic links are with Ecuador and the central Andes. Many pieces have a pale colour, indicating an alloy with a good deal of silver. The finest Nariño objects are not three-dimensional castings, but are large items made from heavy sheet metal, burnished to a brilliant finish. Characteristic Capulí shapes are the matching pairs of ear discs with repoussé patterns and the ornaments decorated with cut-out monkeys. From the Piartal period come the finest nose ornaments of sheet metal (*see* nos. 493–496), a series of bi-coloured or bi-metallic pieces, and a group of discs, each with a central hole. Traces of knotted cords indicate that these discs may have been suspended as decorative 'mobiles' (*see* no. 487) (*Clemencia Plazas de Nieto*: personal communication).

Fig. 44 Plan of a village of circular houses, El Arrayán, Ipiales, Nariño, Tuza period. From Uribe 1977.

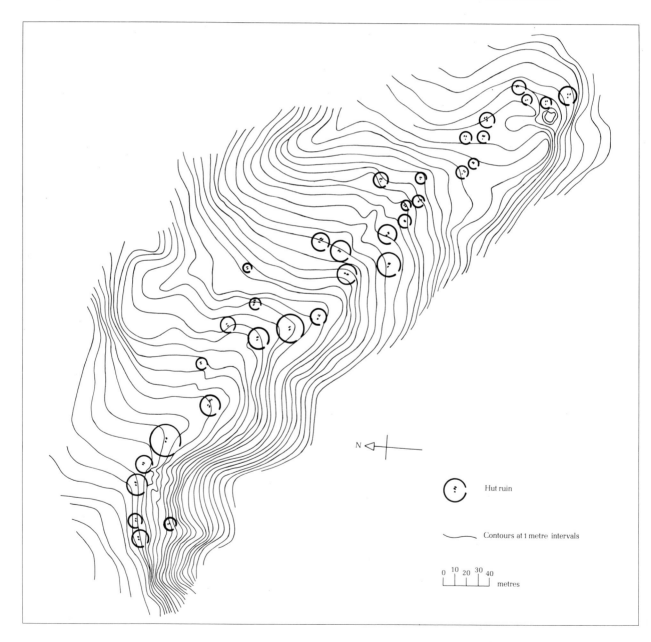

N

⊙ Hut ruin

Contours at 1 metre intervals

0 10 20 30 40
metres

15 Tumaco and Lowland Nariño Region

Before we, the negroes, arrived, the Indians
lived here, in this same place. The Indians lived
under the ground, and ate gold from golden plates
and drank gold from golden cups, and their children
played with dolls made of gold. When we arrived
the Indians fled, under the earth towards the
mountains where the rivers have their sources . . .
But before fleeing, the Indians took all the
gold, the cups full of golden pineapples and the
golden dolls, and broke everything up with their
hands and feet, turning it all into gold dust . . .
And now we, the negroes, must break our bodies
to find the gold dust and to keep ourselves alive
in the places where the Indians used to live before.
Myth of the miners of Güelmambí, Barbacoas; from
Friedemann, 1974

Before the creation of modern national boundaries, the Tumaco region of Colombia formed a single cultural province with the adjacent Ecuadorian department of Esmeraldas. Inland from the coast, the district around Barbacoas has been an important centre of goldmining and jewellery-manufacture since early Colonial times (*Friedemann, 1974*). No systematic excavation has yet been carried out near Barbacoas, but the general region has yielded gold fish-hooks and simple ornaments (see no. 502), and also a few more elaborate pieces in an Ecuadorian style (*Pérez de Barradas, 1954*, Pls. 260–1).

The coastal strip was first explored in 1526–7 by the ships of Pizarro, on his way to the conquest of Peru, and the province was described as populous and rich:

All the houses are fortresses, built over trees, or on very high wooden pillars, and they go up by steps that can be put up or down.
Pascual de Andagoya on Tumaco

They wear short shirts which do not cover their shameful parts, and they are tonsured like friars, except that they cut all their hair in front and behind, but let it grow at the sides. They wear emeralds and other things in their nostrils and ears, and strings of gold, turquoises, white and coloured stones.
Francisco López de Gómara on Esmeraldas, 1552

From the eroding beaches, rubbish heaps and artificial mounds (called *tolas*) of this whole region has come a remarkable series of figurines modelled in greyish clay and originally painted in bright but fugitive colours. The subject-matter includes realistic animals, fantastic and imaginary beasts, human warriors, women with children, musicians, embracing couples, masked individuals and ordinary people. Details of costume and jewellery are faithfully depicted, and closely match the early Spanish descriptions:

The people wear many gold studs in their faces. They pierce the flesh in many places, and in each hole they put a grain or stud of gold, and many of them put turquoises and fine emeralds.
Francisco López de Gómara on Esmeraldas, 1552

Not all this archaeological material is of the same age. There were villages along the banks of the Rio Mataje well before 400 BC, while, further north, a mound at Imbilí is dated AD 1000 (*Reichel-Dolmatoff*, 1965, pp. 111–14, 132). Other finds, including coastal trade pieces from sites in highland Nariño, continue the story down to the Spanish Conquest (*Uribe*, 1976).

Some of the archaeological sites (like the one at Isla del Morro, near the port of Tumaco) are very large, stretching for a kilometre or more along the beach. At the beginning of the century, before treasure-hunters devastated the site, La Tolita had some forty mounds scattered along the river bank and arranged around an open square. Lesser sites, like the little hamlet of Monte Alto, consist of small rubbish heaps, low mounds, and a few simple pit graves (*Cubillos,* 1955).

These sites have yielded a rich haul to treasure-hunters, who wash and sieve the earth in search of the little studs, nose rings and tiny gold ornaments which are the stock in trade of the Tumaco jeweller. At Monte Alto, a minor site by comparison with La Tolita, there were once four hundred people engaged in this activity. Most of these finds never reach museums, and (in the absence of archaeological background information) the development of Tumaco metallurgy is still poorly understood, though it may be among the earliest in Colombia.

Fig. 45 Mangrove vegetation on the Pacific coast near Tumaco

Both men and women have their noses pierced,
and wear a sort of twisted nails in them, of
gold about the thickness of a finger, called
caricuris. They also wear necklaces of fine
gold, beautifully worked, and earrings of
twisted gold.

Pedro de Cieza de León, 1554

With the founding of the towns of Restrepo and Darién in the twentieth century, the upper Calima valley became famous for its rich graves. Wherever recent colonists have cleared the forests, traces of ancient occupation have been revealed, in the form of rock carvings, house platforms, shaft tombs, ridged fields in the valley bottom and mosaics of little square fields on the slopes.

Archaeologically, the peoples encountered by the Conquistadors are represented by material of the *Sonso phase* (AD 1200 to the Conquest), in Calima and the nearby parts of the Cauca valley. The tombs consist of deep shafts with side chambers containing offerings of resist-painted vessels, stone axes, wooden objects (coffins, troughs, stools, spoons, weapons), spindle whorls, terracotta roller stamps for printing textile patterns (*see* nos. 560, 561), crystal beads, stone pendants and a few rather simple gold objects (*Bray and Moseley*, 1969–70; *Pineda*, 1945; *Wassén*, 1936; *Caldas et al.*, 1972). The 'twisted nail' nose ornaments and ear pieces described by Cieza can be exactly matched in tombs of this period (*see* nos. 547, 548).

Cieza does not mention any spectacular gold items from this area, and the excavated Sonso tombs have all been poor in gold. Instead, the more elaborate gold items – the ones which are characteristic of the 'Calima style' as it is generally defined – are found in shaft graves with much richer contents and with a different style of pottery (*Pérez de Barradas*, 1954; *Dussan de Reichel*, 1965–6). The finest vessels are unpainted, dark-surfaced jars or double-spouted effigy vessels modelled in the shapes of human beings or fantastic animals, and covered with finely incised patterns (*see* nos. 551–554). The faces on the human effigy pots are heavy and brooding, with slanted eyes, thick lips, puffy cheeks, and deep furrows at the sides of the mouth.

The gold objects found with this pottery are masterpieces of hammering and casting. From sheet metal were made ear spools, nose ornaments, masks, lime-flasks and pectorals with human faces in high relief – all of them further decorated with repoussé designs and dangling elements. Characteristically, these items are large and made of relatively pure gold. In contrast, the finest cast pieces are miniatures – the pins or lime-dippers topped with birds, human figures and imaginary animals.

This pottery and goldwork are in a well-defined style which, for want of a better term, we can call 'Early Calima'. Since all the material comes from illegal excavations, its precise age is unknown, though there are hints that it may be very early.

Near the mouth of the Rio Calima, in the rain forest of the Pacific lowlands, is a site called Catanguero, with a date of about 250 BC. Catanguero pottery is said to include incised wares and also figures with Early Calima-like faces. Further south, on the Rio Mataje, which forms the border with Ecuador, is an archaeological mound with pottery similar to that of Catanguero (including double-sprouted vessels), dated between *c.* 300 BC and the start of the Christian era. The excavator of these sites suggests that people from the coastlands moved up the rivers into the hills of the western cordillera during the final centuries BC, bringing with them certain pottery forms and the knowledge of metallurgy (*Reichel-Dolmatoff,* 1965, pp. 85, 100, 114). Since a few gold pins of 'Early Calima style' have been found in coastal Ecuador, near La Tolita, it seems that ideas and products were exchanged in both directions. If these speculations are eventually confirmed, the goldwork of the 'Early Calima style' may be some of the oldest in Colombia.

Fig. 46 Calima Valley, engraved boulder

COLOUR PLATES

Lake Guatavita
Previous page

11 Portrait of
Gonzalo Jiménez de
Quesada
Top left

13 The Codex Köler
Bottom left

16 Muisca tunjo
depicting the
ceremony of El
Dorado
Top right

31(e) Pectoral, with
human face
Bottom right

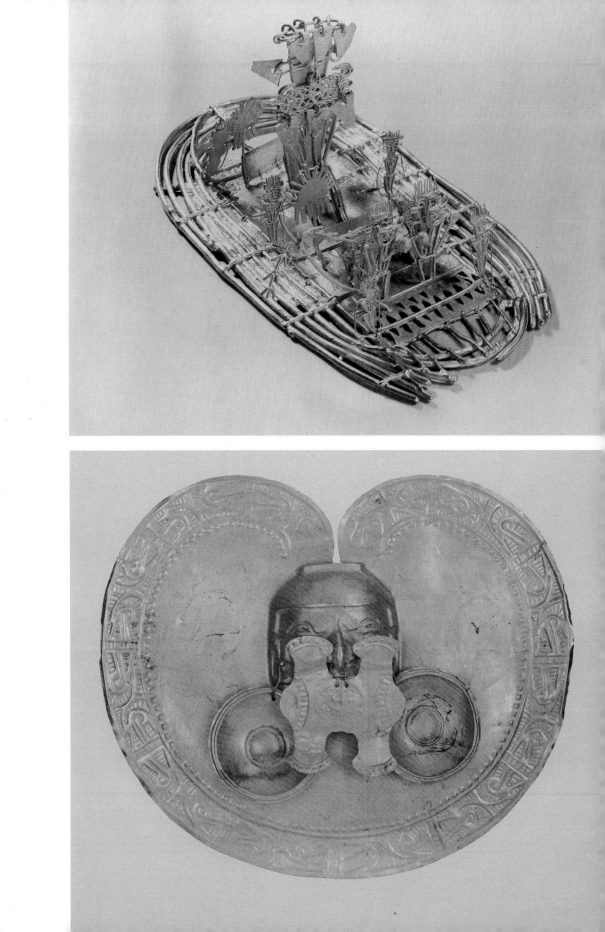

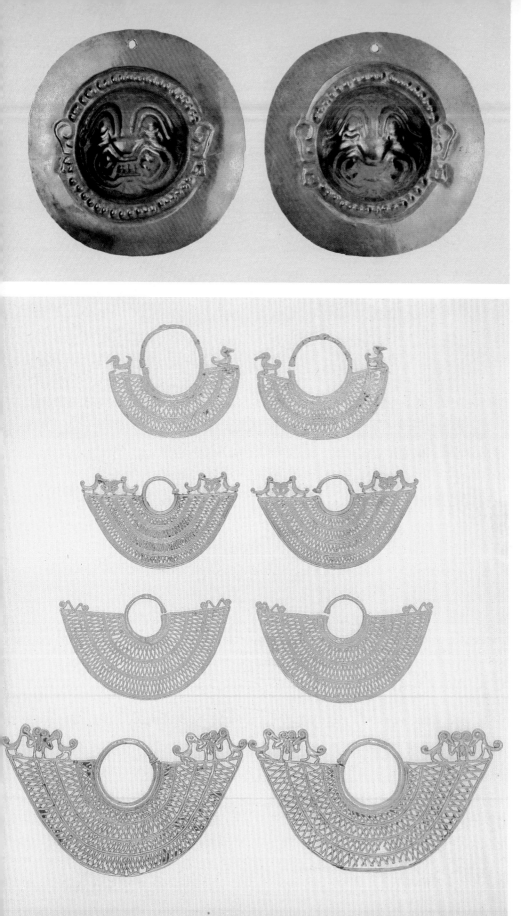

50 Pair of ear
danglers
Top left

72, 73, 74, 75 Pairs
of Sinú ear
ornaments
Bottom left

79 Bi-coloured
plaque
Top right

87-90 Four fish
hooks
92 Spatula
93-97 Chisels
98-100 Needles
Bottom right

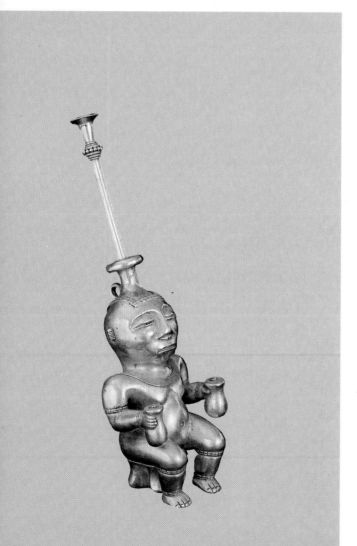

138 Tairona miniature jar
Top left

143(a) Lime-flask
Bottom left

170 Painted mantle
Right

231 Jaguar pendant
Top left

235 Sinú staff head
Right

236 Sinú staff head
Bottom left

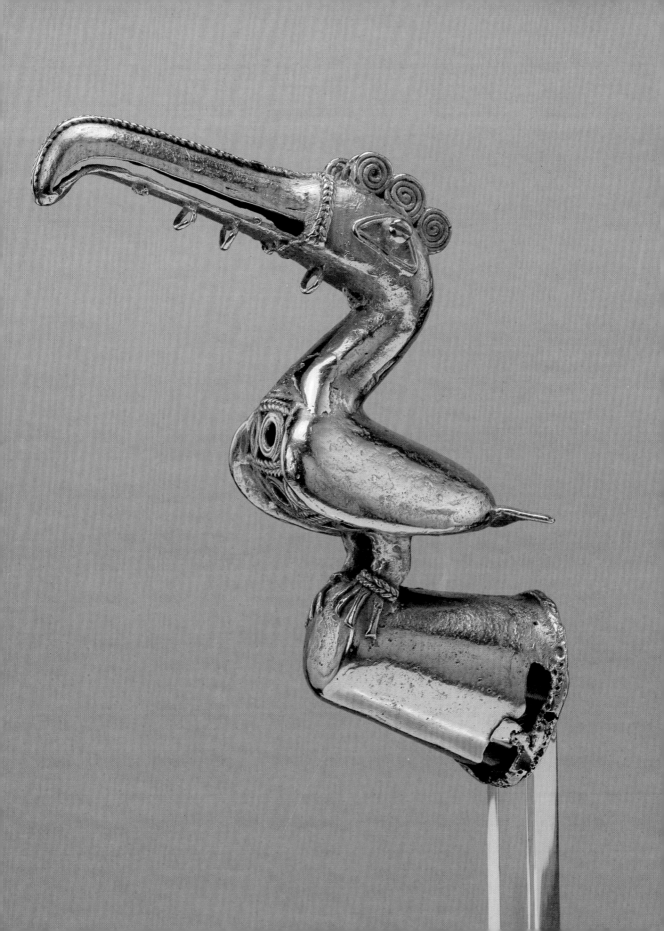

246 Bowl with
modelled pedestal
Left

252 Lid of burial urn
Right

Overleaf
256 Darien pectoral
Top far left

299 Tairona bird
pectoral
Top left

308 Tairona pectoral
with human figure
Bottom left

263 Tairona figure
pendant
Top right

309 Tairona pectoral
with three birds
Bottom right

310 Tairona pendant
Bottom far right

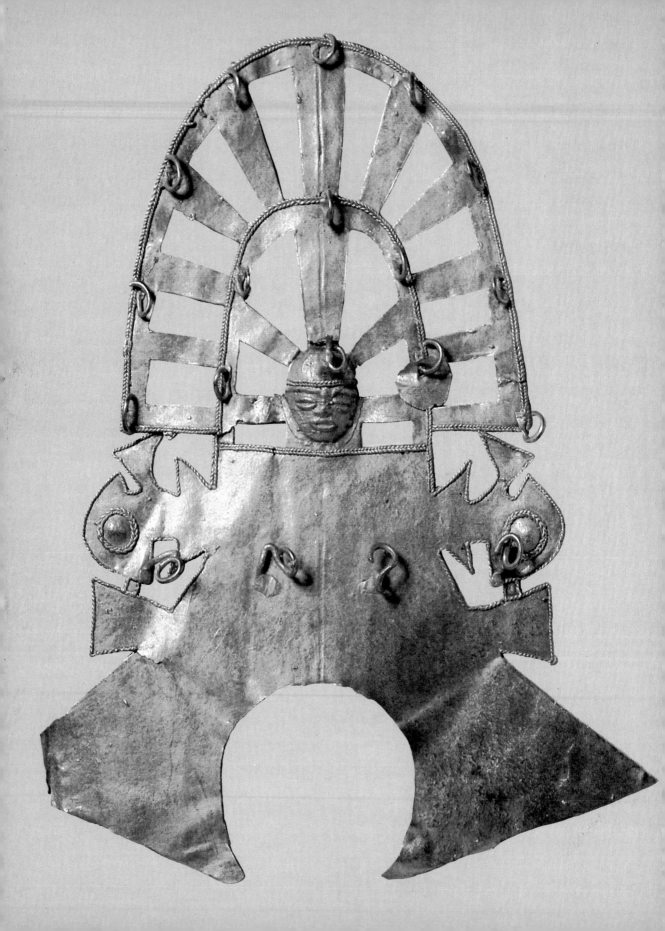

329 Muisca pectoral
Left

339 Openwork
Muisca nose
ornament
Right

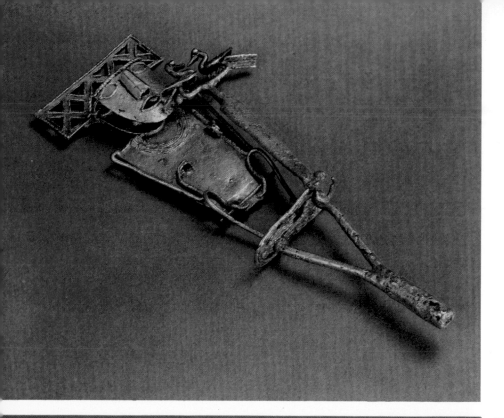

346 Muisca tunjo
Top left

363 Pendant
Bottom left

366 Shallow bowl
Right

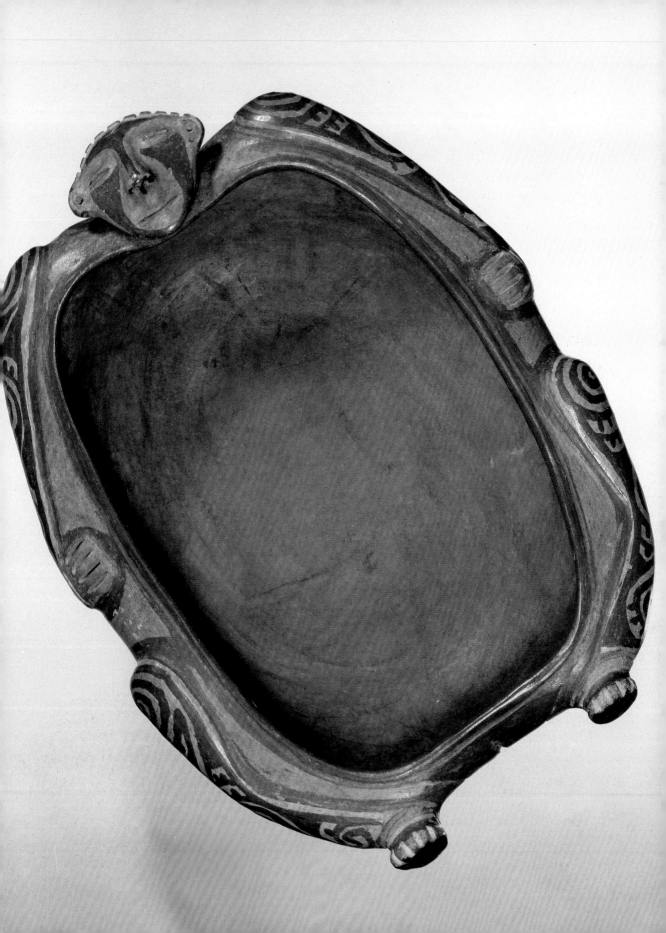

377 Lime-container
Left

382 Pectoral disc
Right

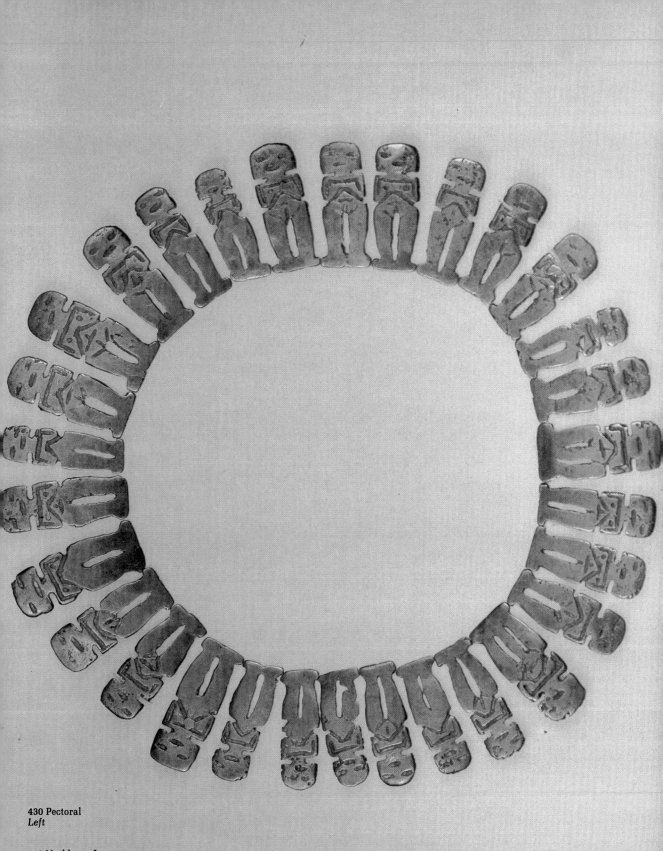

430 Pectoral
Left

440 Necklace of
Tolima figure
pendants
Right

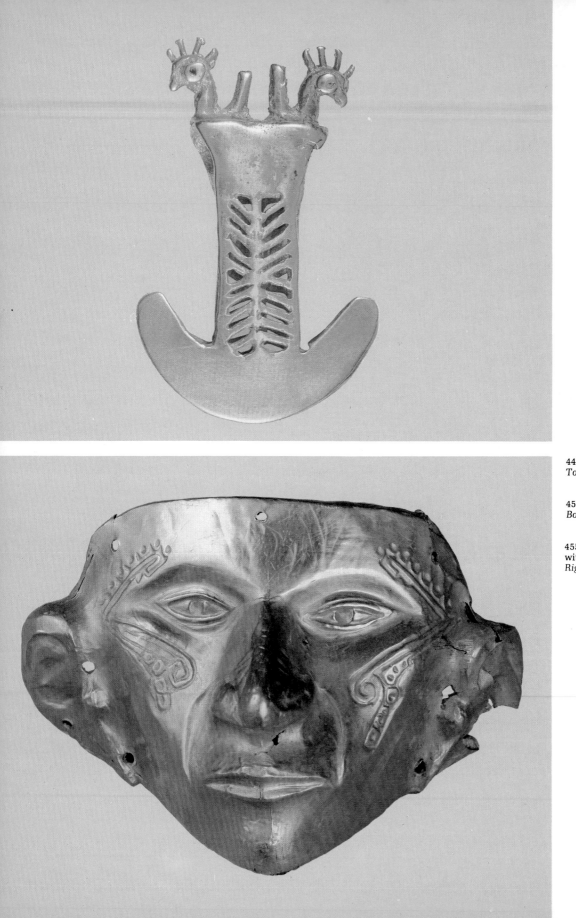

448 Tweezers
Top left

458 Mask
Bottom left

455 Pectoral, figure
with head-dress
Right

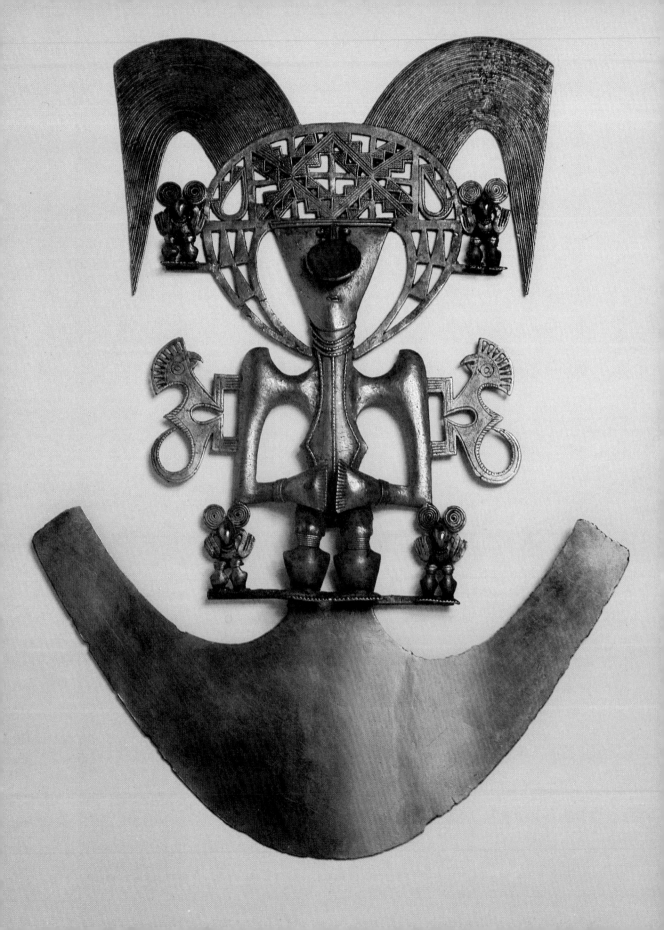

489 Embossed
disc pendant
Left

496 Nose
ornament
Bottom right

529 Nose
ornament
Top right

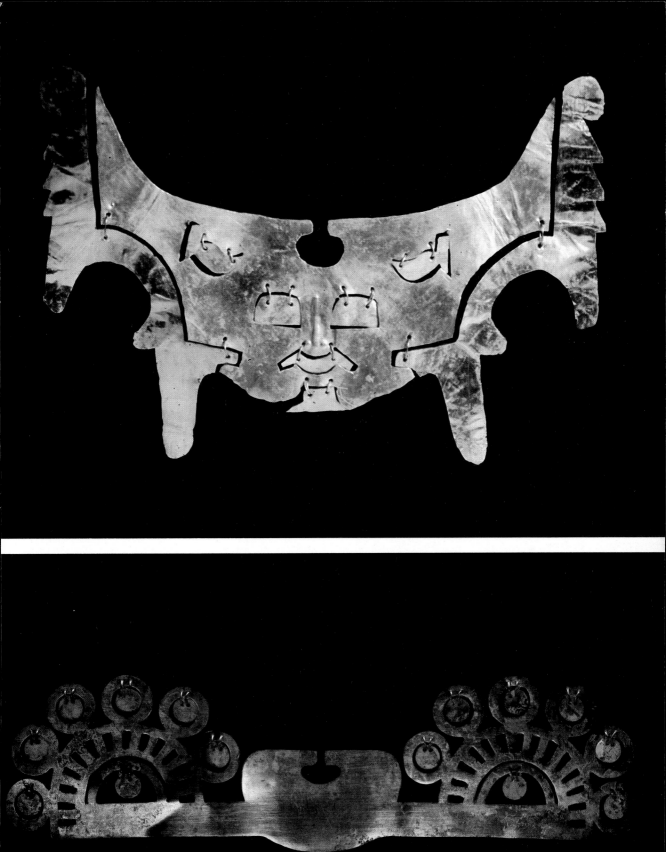

514 Male seated
figure
Left

512 Female seated
figure
Right

540 Lime-dipper
Top left

571 Burial urn
Bottom left

550 Calima alcarraza
Right

573 Painted burial
urn

CATALOGUE OF EXHIBITS

Spain and the First Voyages

1 Model of Columbus's flagship, the Santa María

The largest of the three vessels during the voyage of 1492 which led to the discovery of America. The ships used in the great voyages of discovery were the ordinary merchantmen of the day, many of them (like the *Santa María*) built in the Atlantic ports of Spain and Portugal. No detailed description exists of the *Santa María*, and the model represents a generalized version of a typical small merchant ship of the late 15th century. Recent research indicates that the square transom stern shown on the model was not introduced until the start of the 16th century (*see* the ship drawings in the Ribeiro chart and the Codex Köler, nos. 2 and 13). The *Santa María* would have had the older, round stern.

Surprisingly, we have more information about the crew than about the *Santa María* herself. Ninety men sailed with Columbus; about forty in the *Santa María*, and the rest divided between the two smaller caravels. Each ship carried a master (who commanded the crew and looked after the cargo) and also a pilot, responsible for navigation. These two officers received the same wage, twice that of an ordinary seaman. In addition each ship had a boatswain (responsible for anchors, sails and rigging), a steward (for provisions and stores), a carpenter, a caulker, a cooper and a 'surgeon'. There was no specialist sailmaker or cook. The crew slept on deck, for hammocks (a native American invention) were unknown to Europeans until Columbus's landfall in the West Indies. All cooking was done over a firebox on the deck. Besides wine and fresh water, the stores included beef or pork in brine, barrels of salt fish, ship's biscuit, flour, onions and garlic, cheese, and dried peas or beans (Gould 1924–43; Parry 1973: 96–101).

The model is at a scale of 1/20, and represents a ship just over 30 m long, with part of the planking removed to show the construction.
Science Museum, London *1923.26*

1

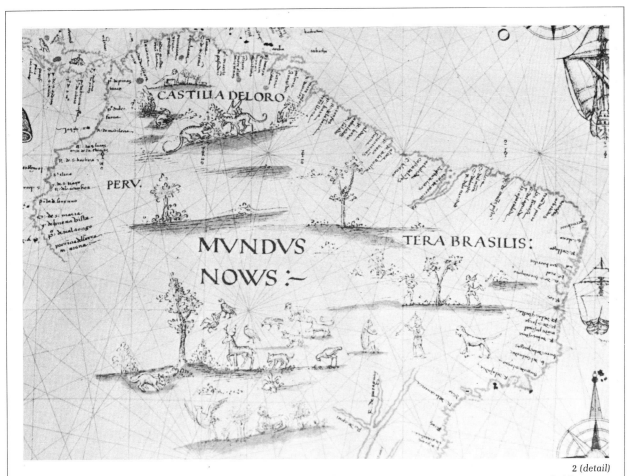

2 World chart, 1529

The text along the upper and lower borders reads: 'Universal chart in which is contained all that has been discovered in the world until now. Diogo Ribeiro, Cosmographer of His Majesty, made it in the year 1529 at Seville. Which is divided into two parts according to the capitulation which took place between the Catholic Kings of Spain and King John of Portugal at Tordesillas in the year 1494.' The Treaty of Tordesillas defined the Spanish and Portuguese spheres of influence, allowing Spain to control all lands lying westward of an imaginary north-south line fixed at 370 leagues west of the Azores. This treaty eventually gave the Spanish Main and the West Indies to Spain, and Brazil (then undiscovered) to Portugal. The Tordesillas line is drawn on Ribeiro's chart, with the domains of the two powers marked by their national flags.

Although born in Portugal, Ribeiro was cartographer and instrument-maker to the Casa de la Contratación (House of Commerce) in Seville, founded in the early 16th century by the Spanish government to train and license navigators for the America trade. Both the Spanish and the Portuguese tried to prevent cartographical information passing to their competitors, and world charts were not therefore carried on normal voyages. From 1508, the Casa began to keep a record of all discoveries, incorporating information provided by individual captains into a series of master charts that were continuously amended and revised.

The Ribeiro chart is the finest of these. In the corners are pictures of an astrolabe (see no. 5) and a pilot's quadrant. In the centre is a wind rose or compass, surrounded by drawings of the signs of the Zodiac. The principal coat of arms is of Pope Julius II (1443–1513). There are several drawings of 16th-century ships, including (on either side of South America) a group accompanied by the legend *voy a Maluco* ('I go to the Moluccas') – a reference to Magellan's 1522 discovery of the western route to the Spice Islands by way of Cape Horn. By 1529 the Caribbean coast of Colombia was well known. The chart marks, among other places, Santa Marta, Cartagena and Cenu (the Sinú region).

The original chart, on parchment, measures 85 x 204.5 cm and is in the Vatican Library, Rome (Cortesão and Teixeira da Mota 1960: 101–3). On exhibition is a slightly reduced facsimile (61 x 141 cm) by W. Griggs, published in 1886.
BL *Maps S.T.W.1*

3 Navigator's dividers

Bronze. Augsburg: German, 16th century, with the town mark of a wheel. Found in the river Rhine.

Dividers, used with a straight edge, were the basic equipment for navigating by means of a plane chart, with no indication of latitude or longitude. The pilot used his dividers to calculate distance against a scale, and to plot the ship's course along a compass bearing, marking the vessel's position by pricking the parchment of the chart with the point of the dividers.
Length 29.7 cm
BM/MLA (Horology) 1903.2–18.1

4 Mariner's compass

Late 16th century; perhaps Italian. Probably the oldest surviving compass in Europe.
'And for eleuations, a plaine Astrolabe exactly made, and a crosse staffe, are sufficient . . . Vnto the whiche maie bee added the Topographicall Instrument for taking of distances, and making descriptions vpon the land. With these Instrumentes, and the Sailyng Cumpasse and Marine plat [chart] . . . the whole worlde maie bee trauelled, discouered & described.'
(William Barlow, Discours of the Variation of the Cumpas or Magneticall Needle . . . 1581)
The needle is a magnetized iron wire, bent double and glued to the underside of the card, orientated from north to south. The wire and card pivot on a brass pin, and the compass is mounted in two brass gimbals (pivoted rings which hold it steady against the roll of the ship). The card is graduated in thirty-two points, with north indicated by a fleur-de-lis. The bowl is of ivory. Being made of soft iron, 16th-century needles tended to lose their magnetism, and every navigator's kit would include a lodestone with which the needle could be 'fed' from time to time.
Diameter 10.8 cm
National Maritime Museum, London
C.82/52–126

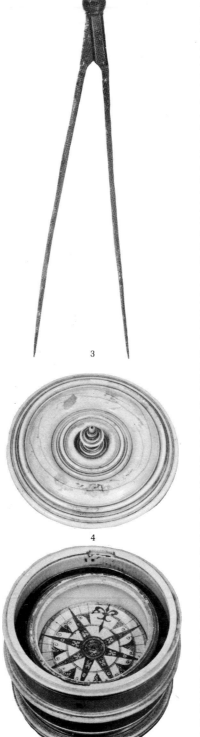

3

4

5a–b Mariner's astrolabe

The mariner's astrolabe is an instrument for calculating latitude by measuring the angle of the sun or of the Pole Star above the horizon. Probably developed during the closing years of the 15th century, it was specially designed for use at sea, on a moving ship. It consisted of a brass openwork ring in the shape of a spoked wheel, with angles of elevation marked on the circumference. In the centre was pivoted an alidade (sighting device) which moved over the scale. The body of the astrolabe was made thick and heavy, so that it hung steadily from its suspension swivel, and the spoked form offered less wind resistance than a solid disc. Projecting from the alidade were two vanes, or sights, each vane usually provided with both a small and a large hole. The Pole Star was directly observed by sighting through the large holes, but the sun's altitude was measured by projecting the sun's rays through the smaller holes, as in the drawing (b).

(a) Mariner's astrolabe of 1555
This is the oldest dated example surviving to the present (though a slightly earlier one, dated 1540, disappeared during World War II). Unlike most astrolabes, which measure the angle above a horizontal horizon, the scale on this example measures zenith distances, i.e. the angle measured downwards from the vertical zenith line. This peculiarity may indicate Portuguese manufacture, and it has been suggested that the five stamped circles (present also on the 1540 astrolabe) are the mark of the Portuguese cartographer and instrument-maker Lopo Homem. On the reverse is crudely stamped ANDROW SMYTON 1688. Smyton (or Smieton) was a Dundee shipmaster in the 1680s, a time when there was much trade in salt between the Bay of Biscay and Dundee. (Anderson 1972: 10).
Diameter 22.2 cm
City of Dundee District Museums and Art Galleries Dept.
(b) Woodcut showing the use of the

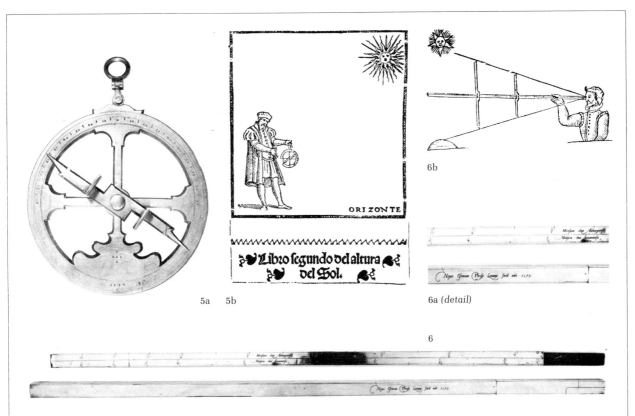

5a   5b

6b

6a (detail)

6

mariner's astrolabe
The navigator is using the astrolabe to determine the meridian altitude of the sun. From Pedro de Medina, 1563. *Regimiento de navegación*, Seville. BL *C.125.b.4*

6a–b Cross staff

Like the astrolabe, the cross staff is basically a device for measuring the angular elevation of the sun or of a star above the horizon. It was first described in 1328 by the Provençal Jewish scholar Levi ben Gerson, but seems not to have been used by seamen until the early 16th century. Because of its crossbow-like shape, it was also called *balestilha*, *arbalista* etc. (hence the phrase to 'shoot' the sun). Under this alternative name it is listed in a legal document of 1533 concerning a certain John a Borough (Master of the *Michal* of Barnstaple), whose possessions included 'a Balestoio, a Quadryant and a lodestone and a Rynning glasse' (Maddison 1969: 46–51; Wynter and Turner 1975).

The device consists of a square-sectioned rod, usually of box wood, on each face of which are scales of degree from 0° to 90°, which can be read off when the sliding cross-piece is aligned. The manner of use is shown by a diagram in a manual of navigation, first published in 1595 (b). The navigator fits the appropriate cross-piece, places the staff to his eye, then moves the cross-piece along the shaft until the lower edge appears to touch the horizon and the upper edge aligns with the bottom of the sun. In the late 16th century a second cross-piece was often added, to increase the accuracy of measurement. From the angle of the sun (or, alternatively, of the Pole Star) above the horizon, the navigator can compute his latitude.
(a) Cross staff of 1571
Brass on a wooden core. The cross-piece is a reconstruction. This is the second oldest surviving cross staff, and was probably not intended for use at sea. On one of the brass plates is the inscription: *Nepos Gemmae*

Phrisy Louanÿ fecit año 1571 (Made by the nephew of Gemma Frisius at Louvain in the year 1571). Frisius and his nephew Gualterus (Walter) Arsenius were famous instrument-makers to the European astronomical world, and Tycho Brahe records that he once owned an Arsenius cross staff of just this kind, and was not too well pleased with it because the wooden core began to warp (Maddison 1969: 49). The staff is made in two joining sections and is engraved on three sides. It has a scale of degrees of arc, a linear scale of equal parts, and separate scales of Antwerp and Louvain linear measure.
Length 139.2 cm
BM/MLA (Horology) 86.6–30.1
(b) Diagram to show the use of the cross staff
From *The Seaman's Secrets, devided into 2 partes, wherein is taught the three kindes of Sayling. . . .* By Iohn Davis. London 1595.
Second edition 1626.
BL *533.f.30*

7

7 Portrait of the Emperor Charles V
(1516–58)
Oil on panel. Studio of Bernart van
Orley (1488–1541). Probably in the
collection of Henry VIII, for an
inventory of 1542 lists a portrait of
Charles V, 'his doublet being cutt
and a rosemary braunch in his
hande'. Painted c. 1520–5, and
thought to have been presented by
Charles to Henry VIII, whose first
Queen, Catherine of Aragon, was
the Emperor's aunt. The King and
the Emperor met in 1520 (Millar
1977, exhibit no. 6). It was during the

reign of Charles V that the interior
of Colombia was explored and
colonized.
Dimensions 43.4 x 32.2 cm
Coll. H.M. The Queen

8a–j Gold coins of Charles V
(1516–58)
Although the Caribbean coast was
colonized during the joint reign of
Ferdinand II and Isabella, the
exploration of interior Colombia
took place under their grandson,
Charles I, better known as the

Emperor Charles V. Charles was the
most powerful monarch in Europe,
and (as this selection of coins shows)
his domains were spread over the
entire continent. He was Holy
Roman Emperor, ruler of the
Spanish kingdoms, the Netherlands,
Austria, Naples and Sicily, and parts
of northern Italy. Gold coins were
not yet minted in the colonies of
Spanish America, though metal was
refined and smelted in the major
New World cities for shipment to
Spain.
(a) ducat (3.60 g. gold). Valencia.
    BM/CM 1853–9–28–1
(b) ducat. Majorca. BM/CM 1893–10–
    3–9
(c) ducat. Sicily. The obverse (with
    cross) labels Charles as King of
    Spain and Sicily. BM/CM 1856–
    9–1–35
(d) ducat. Naples. The obverse has a
    portrait of Charles, and the title
    Roma.R.Carolus (Charles, King
    of the Romans). BM/CM 1849–
    11–21–632
(e) ducat. Naples. A little later than
    (d). Charles is shown in Roman
    style, and the inscription now
    reads *Carolus IIIII. Rom. Imp.*
    (Charles V, Emperor of the
    Romans). BM/CM 1919–2–14–295
(f) double ducat. Aragon. Double
    portrait of Charles and Joanna,
    with the shield of Aragon on the
    reverse. BM/CM 1909–10–6–14
(g) double ducat. Barcelona. BM/CM
    Sarah Banks 149–109
(h) escudo (a coin of 3.4 g.). Castille
    and Leon. Segovia mint, with a
    mint mark depicting the Segovia
    aqueduct.
    BM/CM 1926–9–1–1
(i) double scudo. Milan. The obverse
    shows Charles as Holy Roman
    Emperor. The reverse depicts the
    pillars of Hercules, thought in
    classical times to stand on either
    side of the Straits of Gibraltar.
    BM/CM 1853–8–15–23
(j) crown (*couronne d'or*). Brabant,
    Netherlands. Dated 1553. The
    symbol on the obverse incor-
    porates the fleur-de-lis motif of
    French coinage, since Charles
    was the descendant of the Dukes
    of Burgundy. BM/CM 1928–1–9–1

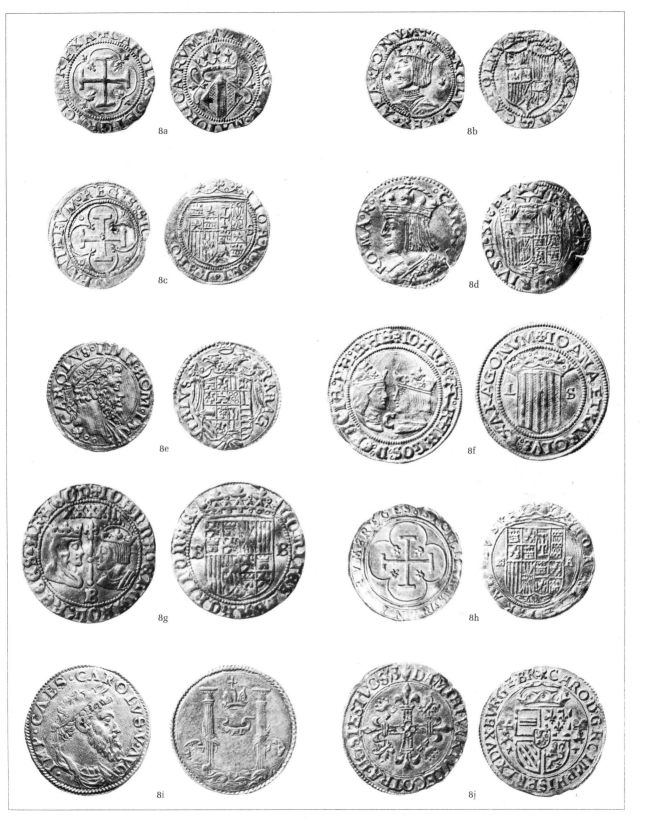

8a

8b

8c

8d

8e

8f

8g

8h

8i

8j

9c

9a–d Spanish Majolica

In the early years of the 16th century, the new Spanish colonies were not yet self-sufficient in manufactured goods. Trade with the Americas was an official monopoly of the merchants of Seville and Cadiz, and records of their cargoes were carefully filed away in Spain. From these shipping manifests there is evidence that both plain pottery (notably jars for oil, wine and olives) and also decorated Spanish wares were exported to the Caribbean ports. Archaeologically, fragments of plain, green-glazed, wheel-made pottery are common on Indian sites of the contact period. Expensive fine wares, like the majolicas, are rare outside the Spanish cities, but have been found in Indian villages near the coast of Colombia, and also inland, in Muisca territory (Goggin 1968).

The term *majolica* is used for tin-enamelled earthenware. In the *cuerda seca* technique of decoration, the outline of the design was drawn on the vessel with a greasy substance, and the intervening areas filled with coloured glazes or enamels. The grease line prevented the colours from running into each other during firing. After the grease had burned away, the underlying terracotta was exposed in these protected areas. The colours are thus outlined, in relief, by unglazed lines.

(a) Dish; Seville, first half of the 16th century

Enamelled earthenware; *cuerda seca* technique. On a white field is a rather gormless unicorn in brown and green, surrounded by floral forms.

Diameter 44 cm

Victoria & Albert Museum, London (*Dept. Ceramics*) 300–1893

(b) Dish; Seville, first half of the 16th century

Enamelled earthenware; *cuerda seca* technique. Blue-and-yellow bird, on a white background. The remaining surface is filled with conventional devices, and round the rim is a green border.

Diameter 22.7 cm

Victoria & Albert Museum, London (*Dept. Ceramics*) 1461–1870

(c) Dish; Talavera, mid-16th century

Majolica, painted in blue with a deer; the border has the so-called *mariposa* (butterfly) pattern. This type of pottery was one of the standard 16th-century wares of Spain, produced at both Talavera de la Reina and at Puente del Arzobispo (Castille). The designs derive ultimately from Hispano-Moresque pottery, and Moorish potters were probably employed at this time to paint the wares. The quality of such pieces varies considerably, but this is a particularly fine and bold specimen. (Martínez Caviro 1969, pl. 1A and Ainaud de Lasarte 1952, fig. 679)

Diameter 34.5 cm

Private collection

(d) Dish; Talavera or Puente del Arzobispo, c. 1600–25

Majolica, painted in blue and orange, with manganese outlines and details, depicting a Spanish warrior on a stylized floral ground. Wares painted in these colours show a wide variety of designs and were popular over a long period (c. 1550–1675). They were made at Talavera de la Reina and Puente del Arzobispo, but quite similar wares were made in Seville and it is not always easy to differentiate them. At some time during its long life, the edge of this dish was damaged and ground down in order to preserve the piece. (Frothingham 1944, fig. 28 and Martínez Caviro 1969, fig. 14A)

Diameter 28.5 cm

Private collection

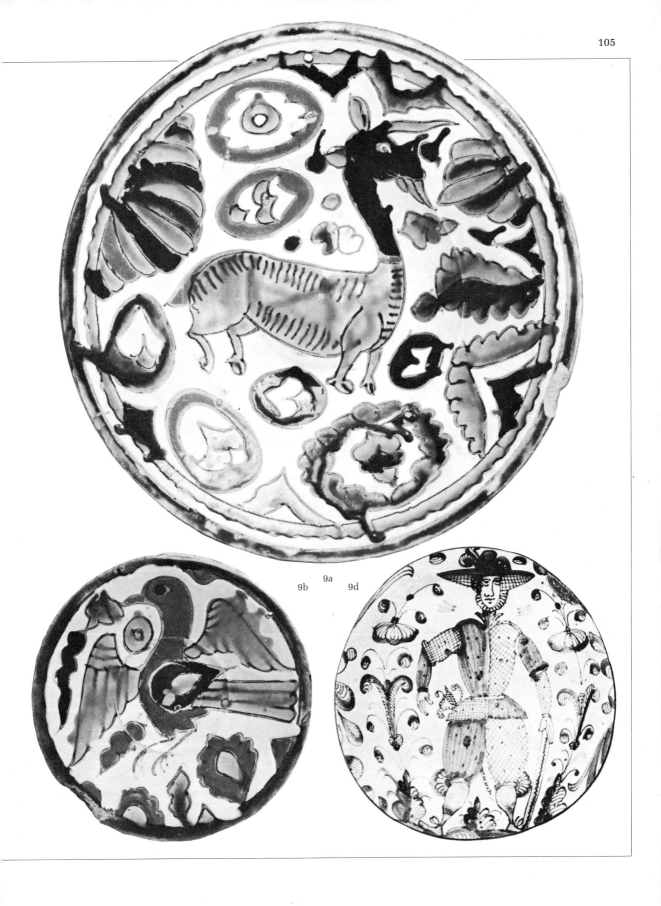

9b   9a   9d

10a–c Spanish trade goods

Relations between the Spanish and Indians were not always unfriendly, and European goods reached native settlements in fairly large quantities as presents or as a result of trade. As early as 1529, an expedition under Pedro de Lerma was offering the Taironas agricultural tools of iron, and also 'many beads, many combs, knives and scissors, coloured hats, caps, and shirts finely worked at the neck' (Castellanos, II: 359). Another list of 1536 included shirts, doublets, coloured caps, axes, spades and hoes (Castellanos, II: 437). Wine was also a popular article of trade. By 1572–3 the Indians were becoming more sophisticated in their wants, and we find a Tairona chief from the Bonda region (who already wore a sword and dagger) asking for arquebuses, gunpowder and shot (Castellanos, II: 625). Like any other prized possessions, European articles were placed in Indian tombs as funerary offerings.

(a) Bronze scabbard tip
From a tomb at Colosó, Sucre, in the Sinú region.
Length 5.2 cm
Galería Cano, Bogotá

(b) Iron axe
A permit written in Toledo on 10 August 1529 grants a certain Alvaro de Torres a licence to barter up to 200 iron axes with the Indians of Santa Marta (Suárez 1913: 19).
From the same tomb as (a).
Length 10 cm
Galería Cano, Bogotá

(c) European glass beads
Glass beads, especially the blue and green Venetian types, were a standard article of trade on European voyages of discovery. Of the very first European contact with native Americans (in the Bahamas), Columbus wrote in his log book: 'I gave some of them red caps and glass beads which they hung around their necks, also many other trifles . . . They afterwards swam out to the ship's boats in which we were sitting, bringing us parrots and balls of cotton thread and spears and many other things, which they

exchanged for such objects as glass beads, hawks and bells.' These glass beads occur all over Spanish America on Indian sites of the contact period. In Colombia they are found with Sinú, Tairona and Muisca materials, proving that the goldwork of these styles was still flourishing when the Spaniards arrived.

The long beads of rectangular or twisted section vary in colour from greenish-blue to dark blue. The small beads are white, black, blue and dark red. There are also some globular, multicoloured beads, and a few tubular, striped ones.
From a tomb at Kilómetro 1 – Apartado, Antioquia.
Longest blue beads c. 4 cm
Galería Cano, Bogotá

10a

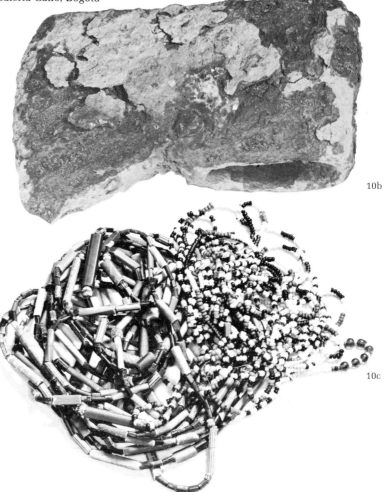

10b

10c

Lake Guatavita and the Legend of El Dorado

11 Portrait of Gonzalo Jiménez de Quesada
Oil on canvas. Quesada led one of the three expeditions which converged on the Muisca homeland in 1538–9, and he was joint founder of the national capital at Sante Fe de Bogotá. The inscription on the painting reads: 'Gonzalo Ximenez de Quesada, Commander of the Order of Santiago, Cavalier of His Highness the King of Spain in the Conquest and Foundation of the Kingdom of New Granada. He was a very famous soldier.' By an anonymous 18th-century painter, but believed to be an authentic likeness.
Dimensions 88 x 65 cm
MN *557*
Colour plate

12 Quesada's coat of mail
Belonged to the Conquistador Gonzalo Jiménez de Quesada.
16th century.
Weight 4.72 kg
MN *1*

13 The Codex Köler
Papers of the Köler family of Nuremberg, containing an illustrated account by Hieronymous Köler of the expedition that left for Venezuela in 1534, and led to the opening up of interior Colombia. Under Charles V, the German banking and trading house of Welser was given a concession to colonize what is now Venezuela. The city which they founded at Coro, on the Caribbean coast, was the base from which Nicolaus Federmann set out in 1537 on the march that took him to the Muisca homeland. Hieronymous Köler, then a young man of twenty-seven, did not take part in Federmann's expedition, but he left an eyewitness description of the way in which the undertaking was organized in Spain. Each member had to be approved by the Casa de Contratación in Seville, and registered in its books. The men then collected their equipment, heard Mass, and marched in procession to the port. The sailors were a surprisingly mixed lot. The crew of Köler's own ship was 'part Scots,

part English, some Flemings, but the greater number Biscayans, Spanish and Italians, about 30 persons, who could hardly understand each other. There were also some orientals among them.' Köler's pictures of the *islands* of Venezuela show Indians with golden plates and vessels, drawn in a naive and inaccurately European style (Friede 1961; von Hagen 1974).

This illustration shows a part of the procession in Seville, accompanied by drummers and by the red-and-white banner of the Welsers.
BL *Add. Ms. 15217*
Colour plate

14 Nicolaus Federmann's sword
Steel. Once belonged to the Conquistador Federmann. On one side of the blade is the inscription *Viva el Rey de Portugal*, and on the other is engraved *Domini Causa Vencio 1539*.
Found at Pasca, Cundinamarca
Length 99 cm
MN *28*

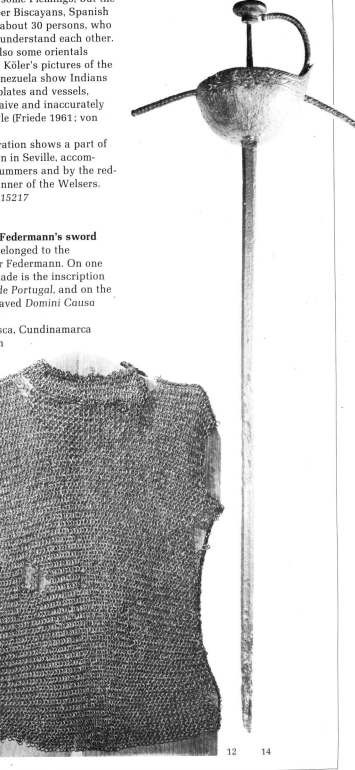

12   14

15a–f Spanish Footsoldier *c.* 1535
The explorers of New Granada were
not a hand-picked elite. Cieza de
León recorded in 1554 that *'scarcely
a year elapsed without seeing an
expedition fitted out . . . People of all
ages and every grade of society
flocked . . . but the majority were
either coarse and avaricious
adventurers, or disappointed
courtiers.'* Their equipment would
have reflected this, varying from the
full armour of the few horsemen or
caballeros who accompanied the
infantry, to makeshift defences used
by the majority.

Among the alternatives for armour
were cuirasses and quilted cotton
'jacks', both popular in the previous
century. The Cortes and Pizarro
expeditions recorded only jacks
(often referred to as the poor man's
substitute for armour), but Heredia's
Colombian expedition considered
cuirasses initially, taking on board
*'leather cuirasses which had been
prepared as a protection against the
poisoned arrows'.* (*Pedro de Cieza de
León*, 1864) However, these were
subsequently rejected in favour of
*'cotton for defensive armour, the
moisture not being suitable for
cuirasses.'* (*Pedro de Cieza de León*,
1864)

Although worn in 16th-century
Europe by sailors and soldiers – as
here, with mail sleeves and helmet –
the quilted cotton defence seems to
have been particularly suited to the
conditions of the Americas, where it
was principally accompanied by
swords and lances. By 1573 cotton
armour was so accepted for the
American expeditions that it was
issued to every soldier on de Soto's
Florida expedition.
(a) Reproduction of a quilted cotton
doublet *c.* 1530. (Not illustrated)
(b) Italian sword *c.* 1480
V & A M43 1947
(c) Spanish helmet and bevor
TL IV-500
(d) Mail sleeves
TL III-1428
(e) Gauntlets *c.* 1500
TL III-1197-8
(f) German halberd *c.* 1520
TL VII-1516

15b

15f

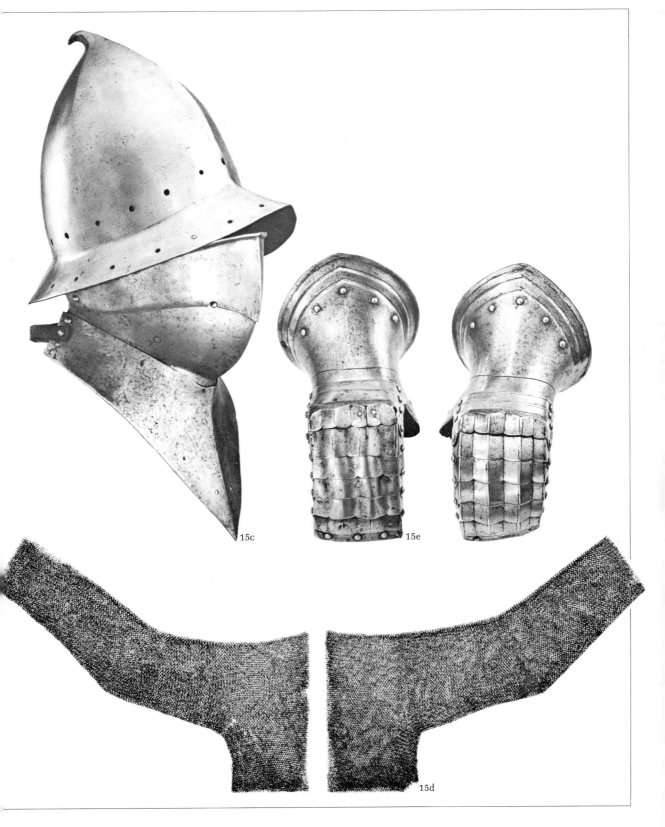

15c

15e

15d

16 Muisca tunjo (votive offering), depicting the El Dorado ceremony
Cast gold. This, the most elaborate tunjo ever found, shows several figures on what appears to be a raft. The main participant in the ceremony is much larger than the subsidiary figures, and is the only one who is seated (on a high-backed stool placed between two panels surmounted by semicircular emblems). He also wears more complicated jewellery, including a typical Muisca nose ornament. Just in front of the forward panel are two small figures carrying lime-gourds and lime-dippers. In front of them stand two slightly larger figures holding rattles and with masks in front of their own faces. Beside them is a branch-like object. Around the edges of the raft are six simple figures.
Pasca, Cundinamarca
Length of base 18.3 cm
Replica; Galería Cano, Bogotá
Colour plate

17 The Golden Man; engraving by Theodor de Bry, 1599
This engraving is a good example of the way in which the legend of El Dorado, the Gilded Man, was presented to the European public. De Bry never went to America, and his drawings are based, at second hand, on the works of other travellers. The details are taken from reliable accounts, and the essentials of the story are shown. The new Muisca ruler is being anointed with gold dust, ready for the ceremony in which he washed himself clean and made precious offerings in the waters of Lake Guatavita. One assistant smears him with resin, while another blows gold dust through a tube. The golden goblets of maize beer are a reality (though their shape is more Peruvian than Colombian), but the costumes are pure fantasy. Hammocks were used in lowland Colombia, but not in Muisca territory. The entire scene has been transformed into something more akin to European Classical art than to the ethnographic reality.
From Theodor de Bry, *Historia Americae, Pars VIII*, pl. XV. Frankfurt 1599.
BL C.115.h.3

18 The Discoverie of Guiana by Sir Walter Ralegh (First edition, London 1596)
The discovery of Lake Guatavita in the 1530s left the European imagination still unsatisfied. Travellers' tales, reinforced by half-understood Indian legends and by pure wishful thinking, placed the city of the Gilded Man, the kingdom of El Dorado, in various unexplored regions of South America. El Dorado quickly became a part of European mythology (no. 17). One persistent Spanish story located a golden city called Manoa on the shores of a (non-existent) inland sea in the interior of Guiana. As the title page of his account indicates, Ralegh equated Manoa with the city of El Dorado, and this belief prompted his unsuccessful voyage of exploration in 1595. His expedition obtained a few gold trinkets from the Indians, but found neither gold mines nor the mythical kingdom. A second voyage to the River Orinoco, in 1617, was a fiasco, and Ralegh was executed soon after his return to London in the following year.
BL C.32.g.25

17   18

19 Goldsmiths of Guiana; engraving by Theodor de Bry, 1599
'How the Guianians are accustomed to cast their golden images' – aboriginal technology, as interpreted by an artist who never set foot in America. In the background, workmen are scraping up gold, and melting it in a cauldron (rather than a crucible or brazier). The images are being cast in two-part moulds instead of by the more usual lost-wax method. The composition, dress, and even the shapes of the gold statues, owe more to the European Classical tradition than to South American reality. The caption below the engraving is taken almost word for word from Sir Walter Ralegh's book (no. 18), and begins: 'The inhabitants of the kingdom of Guiana cast their statues and images in general from little grains of gold which they collect from a certain lake not far from the royal city of Manoa . . .' The rest of the caption is a close paraphrase of Ralegh's description (quoted on p. 28). (*See* fig. 8) From Theodor de Bry, *Historia Americae, Pars VIII*, pl. XVII Frankfurt, 1599. (*See also* no. 17)
BL *C.115.h.3*

20 Muisca tunjo, man with shield
Cast gold. The figure wears big ear spools and a plate (?armour) over his chest (Empson 1832, pl. IX, 1). Lake Guatavita. In Empson's words: *'These golden figures were obtained at Bogotá . . . I believe them to have been found in the Lake of Guataveta . . . Persons have been constantly diving for, and seeking by other means, these Indian remains; but as they were only valued as gold, and as the precious metals are always preferred in grains or ingots, it was common for the persons into whose hands they fell, to put them immediately into the crucible . . . I was upwards of three years in the country before I could obtain any, or even a sight of them. The gentleman, who procured these interesting objects for me, was intimately connected with the parties who caused the lake of Guataveta to be drained, doubtless with the*

expectation of meeting with treasures that would repay them for the outlay of many thousands of dollars. The speculation was ruinous to the projectors.'
Since Empson had returned to England with his collection before February 1828, he is almost certainly referring to the drainage efforts of José Ignacio Paris, which began in 1823 (see p. 21).
Height 5 cm
MM *95–17*

21 Brochure issued by Contractors Ltd in 1911
Under the title *Description and Details of Articles recovered from the Sacred Lake of Guatavita*, this pamphlet was issued to shareholders and would-be investors by Contractors Ltd, then engaged in trying to drain the lake (see p. 22). The items listed here were said to have been found on the sides of the lake bed, with the main treasure still remaining to be discovered in the centre. Besides Muisca pieces, the brochure illustrates objects (such as a Calima diadem) which would hardly be expected at a Muisca votive site. This raises the possibility that the Company deliberately added a few spectacular gold pieces to its own items, with the intention of appearing more attractive to investors. The introductory letter announces that the collection would be sold at auction in December of that year (see no. 22). But there was a special offer to shareholders: 'A few of the lesser grade emeralds have been withheld from the sales made, so as to give Shareholders of the Company an opportunity, should they desire to do so, of acquiring an interesting memento of the operations at the Lake, as it is possible that some shareholders may prefer to purchase a small emerald rather than a gold ornament or a piece of pottery.'
MM *Am. A21/13*

20
21

DESCRIPTION AND DETAILS

Of Articles recovered

——— from the ———

SACRED LAKE OF

GUATAVITA,

Republic of Colombia, South America,

Through the operations of

CONTRACTORS, Ltd., 65, London Wall, E.C.

22 Sale catalogue, December 1911
The sale of objects promised in the
Contractors' brochure (no. 21) took
place at the rooms of Sotheby,
Wilkinson & Hodge on 11 December
1911. Sixty-two items of gold and
pottery from Guatavita were sold,
many of the pieces going to
ethnographical museums in Britain,
where they still exist (nos. 23–27).
This annotated catalogue accompanied the pieces bought at the sale
by the British Museum, and gives
details of the buyers and the prices
they paid.
MM *Eth. Doc. 1493*

**23 Hollow vessel, nude man
reclining on a stool**
Pottery, possibly for offerings.
Lake Guatavita. One of the objects
found by Contractors Ltd, and sold
at auction in 1911. Listed (item 35)
and illustrated (pl. V) in the sale
catalogue, no. 22. In 1911, this
unique piece sold for £3.
Height 15.3 cm
CMAA *24.185*

23

CATALOGUE

OF

ANTIQUE GOLD ORNAMENTS

and Pottery

RECOVERED FROM LAKE GUATAVITA, IN THE REPUBLIC OF
COLOMBIA, SOUTH AMERICA,

DURING THE OPERATIONS OF

"CONTRACTORS LTD." OF 65, LONDON WALL, E.C.

AND OTHER PROPERTIES

INCLUDING

A PAIR OF EGYPTIAN GOLD BRACELETS,

AN ANTIQUE MARBLE BUST OF SENECA,

ANTIQUE GOLD RINGS AND ROMANO-SYRIAN GLASS.

WHICH WILL BE SOLD BY AUCTION,
BY MESSRS.

SOTHEBY, WILKINSON & HODGE
Auctioneers of Literary Property & Works illustrative of the Fine Arts.

AT THEIR HOUSE, No. 13, WELLINGTON STREET, STRAND, W.C.
On MONDAY, the 11th of DECEMBER, 1911,
AT ONE O'CLOCK PRECISELY.

MAY BE VIEWED TWO DAYS PRIOR.   CATALOGUES MAY BE HAD.
DRYDEN PRESS: J. DAVY AND SONS, 8-9, FRITH-STREET, SOHO-SQUARE, W.

10

35 A hollow Vessel, formed as a nude man lying on his back on a curved
     seat with four feet, his arms under his head ; *fine and rare, perfect
     but for one foot missing*
                                                See Illustration. Plate V.

36 Another hollow Vessel, of very similar type, but the man holding a
     trumpet to his mouth with both hands

37 A hollow Vessel, formed as the body of a man holding a mace, or
     sceptre, and wearing an elaborate head-dress and a collar of
     pierced discs
                                                See Illustration. Plate IV.

38 A cylindrical Vessel, shaped as a man holding a sceptre, and wearing a
     head-dress very much like the Egyptian Ureus ; one arm missing

39 Another cylindrical Vessel, shaped as the half-length of a warrior, with
     his elbows resting on two supports, the body crossed by lines of
     pendants

40 Another cylindrical Vessel, a fine head of a chief with lofty winged
     head-dress decorated with the annular ornament known as cup
     marks, and wearing an elaborate nose-ring covering the mouth,
     showing the discretion of silence

41 Another, shaped as a man's head with head-dress incised in horizontal
     lines

42 Another, half-length figure of a man with high winged head-dress ; and
     two small Heads from similar vessels   (3)

43 A large jar-shaped Vessel, in the form of a chief's torso (the head mis-
     sing) holding a sceptre, the body crossed by strings of pendants,
     supported on four busts of human figures

44 A curious globular Vessel, on a hemispherical base, with the head of a
     pelican and two pierced handles appearing like the stumps of the
     cut-off wings
                                                ✱✱ Very rare in form.

45 A small cylindrical Vessel, shaped as a man squatting with arms folded
     resting on his knees
                                                See Illustration. Plate V.

22

24, 25, 26 Three miniature Muisca pots
Hollow vessels; animals with human heads.
Lake Guatavita. Bought by the British Museum at the sale of objects recovered by Contractors Ltd (*see* no. 22).
Length of largest animal 11.2 cm
MM *1911.12–13.8–10*

27 Miniature vessel, with feet
Pottery; four holes round the rim.
Lake Guatavita. Bought by the British Museum at the sale of items recovered by Contractors Ltd. Listed and illustrated in the sale catalogue (no. 22).
Height 5.3 cm
MM *1911.12–13.13*

28 Beads
Selection of beads made from quartzite, agate, cornelian and amber.
Lake Guatavita; 'purchased from Mr. Knowles who excavated them'.
In September 1899 Knowles acquired the rights to drain the lake, and in 1900 became associated with Contractors Ltd for whom he worked as Administrator (*see* p. 22).
Length of largest barrel-shaped bead 7.4 cm
CMAA *26.39A–F, 26.41A–C, 26.43, 26.45*

29 Uncut emerald
Lake Guatavita. Obtained from H. Knowles (*see* no. 28).
Dimensions 1.4 x 0.9 cm
CMAA *26.49*

30a–c Three stone objects
(a) Ball-shaped pendant of green stone. Height 1.8 cm
(b) Button bead in red agate. Width 1.8 cm
(c) Small green bead, either waxed or glazed. Diameter 0.8 cm
Lake Guatavita (Beck Collection)
CMAA *47.2353A–C*

27 ▽   ▽ 28   24 25 26△

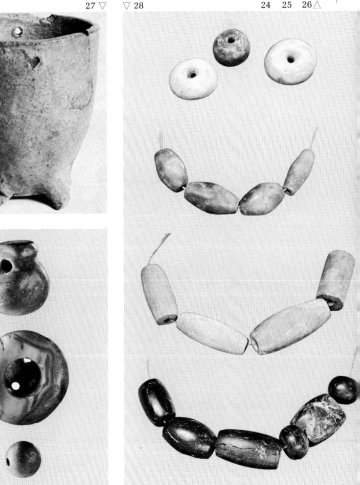

29 ▽   30▷

31a

31h

31f

31a–h Indian in Golden Regalia

(a) **Helmet**
Hammered gold
Rio San Jorge, Ure, Córdoba
Diameter 18.5 cm
MO 8972

(b) **Pair of ear ornaments, with danglers**
Hammered tumbaga with enriched surfaces
Montenegro, Quindío
Heights 10.7, 10.4 cm
MO 24.531/2

(c) **Nose ornament**
Hammered and polished gold
Restrepo, Valle del Cauca
Width 21.5 cm
MO 23.204

(d) **Necklace**
302 hammered gold beads, length 0.2 cm; 7 spiral gold wire ornaments, average length 0.6 cm; 36 green stone beads.
Hacienda Calima, Restrepo, Valle del Cauca
MO 4852

(e) **Pectoral, with human face**
Hammered and repoussé gold, with some detail traced on the front. Nose ornament and ear discs attached by staples. Small hole in the crown of the head.
Restrepo, Valle del Cauca. Early Calima style
Width 30.5 cm
MO 5370
Colour plate

(f) **Pair of sheet metal ornaments**
Hammered gold, with typical Early Calima motifs
Height 22.1 cm
MO 5753/4

(g) **Pair of bracelets**
Hammered gold
Lengths 21.6, 21.4 cm
MO 2784/5

(h) **Ring with stone**
Gold
Diameter 2.3 cm
MO 5575

31b

31c

31d

31g

32 Colossal stone head (cast)
San Agustín (Preuss 1929, I: 35 and
pl. 29, 1; Reichel-Dolmatoff 1972: 34)
Height 2.26 m

33

33 Nose ornament
Hammered gold
Armenia, Quindío
Width 5.2 cm
MO 2403

34 Muisca tunjo, double snake
Cast copper or copper-rich tumbaga
Length 9.6 cm
MO 1122

34

35

35 Nose ornament
Tumbaga with surface enrichment;
hammered. Possible traces of red
paint. The ends of the ornament are
overlapped and bound with thread.
The impression of a woven textile is
preserved by copper corrosion
products near the lower edge.
Highland Nariño
Width 8.9 cm
Coll. Jaime Errazuriz, Bogotá

36 Pendant, seated woman
Coppery tumbaga; open-back
casting. Two suspension holes
through the neck.
Calarcá region, Quindío. (See no. 368)
Height 6.2 cm
MM 1910.12−2.9

37 Ear pendant
Hammered from a cast ingot of
silver-rich alloy. Silver items are rare
in Colombia (in contrast to Ecuador
and Peru), and come mainly from
Nariño on the Ecuadorean frontier.
Miraflores, Ipiales, Nariño
Diameter 6.5 cm
Galería Cano, Bogotá

37

38

38 Platinum eye
Platinum over a gold or tumbaga
base; pupil of green stone. A few
platinum-plated objects are known
from the Esmeraldas region of north
coastal Ecuador, including a mask in
the form of a human face. The style
of these faces resembles that of
Tumaco clay figures. Other masks
from the area are made of gold or
tumbaga, with inlaid platinum eyes.
La Tolita region, Esmeraldas,
Ecuador (eye and pupil from
different sites)
Width of eye 3.1 cm
Coll. Jaime Errazuriz, Bogotá

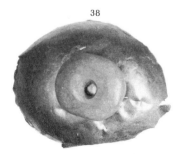

36

39 Pottery crucible
Material scraped from the inside
showed the presence of silver,
copper, tin, zinc and lead; a scraping
from the outside gave traces of
silver and copper (Bray 1972).
Said to have been found in a tomb of
pre-European type at Finca La
Quebrada, near Ginebra, Valle del
Cauca, though a thermoluminescence
date indicates that it was last fired
no more than 120 years ago
(Sampson *et al.* 1972). Possibly, as
often happens, it was heated up by
the finder, in the hope of extracting
gold. (*See* fig. 9)
Height 11 cm
Institute of Archaeology, London
University

40 Mouthpiece of blowpipe
Pottery, with modern cane tube.
Yellow-grey clay, with heavy, incised
ornament. (*See* fig. 11)
Pasca, Cundinamarca. One of several
from this area (Bright 1972).
Length 9.8 cm
MO *CM 5864*

41 Lump of melted gold
The metal still contains quartz
grains and other impurities. (*See*
fig. 12)
From a tomb at La Merced, Restrepo,
Valle del Cauca
Maximum width 5.1 cm
Galería Cano, Bogotá

44

43a–b

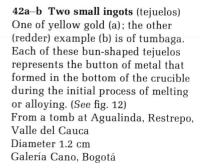

45

42a–b Two small ingots (tejuelos)
One of yellow gold (a); the other
(redder) example (b) is of tumbaga.
Each of these bun-shaped tejuelos
represents the button of metal that
formed in the bottom of the crucible
during the initial process of melting
or alloying. (*See* fig. 12)
From a tomb at Agualinda, Restrepo,
Valle del Cauca
Diameter 1.2 cm
Galería Cano, Bogotá

43a–b Hammer and anvil
Dark, fine grained stone. Gonzalo
Fernández de Oviedo (1535–48)
recorded identical objects among the
Indians of Tamara, at the confluence
of the Cesar and Magdalena rivers:
'. . . *they have forges, anvils and
hammers, which are of hard stone;
some say of black metal like emery.
The hammers are the size of eggs or
smaller, and the anvils the size of a
Majorcan cheese, of another very
hard stone.*'
Santa Marta, Magdalena
Diameter of anvil 18.2 cm
MO *LT 299/300*

44 Foil sheet, funerary vestment
Hammered gold
Ovejas, Sucre
Length of unfolded piece 43 cm;
folded piece 4 cm
MO *24.967/8*

51

45 Tubular nose ornament
Hammered and gilded tumbaga
Minca y Honda, Santa Marta,
Magdalena
Width 12.6 cm
MO *14.929*

46 Pair of Tairona ear ornaments
Sheet tumbaga with enriched
surface. Possibly hammered over a
wooden core, now disappeared.
Bonda, Santa Marta, Magdalena
Height 5.9 cm
MO *24.459/60*

47 Nose ornament
Hammered gold
La Hondura Del Billar,
Ansermanuevo, Valle del Cauca
Width 10.5 cm
MO *19.615*

48 Sinú nose ornament
Hammered gold
Sinú, Sucre
Width 4.7 cm
MO *23.316*

49 Pair of ear danglers
Gold, suspended from hammered
wire. Slightly concave.
Pupiales, Nariño. Capulí period.
Diameters 12.6, 12.8 cm
MO *25.228/9*

**50 Pair of ear danglers with
(?)jaguar heads**
Cast and hammered tumbaga with
enriched surfaces. Probably made
with the aid of a form.
Pupiales, Nariño. Capulí period.
Diameter 9.6 cm
MO *19.492/3*
Colour plate

51 Necklace, with frogs
Composed of objects from two
localities:
(1) Hammered gold. Large frog (with
very clear hammer marks) and
fourteen identical small ones (probably made over a form or template).
From Pereira, Risaralda
Length of large frog 9 cm
MO *2906*
(2) Gold. Twenty-three tubular beads
(Length 1.5 cm) and twenty-six
barrel beads (Length 1 cm).
Finca La Irlanda, Versalles, Quindío
MO *13.157*

46

47

48

49

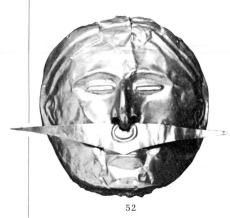

52

52 Mask, with nose ornament
Thin sheet gold; hammered. The nose ornament is made separately, also from hammered metal. The eyes and nostrils are open, and the mask has fastening holes around the edge (Root 1964).
Pereira, near Cartago, Risaralda
Width 16.5 cm
MM *88.7–17.1*

53 Triangular nose ornament
Gilt tumbaga; embossed and hammered sheet.
Stylistically typical of the Quimbaya zone
Width 41.4 cm
MO *1444*

54 Pectoral; disc with human figure
Hammered and repoussé gold
Diameter 14.5 cm
MO *1899*

55 Sinú pectoral with human face
Hammered and embossed gold. The raised circle round the base of the boss is characteristic of the Sinú style, and extends northwards into Costa Rica and Panama.
Palmitas, San Marcos, Sucre
Width 24.8 cm
MO *25.466*

54

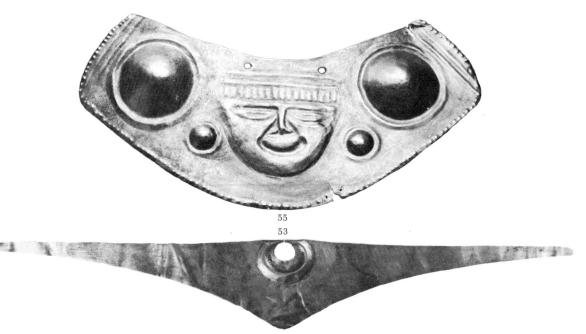

55

53

56a–d Four lost-wax casting moulds
(a) Complete mould, made of porous clay. The nature of the item inside is still unknown. Refilled with modern metal in the laboratory. Height 6 cm.
(b) Complete mould, as found. Shows the pouring channel and two vent holes in the side. Shape of the content still unknown. Height 6.1 cm.
(c) Complete mould, refilled with modern metal and cut open to reveal the content. The section shows the button of metal remaining in the reservoir at the top, below which is the channel through which the metal flowed to replace the wax. The object to be cast was a globular bead, produced by winding wax thread around a core. Height 5.7 cm.
(d) Complete mould, broken into three pieces. The larger piece shows a cross-section of the channel. The two smaller fragments show the content: a little animal. (*See* fig. 23) Part of a larger set found in a tomb at Aguamona, Restrepo, Valle del Cauca (Plazas and Falchetti 1978, fig. 27).
Galería Cano, Bogotá

58

57 Pair of round Sinú ear ornaments, with birds
Cast tumbaga, made by the lost-wax process (*see* p. 32).
Colosó, Sucre
Width 5.7 cm
MO 19.964/5

57

58 Sinú figure pendant
Cast and gilt tumbaga. Two suspension loops behind. On the flat areas of the head-dress are the jeweller's fingerprints, where the original wax model was not completely smoothed before casting. The figure wears a nose ornament of the kind common in Sinú graves (Falchetti 1976).
Ovejas, Sucre
Height 6.3 cm
MO 25.132

59 Muisca tunjo, warrior with spear-thrower and darts
Cast tumbaga with enriched surfaces. Surplus metal from the casting process has not been cleaned off.
Height 7.6 cm
MM *1949 Am 14.1*

59

60 Muisca tunjo, woman
Cast tumbaga. Unremoved excess
metal shows three flow channels,
uniting near the reservoir. The
woman carries a forked staff.
Height. 13.1 cm. (*See* fig. 22)
MO 6370

61 Tolima pectoral
Gold. Cast, with the base stretched
by hammering.
Rio Blanco, Tolima
Height 17.7 cm
MO 6235

**62 Tairona anchor-shaped
ornament**
Cast tumbaga, with enriched surface.
Hollow-cast, by the lost-wax method.
The black core material has not been
removed, and shows through the
damaged metal casing.
San Pedro de la Sierra, Magdalena
Height 2.6 cm
Galería Cano, Bogotá

63 Muisca seated figure
Copper. Hollow-cast by the lost-wax
method. The figure is still full of
black core material, a mixture of
clay with approximately 13% wood
charcoal. Over the core were laid
strips of wax sheet, whose outlines
are still clearly visible in the cast
metal. The face was made by pressing
wax sheet over a stone matrix. The
top of the head is open, and there are
openings in the sides of each leg.
A core sample produced enough
charcoal to give a radio-carbon
date of AD 1055 ± fifty-nine years.
Height 9.4 cm
CMAA 46.22

64 Pair of bells
Gilt tumbaga; lost-wax casting, with
the incised decoration added at the
wax stage. Each bell contains a
metal pellet. This was made first,
and was then incorporated into the
the core material over which wax
was laid to form the bell itself. (*See*
fig. 25)
Probably Quimbaya zone
Height 3 cm
MO 6.172/3

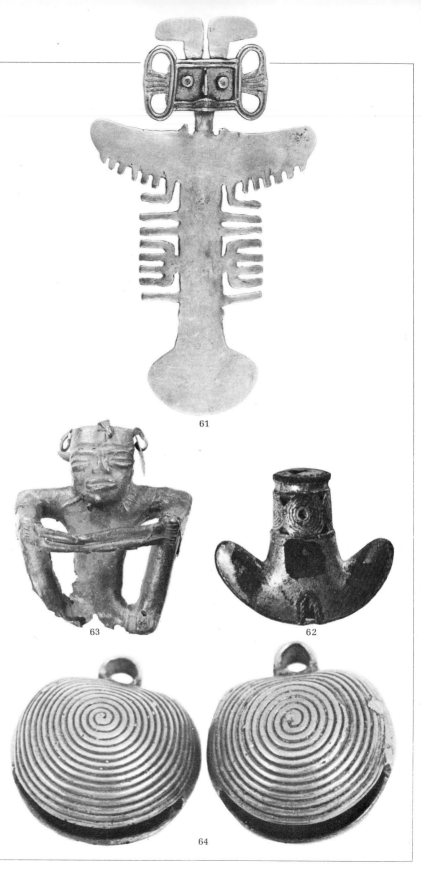

61

63

62

64

65 Muisca stone matrix
Fine grained black stone. These matrices were used to produce matching sets of wax models, which were then cast by the lost-wax method (*see* p. 33). This example has twenty-one different human figures, fish, and insect forms – the latter very similar to no. 66. (*See* fig. 29)
Maximum length 11.5 cm
MM *1925.12–11.1*

66 Muisca necklace pendants
Cast tumbaga. Twenty-six items, including two different insect-like forms. Necklace elements of this kind were mass-produced by using a stone matrix to obtain a series of identical wax models for casting. Similar insect forms are carved on matrix no. 65. (*See* fig. 29)
Length 2.7 cm
MM *1957.7–6.11A–Z*

67 Muisca necklace
Cast gold. The fifty-three elements were produced with the aid of a matrix like no. 65.
Hacienda San José, Carmen de Carupa, Cundinamarca
Height 2.5 cm
MO *8315*

68 Muisca stone matrix
Used to mass-produce wax elements for casting (*see* p. 36). (*See* necklace no. 70)
Maximum length 5.5 cm
MO No number

69 Muisca necklace plaque with spiral ornament
Cast tumbaga. Made with the aid of a stone matrix like no. 68.
Length 1.5 cm
MM *1937.7–6.3*

70 Muisca necklace
Cast gold. The 260 plaques (with their spiral motifs) are a matching set, mass-produced at the wax stage with the aid of a stone matrix like no. 68.
Vereda Santo Domingo, Buenavista, Boyacá
Average width 1.1 cm
MO *10.095*

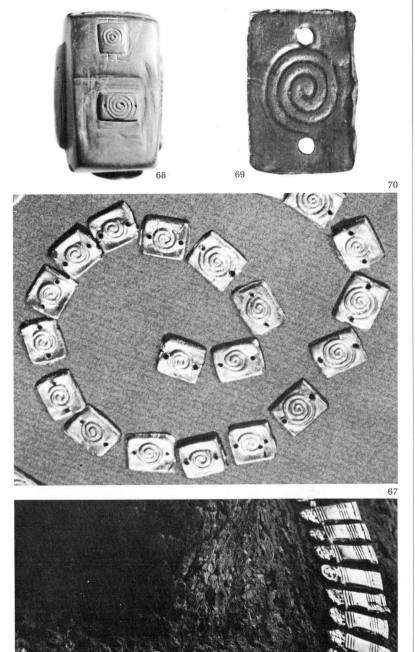

68   69   70

67

71 Sinú nose ornament
Cast gold. Made by the false filigree
process (see p. 36) with wax wire,
and cast in a single operation.
Sinú, Córdoba
Width 13.7 cm
MO 6953

**72 Pair of Sinú ear ornaments, with
animals**
Cast gold. False filigree.
San Marcos, Sucre
Width 5.3 cm
MO 24.798/9
Colour plate

**73 Pair of Sinú ear ornaments, with
animals flanking (?)frogs**
Cast tumbaga with enriched sur-
faces. False filigree.
Bonda, Magdalena. Found in a
Tairona tomb, but of Sinú manufac-
ture.
Widths 6.4, 6.6 cm
MO 13.762/3
Colour plate

**74 Pair of Sinú ear ornaments, with
stylized birds**
Cast gold. False filigree.
Guaranda, lower Cauca Valley,
Bolívar
Width 7 cm
MO 24.733/4
Colour plate

**75 Pair of Sinú ear ornaments, with
animals biting a (?)human figure**
Cast and gilt tumbaga. False filigree.
Palmitas, San Marcos, Sucre
Width 9.9 cm
MO 25.473/4
Colour plate

76 Muisca shell
Cast tumbaga. Produced by winding
wax thread around a core. The
hooks for the danglers were added
at the wax stage. (See fig. 28)
Length 7.8 cm
MO 105

77 Necklace
212 small gold beads. Made by
granulation. (See fig. 19)
Maximum length of individual beads
0.9 cm
MO 3152

78 Pendant, with human face
Cast tumbaga with enriched surface
(now peeling off to reveal the under-
lying copper-rich alloy). The figure
wears a typical Sinú nose ornament.
Belongs to a category of object
widespread in the Sinú and the
Isthmus of Central America
(Falchetti 1976: 85–92).
Sinú region, Sucre
Height 11.2 cm
MO 23.303

79 Bi-coloured plaque
Hammered tumbaga. The colour
contrast is produced by differential
pickling. The gold-coloured areas
were treated with acid plant juices
which removed some of the copper,
to leave a gold-enriched surface (see
p. 38). Elsewhere, the surface was
protected by some acid-resistant
material and still shows the colour
of the original alloy.
Pupiales, Nariño. Piartal period.
Width 6.2 cm
MO 20.996
Colour plate

80 Hanging bi-coloured disc
Tumbaga, with differential surface
pickling. Piartal period.
Miraflores, Pupiales, Nariño
Diameter 14.9 cm
MO 21.223

71

78

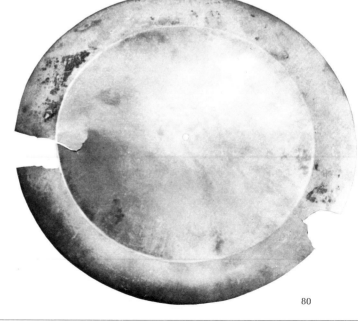

80

81–86 Six fish hooks
Hammered gold
Maximum length 4.7 cm
MO 7086/7, 7089/90/91, 7099

87–90 Four fish hooks
Hammered tumbaga
(87) Length 2.9 cm
MO 1178
(88) Length 3.9 cm
MO 1179
(89) Length 3.5 cm
MO 1172
(90) Length 3.2 cm
MO 3134
Colour plate

91 Spatula
Tumbaga; hammered with enriched
surface.
Tierradentro region
Length 12.8 cm
Coll. Jaime Errazuriz, Bogotá

92 Spatula
Hammered gold. Flat blade, round
shaft. Possibly for wax working.
Length 19.4 cm
MO 5354
Colour plate

93 Chisel
Gilt tumbaga, hammered from a cast
ingot.
Armenia, Quindío
Length 12.9 cm
MO 15.630
Colour plate

94 Chisel
Gilt tumbaga; hammered. It would be
suitable either as a fine chisel or as a
chasing tool.
Length 10.9 cm
MO 327
Colour plate

95 Chisel
Gilt tumbaga; hammered.
Length 7.3 cm
MO 6007
Colour plate

96 Chisel
Gilt tumbaga; hammered.
Minca, Santa Marta, Magdalena
Length 7.8 cm
MO 19.155
Colour plate

97 Chisel
Gilt tumbaga: hammered.
Minca, Santa Marta, Magdalena
Length 4.7 cm
MO 17.995
Colour plate

98, 99, 100 Needles
Hammered tumbaga
(98) Minca, Santa Marta, Magdalena
Length 6.4 cm
MO 10.568
(99) Minca, Santa Marta, Magdalena
Length 9.3 cm
MO 12.851
(100) Manizales, Caldas
Length 11.5 cm
MO 538
Colour plate

101 Trumpet, with a human figure
Embossed sheet gold, folded and
clinched.
San Francisco, Toro, Valle del Cauca
Length 27 cm
MO 393

102 Panpipes
Gilded tumbaga. Piartal period.
Miraflores, Pupiales, Nariño
Length 15 cm
MO 20.104

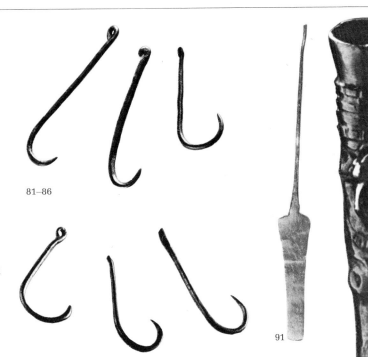

81–86

91

102   101

107

106

103a–h Eight bells
Cast; various alloys.
Pupiales, Nariño. Piartal period.
Heights 5.4–5.8 cm
MO *25.194/8, 25.200, 25.201, 25.203*

104a–d Four bells
Gilt tumbaga; hammered up from
heavy sheet metal. Each bell has a
suspension hole at the top and, when
struck, they give out different notes.
Hacienda El Japón, San Benito Abad,
Sucre, and Majagual, Sucre
MO *7154, 7511, 23.984, 7510* (in
ascending size)

105 Bell
Cast gold
Tairona region, Magdalena
Height 3.8 cm
MO *23.827*

106 Bell, with flange
Cast and gilt tumbaga.
Majagual, Sucre. Also found in the
Tairona area, though this one comes
from the Sinú zone (cf. no. 305).
Height 11.1 cm
MO *7509*

107 Bell, with bird-shaped shank
Cast tumbaga. Contains a metal
pellet and has a hole for suspension.
'Central America'. Stylistically could
be from Caribbean Colombia or the
Isthmus.
Height 3.6 cm
MM *1922.11–4.1*

**108 Bell with long shank and
suspension loop**
Cast tumbaga
Finca Versalles, Vereda Santa Ana,
Armenia, Quindío
Height 6.8 cm
MO *10.493*

103a–h

108

105

104a–d

109 Pair of stars
Tumbaga with enriched surfaces.
Like a button, each star has two
central holes for attachment.
*'Great and valuable banners are
carried before them. I saw one which
was given as a present to Jorge
Robledo. It was a long, narrow
cotton cloth fastened to a pole, and
covered with small pieces of gold in
in the form of stars.'*
*(Pedro Cieza de León on the province
of Carrapa, middle Cauca Valley,
1554)*
Pupiales, Nariño. Piartal period.
Diameter 10.5 cm
MO 20.824/5

110 Circular plaque, star shape
Tumbaga; cut and hammered,
brilliant polish on both faces.
Probably for attachment to textile
backing. (*See* no. 109)
Pupiales, Nariño
Diameter 11.5 cm
MO 20.822

111 Muisca spear-thrower
Hollow cast, in tumbaga with
enriched surface. The hook, which
engages with the javelin butt, is
modelled in the shape of a human
face.
Cogua, Cundinamarca
Length 17.2 cm
MO 24.559

112 Helmet with repoussé ornament
Raised from sheet tumbaga with
enriched surface. The decoration
is embossed from the inside, and
there are details finished on the
outside with the aid of a sharp tool.
A pair of holes at each side for the
attachment of a chin strap.
Quimbaya style (Pérez de
Barradas 1966, I, fig. 13, from the
Treasure of the Quimbayas).
Diameter (longest axis) 19 cm
MM +343

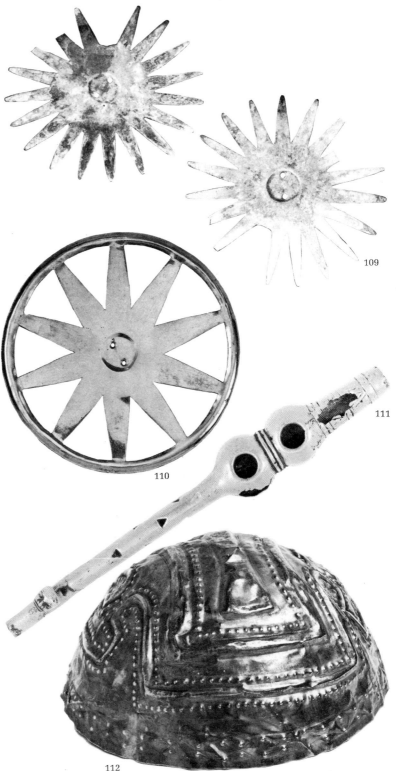

109

111

110

112

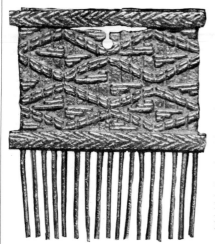

113

115

114

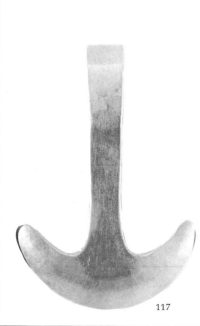

117

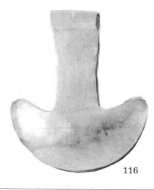

116

118

113 Miniature gold comb
Cast gold. The shape copies the form of comb (with wooden teeth bound together) still used by some Indian groups.
Found by Arthur T. Bennett, a mining engineer (1880–1910), in a shaft about 8.25 m below the surface. Probably from the Quimbaya zone or Antioquia
Width 3.3 cm
AMNH *41.2/496*

114 Depilatory tweezers
Restrepo, Valle del Cauca
Length 9.4 cm
MO *7763*

115 Depilatory tweezers
Hammered gold
Restrepo, Valle del Cauca
Length 6.3 cm
MO *8956*

116 Tweezers
Sheet gold
Restrepo, Valle del Cauca
Height 4.1 cm
MO *24.945*

117 Tweezers
Hammered gold sheet
Restrepo, Valle del Cauca
Height 6.6 cm
MO *24.944*

118 Tweezers, with human figure
Cast and gilt tumbaga. The figure wears a head-dress and earrings. The tweezers have a suspension loop at the top.
Department of Quindío
Height 4.1 cm
MO *3061*

119 Fragment of large Tairona burial urn
Pottery. Red slip. Modelled face with a nose ornament.
Bonda y Gairaca, Santa Marta, Magdalena
Height 16 cm
MO *CT 1031*

120 Tairona nose ornament
Cast tumbaga
Minca, Santa Marta, Magdalena
Width 5.3 cm
MO *15.677*

121 Tairona figure pendant
Cast tumbaga. The figure wears the typical range of Tairona gold jewellery: diadem, crescentic earrings, double-bar nose ornament, and lip plug. All these categories are documented by numerous archaeological specimens (nos. 122–125).
Minca, Santa Marta, Magdalena
Height 6.4 cm
MO *11.445*

122 Diadem
Gilded tumbaga
Minca, Santa Marta, Magdalena
Height 11.9 cm
MO *16.014*

123 Pair of Tairona ear ornaments
Cast gold
San Pedro de la Sierra, Ciénaga, Magdalena
Widths 8.1, 8.3 cm
MO *13.554/5*

124 Tairona double nose bar
Made from a single sheet of hammered tumbaga, with enriched surface (cf. the nose bar worn by figure of no. 121).
Chimichagua, Santa Marta, Magdalena
Length 5.3 cm
MO *11.658*

119

120

122

121

124

123

125 Tairona lip plug
Cast gold
Rio Don Diego, Santa Marta,
Magdalena
Diameter 2.8 cm
MO *24.665*

126 Tairona bird pendant
Cast and gilded tumbaga
San Pedro de la Sierra, Ciénaga,
Magdalena
Height 9.1 cm
MO *14.525*

127 Penis cover
Cast gold. Several Tairona pendants
show figures wearing similar devices.
(*See* no. 236)
Rio Palomino, Magdalena/Guajira
Length 20.4 cm
MO *21.215*

128 Penis cover
Cast gold. The inside is interesting
for the information it gives about the
preparation of the clay core before
this was covered with wax prior to
casting. The sides of the triangles,
and also the base lines on which
they stand, were deeply inscribed in
the core material; then the clay was
removed from the triangular areas
thus delineated. The detail is much
less sharp on the outer surface.
    Bartolomé de Las Casas describes
the use of penis covers among the
Indians of Sinú-Urabá:
*'They walked about . . . in their bare
skins as they were accustomed to in
their own land, their shameful parts
enclosed in tubes of gold shaped like
funnels.'*
The loop allows the object to be tied
to a cord around the waist. The
unimpressive size of this specimen
may arouse doubts about its function
as a penis sheath, but there are other
(and larger) ones from the Sinú
region on which either the testicles
or the glans are indicated.
Majagual, Sucre
Length 10.3 cm
MO *7508*

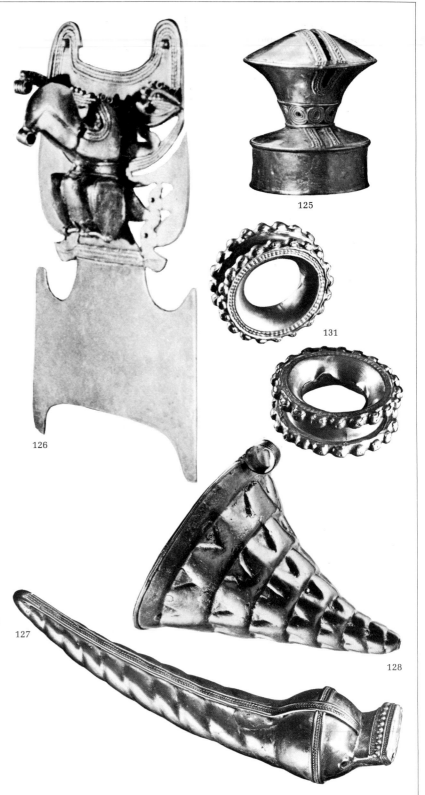

125

126

131

127

128

129 Diadem
Cut and embossed sheet gold. The
nose ornament and ear discs are
stapled to the human face that forms
the centrepiece. The decorative
detail is embossed from the back,
and chased on the front.
Hacienda Calima, Valle del Cauca
Early Calima style
Height 31 cm
MO 4833

130 Plain nose ornament
Hammered gold
Restrepo, Valle del Cauca
Width 22.6 cm
MO 5379

**131 Pair of ear plugs of 'cogged
wheel' type**
Each is made of two pieces of
hammered and embossed sheet gold.
A series of holes shows where the
metal sheets were pinned to each
other and·to the core material.
Finca Grecia, Restrepo, Valle del
Cauca (Pérez de Barradas 1954, I:
58–65). The offerings in this tomb
seem to be the possessions of a
single rich man. Besides the spools,
he had four ear discs (see no. 132), a
breast ornament (see no. 31e), a
necklace, a lime-flask in the form of
an animal, a lime-dipper (see no. 149),
and a gold spoon (see no. 134).
Diameter 8.7 cm
MO 24/25

130

129

132 Pair of concave ear pendants
Hammered gold
Early Calima style
Diameters 16.5, 17 cm
MO *4299/4300*

133 Bowl
Gold, raised from sheet metal. Gold
tableware was reserved for the use
of chiefs:
'. . . . they drink out of golden
goblets, some of which weigh three
hundred castellanos . . . and their
spoons and vessels are of gold.'
(Jorge Robledo, *Description of the
peoples of the province of Anserma*,
1541)
Vereda Calimita, Restrepo, Valle del
Cauca
Diameter 11.7 cm
MO *7528*

134 Spoon
Hammered gold. Finely traced
decoration on the handle.
Finca Grecia, Restrepo, Valle del
Cauca. Found in an Early Calima
grave. (*See* no. 131)
Length 19.2 cm
MO *27*

135 Bowl, copying a gourd vessel
Gold; hammer marks show that it
was raised from sheet metal. The
repoussé design copies the stem scar
on a bowl made from a half gourd.
Campohermoso, Ataco, Tolima
Mouth diameter 17.3 cm
MO *5851*

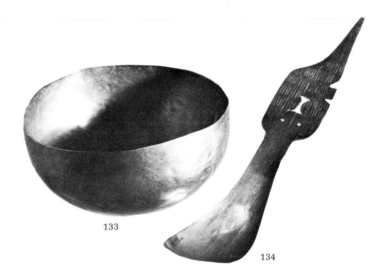

133

134

135

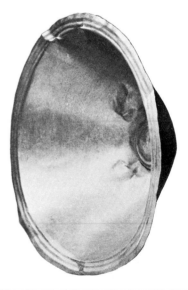

132

136a–b Modern coca bag and lime-gourd

The chewing of the leaves of the coca shrub is widespread in South America today, and for the same reasons as in the past. As one 16th-century conquistador wrote:

'If you ask Indians why their mouths are always occupied with this herb . . . they say that it prevents them from feeling hunger, and gives them great vigour and force.' (Pedro Cieza de León)

Nor has the coca-chewer's equipment changed. The modern objects are of exactly the kind described by Castellanos at the time of European contact:

'Among all the nations of these Indies it is the common custom to chew these leaves called coca . . . With them they use a certain powder or lime made from shells, and they carry it in what they call a poporo, which is a gourd. Into this they put a little stick, and whatever sticks to this they put into the mouth with the leaves.'

The wad, or quid, of coca leaves is kept in the cheek, where it forms a conspicuous bulge, and from time to time small quantities of powdered lime are added. In the Andes, the basic chewing kit thus consists of a bag for carrying the leaves, and a lime receptacle with a mouth just wide enough to take the spatula or dipping stick.

Woven bag, with coca leaves: height without strap 24 cm
Calabash *poporo* with wooden stopper: height 7 cm
Both from San Andrés de Pisimbalá, Tierradentro
Coll. Alec Bright, Bogotá

136

137

137a–b Modern lime-gourd and dipper

From the Kogi Indians of the Sierra Nevada de Santa Marta. At puberty, boys are initiated into the chewing of coca and are given their first lime-gourds. Since the gourd is viewed as female and the spatula as male, the action of inserting the lime-dipper has sexual connotations. The lime-encrusted lip of the gourd is built up by rubbing the spatula around the rim of the container (Reichel-Dolmatoff 1949–50; 1951). (*See* fig. 34)
Height of gourd 14.5 cm
MN *No number*

138 Tairona miniature jar, seated figure

Grey-black pottery, carved as if it were wood. The figure wears a jacket, and over the left shoulder he carries a woven bag similar to the *mochila* in which present-day Kogi Indians carry their coca paraphernalia. The ends of the stool are in the form of animal heads.
Minca, Santa Marta, Magdalena
Height 7.3 cm
MO *CT 1040*
Colour plate

139 Muisca tunjo

Cast tumbaga. In his right hand the figure holds a lime-flask and stick; in his left hand he carries a cup or dish. On his back is a shield. Castellanos notes that Muisca men were buried with their coca bags and lime-gourds. (*See* frontispiece)
Pasca, Cundinamarca
Height 7.9 cm
MO *25.614*

140 Lime-container

Heavy sheet gold with repoussé ornament. The object was made as two hemispherical units, joined around the 'equator'.
Height 7.6 cm
MO *5563*

141 Flask with lid

Cast tumbaga with enriched surface. Probably a lime-container. The flattened oval shape allows the flask to be carried comfortably on a cord. Matching rectangular holes in the body and lid were presumably for the attachment of a carrying device.
Height 15.5 cm
MM *1910.12–2.7a* and *b*

142 Lime-flask, in the shape of a human figure

Made from three separate sheets of hammered gold, welded together. Nose ornament tied on with hammered wire. There is a small hole in the back.
Restrepo, Valle del Cauca
Height 6 cm
MO *5423*

140

142

141

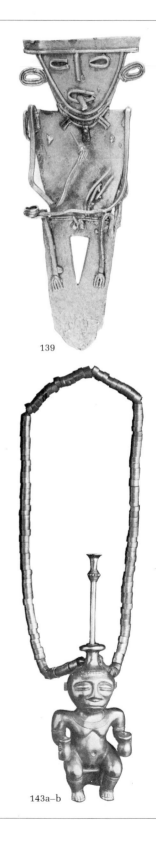

139

143a–b

143a–b Lime-flask and necklace
(a) Lime-flask
Cast gold. A classic Quimbaya
piece. Typically, the figure is nude
except for ornaments and jewellery.
In her hands she holds a pair of
vessels of the kind which figure in
the Treasure of the Quimbayas
(cf. no. 361). Suspension loop on the
head.
Hacienda Las Margaritas, Sevilla,
Valle del Cauca
Height 11.4 cm
MO *21.212*
Colour plate
(b) Necklace
Cast gold. 146 beads.
Puerto Tejada, Cauca
Average length 0.4 cm
MO *16.819*

144 Lime-dipper, with warrior
Cast gold
Early Calima style
Length 24.6 cm
MO *6164*

145 Lime-dipper, with bird
Cast gold
Restrepo, Valle del Cauca
Length 17.7 cm
MO *13.365*

**146 Lime-dipper, funnel-shaped
head**
Cast gold
Length 16.5 cm
MO *5762*

147 Lime-dipper, with a bell head
Cast gold
Rio Blanco, Tolima (though probably
made in the Calima zone)
Length 44 cm
MO *5909*

**148 Lime-dipper, with a funnel-
shaped top**
Cast gold
Restrepo, Valle del Cauca
Length 24.4 cm
MO *24.933*

**149 Lime-dipper, with masked figure
holding a staff**
Cast gold. The mask, staff, the fan-
shaped object in the left hand, and
the *alter ego* animal figure behind
the shoulders can all be matched in
San Agustín statuary.
Finca Grecia, Restrepo, Valle del
Cauca. From an Early Calima grave.
(*See* no. 131)
Length 30 cm
MO *26*

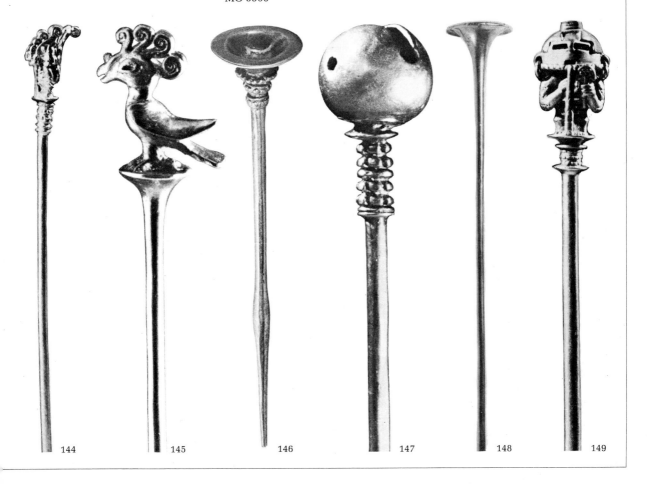

144   145   146   147   148   149

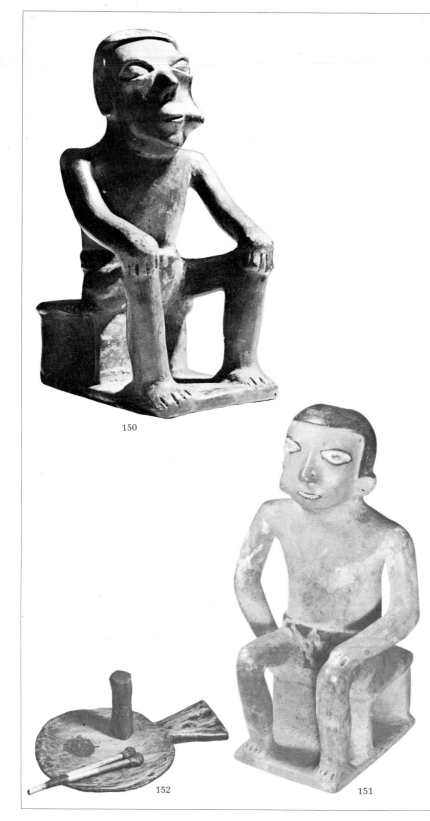

150

152   151

150 Seated figure of a coca-chewer
Painted pottery
Capulí style,
c. AD 800–1250 (Uribe 1977).
Finca Santa Lucia, Pupiales, Nariño
Height 20 cm
MO *CN 3115*

151 Seated figure of a coca-chewer
Pottery; smooth buff-coloured slip,
with details of features and clothing
picked out in white and black. The
figure wears a loincloth and belt.
One cheek distended by a quid of
coca leaves.
Capulí style of Andean Nariño
AD 800–1250 (Francisco 1969;
Uribe 1977)
Height 21 cm
BP *N-8511*

152 Apparatus for yopo-snuffing
From 16th-century chronicles it is
apparent that drug-induced halluci-
nations and altered states of
consciousness played a key part in
the religion of many Colombian
Indian tribes. Tobacco, datura and
yopo snuff were used by priests and
shamans to induce visions and to
'speak with the devil' (as the
Spaniards usually put it). The
narcotic snuff called *yopo* is
prepared from the seeds of a
leguminous tree (*Anadenathera
peregrina* or *Piptadenia peregrina*).
The toasted seeds are placed on a
shallow hardwood tray and crushed
into powder by means of a wooden
pestle. An alkaline substance (lime
from snail shells, or the ashes of
burned plant material) is usually
added to the *yopo* powder. The
resultant snuff is inhaled through a
hollow tube made of bird bones, with
nostril-pieces carved from palm
seeds. The kit is completed by a
feather 'pipe-cleaner'. The effects
include twitching muscles, slight
convulsions, nausea, visual halluci-
nations, disturbed sleep, and often
an exaggeration of the size of objects
(Schultes 1976: 86–91).
Modern Cuiva Indians, region of
Cravo Norte, in the eastern llanos
Width of tray 18 cm; length of
snuffing tube 16 cm
Coll. Alec Bright, Bogotá

153 Snuffing pipe
Pottery; red slip. Head and two feet of some kind of animal. Pipes of this kind never show signs of burning, and (with their round, stubby, and curved stems, and wide bores) are awkward to handle as tobacco pipes. The shape is ideal for use as a snuffing tube, with the powder placed in the bowl and the end of the stem held to the nostril (Schultes 1976: 92).
Restrepo, Valle del Cauca
Length 11.8 cm
MO CC 3972

154a–b Pair of Muisca snuff trays
Comparison with wooden examples from other parts of South America suggests that these little trays were used to hold narcotic snuffs (cf. Schultes 1976: 92). Oviedo records that the Muiscas used two substances 'yop' (i.e. yopo – see no. 152) and 'osca' as a means of taking omens. *'They will not set out, nor make war, nor undertake anything important without knowing how the affair will turn out . . . They say that the Sun will tell them how they should proceed in what they ask. And if you ask them how the sun tells them this, after they have taken certain herbs, they reply that if certain joints move after the Indians have eaten herbs, it is a sign that their affairs or their wishes will come out well. And if certain other joints move, it is a sign that things will not turn out well, but badly. And for this absurdity, all the joints of their body are categorized, named, and known for either good or bad.' (Gonzalo Fernández de Oviedo)*

The phenomenon described by Oviedo matches the twitching effects induced by yopo-snuffing. (See no. 152)
(a) Tray with bird figure
Cast gold
Length 10.2 cm
MO 7340
(b) Tray with two animals
Cast gold
Vereda El Roble, Gachancipá, Cundinamarca
Length 12.4 cm
MO 6784

155 Muisca effigy vessel
Pottery, with remains of light-red paint. Hollow, with a small hole in the top. The figure wears ear spools and holds a snuff tray similar to the gold examples no. 154a–b.
Height 25 cm
BP M-10754

153

155

154

156, 157, 158 Spear-thrower and two javelin heads

Palm wood.

'The most common weapons used in their wars are certain throwing spears of light material, such as reeds, with points made of hardwood. They hurl these . . . with the aid of sticks . . . The device has two hooks of different kinds, one fixed at each end of the tool. One hook engages with the butt of the dart, and the index finger is crooked round the other . . . And, since they had neither defensive weapons nor clothing sufficient to resist them, these darts were dangerous weapons, even though they were not poisoned.'
(Castellanos)

Many of the Muisca tunjos depict warriors carrying a spear-thrower and a pair of javelins. These actual javelin heads, and the spear-thrower (with its wooden finger grip and stone hook attached by cotton twine) perfectly match the chronicle description. The English traveller Cochrane (1825) commented that, in his day, hardwood javelins were still used for hunting alligators, and easily penetrated the tough hide.

(156) Length 66 cm
MN *AII*
(157) Length 63 cm
MN *38–1–925*
(158) Cueva de los Indios, a dry burial cave on the Mesa de los Santos, in Guane territory (Schottelius 1946).
Length 54 cm
MN *41–III–2432*

159 Muisca tunjo, warrior with spear-thrower

Cast tumbaga. On his right arm he carries a shield (or possibly a quiver).
Height 11.6 cm
MO *3046*

160 Muisca tunjo, warrior carrying a severed head

Cast tumbaga. The Muiscas took the heads of their enemies as trophies:
'. . . if the men of Bogotá kill or take prisoner any Panche Indians, they take the heads back to their homeland and put them in their oratories.'
(Oviedo).

The object in the left hand may be a *macana*, described by the Spanish as a sword-club of polished palm wood *'more or less the size of a hand in breadth, and with the edges thin and sharp. With this they used to cut, and even chop up, an Indian.'*
(Oviedo)
Height 10.6 cm
MO *6255*

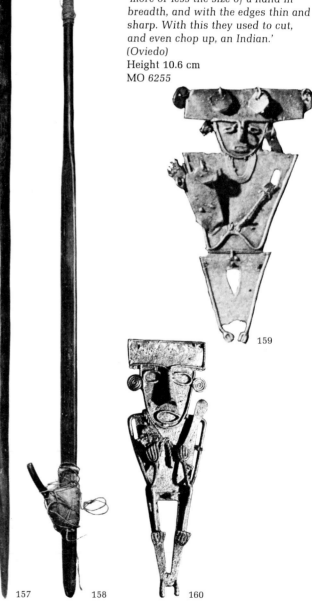

159

156

157

158

160

161 Muisca female idol, with a hollow in the stomach

Carved wood.

'In their houses they also have their idols of gold, and whoever cannot afford this has them of wood. And in the hollow of the stomach they used to put the gold and emeralds that they obtained. They were not bigger than half a Spanish yard.'
(Antonio de Herrera)
Ramiriquí, Boyacá (Restrepo 1972, pl. 1)
Height 24 cm
MN *38–I–736*

162 Muisca effigy jar

Pottery; rough brown clay. The lid, in the shape of a human face, was originally painted in dark red over cream. Possibly an offering pot.
Pasca, Cundinamarca
Height 20 cm
MO *CM 1075*

163, 164 Votive figures, snakes

Cast gold. No. 164 terminates in a casting button.

'. . . there used to appear in these same waters [of Lake Guatavita] a small dragon or large serpent, and when it appeared they had to offer it gold or emeralds . . .' (Pedro Simón)
(163) Length 14 cm
MO *2128*
(164) Length 13 cm
MO *1124*

165 Muisca 'dragon'

Cast and gilt tumbaga. The very large dendrites indicate slow cooling after casting.
El Chocho, Fusagasugá, Cundinamarca
Length 5.7 cm
MO *6303*

166 Miniature Muisca animal

Cast tumbaga
Length 2.1 cm
MM Ⓢ*1329*

161

162

166

165

163

164

167 Muisca, miniature pot
Cast tumbaga. Representation of a
jar with four handles.
Height 1.8 cm
MM *1949 Am. 14.5*

168 Muisca shell
Gold; hollow cast, and still full of
black core material.
Length 9.3 cm
MO *103*

167

168

170 *(detail)*

**169 Muisca tunjo, figure on a
wooden platform**
Cast tumbaga. The scene may refer
to a form of sacrifice described by
Castellanos and Simón, in which the
victim was tied to a tall pole and
shot to death with arrows from
below.
Height 9.5 cm
MO *4832*

170 Painted mantle
Cotton cloth; plain weave, with
double warps and single wefts. The
decorative borders at each side
employ yarn of three different
colours (natural, and two shades of
brown), and have warpfloat patterns
which incorporate panels of
geometric ornament and also
stylized figures with triangular kilts
and fancy head-dresses. These
patterns appear (with the colours
reversed) on the back of the cloth.
The central part of the mantle is
painted, on one face only, with
stylized figures and panels of
geometrical ornament in blue-green,
beige, light brown (perhaps
formerly red) and dark brown
(which may originally have been
black). The spiral and interlocking
patterns are matched on Muisca
pottery and stone objects (*see* no.
182).
   These mantles were used throughout Muisca territory and were widely
traded. At La Tora, on the River
Magdalena (*see* p. 16) the Spaniards
encountered Muisca textiles '*of very
fine cotton, well woven, and painted
by means of brushes (in the fashion
of the Indians of this Kingdom), with
narrow coloured bands, which they
call* maures, *running the length of
the cloth, and with other little
designs . . .*' (*Pedro Simón* 1625).
Simón goes on to say that such
textiles were highly valued, and
were sold at fixed prices. An old
label, now missing, gave the
provenance as 'Gachansipá',
(with no. 568).
(Broadbent 1970: p. 9).
Width 137 cm
MM *42.11-12.3*
Colour plate

171

169

171 Human skull, artificially deformed

Many Colombian Indian tribes altered the shape of their skulls for cosmetic reasons. Pedro Simón wrote of the Panches at the time of European contact, describing their *'terrible countenances, with the foreheads and the backs of the skulls flattened . . . because, at the birth of an infant, they put a little board behind the head and another at the forehead. They compress both parts, and make the head stick up, with the forehead and the back flattened.'* This was not normally a Muisca custom, though there are a few deformed skulls from Muisca cemeteries.
MN *No number*

172 Hollow figure
Grey pottery; remains of orange paint. Mould made. The skull is artificially flattened (see no. 171).
Tumaco style of south coastal Colombia
Height 21 cm
BP *T-2374*

173 Muisca jar
Pottery; dark red and white paint over a buff background. Storage vessel for water or *chicha* (maize beer).
Height 41 cm
BP *M-2818*

174 Muisca bowl, with two handles
Dark grey ware. Inturned rim decorated with impressed dots and designs in relief.
Diameter 20.5 cm
MN *38-I-91*

175 Muisca jar
Pottery; painted decoration in white and dark red over a buff-orange slip. A typical *múcura* (jar for liquids) of the period just before the Spanish Conquest (Perdomo 1977).
Height 53 cm
BP *M-3810*

172

175

173

174

176–196 Reconstruction of the home of a Muisca peasant family
Each family had its own hut which was round, thatched with grass, and had walls made of a timber and cane framework covered by a mixture of mud and straw. The cane door, the interior partition, and the bed with its reed mattress and cotton blanket, are all described in Spanish chronicles.

176a–b Stones for grinding maize
The lower one (the *metate*) rests on three small legs; the upper stone (the *mano*) was held in the hand.
Metate Length 40 cm
MN *42–V–3900 (mano), 2876–A–2876 (metate)*

177, 178, 179 Axes of polished stone
(reconstructed hafts)
(177) Length of blade 7.5 cm
MN *691–A–691*
(178) Rio Tumara, Chocó
Length of blade 11 cm
MN *XXII*
(179) Tierradentro Tomb 8
Length of T-shaped blade 10 cm
MN *38–I–1540*

180, 181 Perforated discs
Polished stone; probably digging-stick weights or clod-breakers used in agricultural work.
Diameters 8.5, 5.9 cm
(180) MN *40–II–2376*
(181) MN *38–I–317*

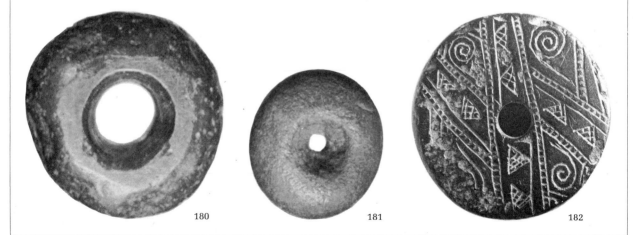

176

177

178

179

180

181

182

182 Muisca spindle whorl
Fine-grained black stone, with
incised geometric designs similar to
those found on Muisca pottery and
textiles (*see* no. 170). The palm wood
spindle, with its cotton thread, is
modern. Father Zamora noted that
'the women are continually spinning
yarn for the mantles which they
wear, and for those of their sons and
husbands'.
Diameter 3.2 cm
Private collection

183 Lime-container (*poporo*)
Calabash
Modern Páez Indians, Tierradentro
region
Height 10 cm
MN *44–I–4618*

184 Bag with coca leaves
Modern Guambiano Indians, Santa
Rosa sobre Caquetá, Cauca
Height without strap 14 cm
MN *46–V–6533*

**185, 186 Two necklaces of Oliva
shells**
Conch shell trumpets and ornaments
made of sea shell are found on
archaeological sites all over Muisca
and Guane territory. They were
traded from the Caribbean coast
'passing from hand to hand, at very
high prices' (Pedro Simón 1625). In
return, the coastal peoples received
emeralds and Muisca products.
Vereda Salitre, Paz del Rio, Boyacá
(185) MN *2912–A–2912*
(186) MN *2913–A–2913*

185 186

183   184

191

192

193

187

187 Muisca jar
Pottery; dark red paint over buff-orange background. One large handle and six little lugs at the junction of neck and shoulders.
Height 31.5 cm
MN *686–A–686*

188 Muisca jar, three handles
Pottery; blackish-brown paint over a cream base. The largest handle is divided at the base and has two nipples in relief. Vertical ribs from neck to shoulders.
From a burial at Ubaque, Cundinamarca
Height 40 cm
MN *213*

189 Four-handled jar
Pottery; traces of dark red painted lines over an orange slip.
Escuela de Mercadillo II, Cáqueza, Cundinamarca
Height 13.6 cm
MN *211*

190 Jar, single handle
Pottery; yellow, gritty clay, with red slip.
Cáqueza, Cundinamarca
Height 16.4 cm
MN *210*

191 Muisca jar, single handle
Pottery; decorated on neck and shoulders with designs in dark red paint. *Múcura* (vessel for liquids).
Height 23 cm
MN *38–I–35*

192 Painted jar
Pottery, with eyes and nose modelled in relief on the neck. One large handle and two small ones. Neck and shoulders painted with dark red designs over a cream slip. Valle de Tenza style; Muisca.
Height 23 cm
MN *59–I–668*

193 Painted jar
One large handle and two small ones; dark red decoration over a buff field.
Tomb 1, Oiba, Santander. One of a group of forty-seven pots found in the funerary chamber. Oiba is in the territory of the Guane Indians, northern neighbours of the Muisca, and the other vessels from the tomb were of local Guane manufacture. This item is Muisca in style, and its presence in a Guane cemetery shows that pottery was traded between the two groups (Sutherland 1971).
Height 26.5 cm
MN *70–IV–3402*

194 Cotton cloth
Cundinamarca, present day. (Not illustrated)
MN *219*

195, 196 Reed mattresses (modern)
Cundinamarca. (Not illustrated)
MN *220/21*

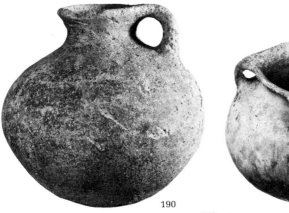

190

189

188

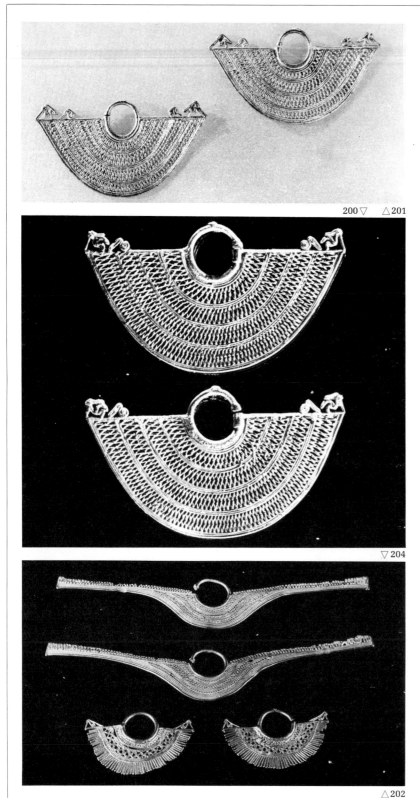

200 ▽   △ 201

▽ 204

△ 202

197 Pair of Sinú ear ornaments, with birds
Cast tumbaga
San Benito de Abad, Sucre
Widths 3.6, 3.8 cm
MO 24.174/5

198 Pair of Sinú ear ornaments, with stylized birds
Cast gold
Colosó, Sucre
Width 3.9 cm
MO 22.549, 22.551

199 Pair of Sinú ear ornaments, with alligators
Cast gold
Guaranda, Sucre
Width 5.6 cm
MO 24.737/8

200 Pair of Sinú ear ornaments, with birds
Cast gold
Guaranda, Bajo Cauca, Bolívar
Width 9.5 cm
MO 24.729/30

201 Pair of Sinú ear ornaments, with birds
Cast tumbaga, enriched surfaces.
San Marcos, Sucre
Width 8.7 cm
MO 24.792/3

202 Pair of Sinú ear ornaments
Cast gold
Colosó, Sucre
Width 3.1 cm
MO 22.554/5

203 Pair of Sinú ear ornaments
Cast gold. (Not illustrated)
Betancí, Córdoba
Width 4.2 cm
MO 22.409/10

204 Pair of Sinú ear ornaments
Cast gold
Colosó, Sucre
Width 9.9 cm
MO 22.352/3

205 Pair of Sinú ear ornaments, with row of stylized birds
Cast gold
Guaranda, Majagal, Sucre
Widths 7.7, 9.7 cm
MO 24.615/6

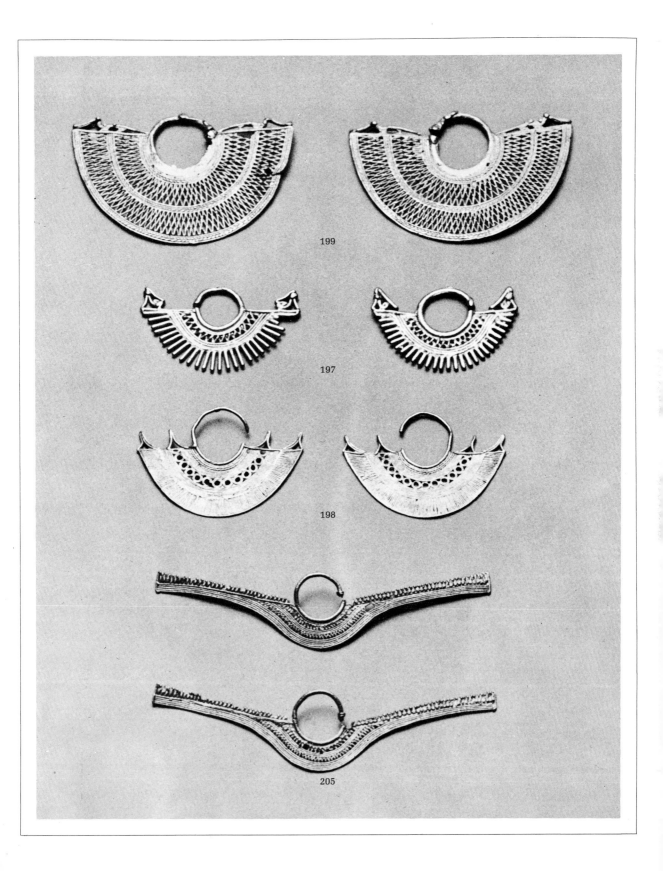

199

197

198

205

206 Pair of Sinú ear ornaments
Cast and gilt tumbaga. Geometric
panel surmounted by stylized birds.
Colosó, Sucre
Width 5.9 cm
MO 22.345/6

207 Sinú nose or ear ornament
Cast gold
Width 13.7 cm
MO 2283

208 Sinú nose or ear ornament
Cast gold
Width 15 cm
MO 2282

209 Sinú nose or ear ornament
Cast gold
Sinú, Córdoba
Width 10.3 cm
MO 6382

210 Sinú nose ornament
Gold; cut out, hammered and
embossed.
El Anclar, Montelíbano, Córdoba
Width 10.8 cm
MO 24.399

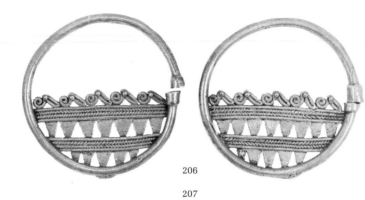

206

207

208

209

210

211 Sinú nose ornament
Hammered gold
Palmitas, San Marcos, Sucre
Width 23 cm
MO *25.472*

212 Sinú nose ornament
Hammered gold
Betancí, Córdoba
Width 23.7 cm
MO *22.097*

213 Sinú nose ornament
Hammered gold
Betancí, Córdoba
Width 20.9 cm
MO *22.098*

214 Sinú nose ornament
Hammered gold
San Marcos, Sucre
Width 7.3 cm
MO *24.811*

215 Sinú nose ornament with elongated ends
Hammered gold
San Marcos, Sucre
Width 9.3 cm
MO *24.810*

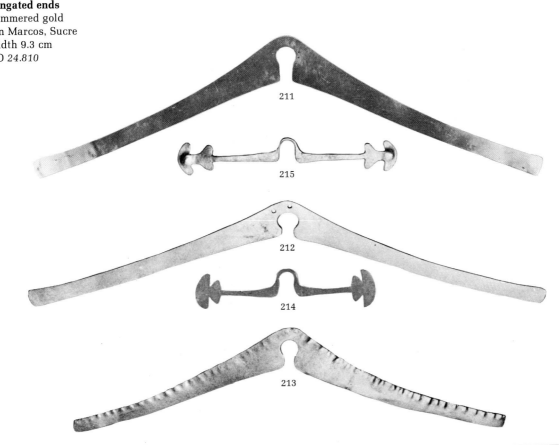

211

215

212

214

213

**216 Sinú nose ornament with
elongated ends**
Cast gold
San Marcos, Sucre
Width 11 cm
MO *24.805*

**217 Sinú nose ornament with
elongated ends**
Hammered gold
Alto Sinú region, Córdoba
Width 22.8 cm
MO *7809*

**218 Sinú nose ornament with
elongated ends**
Hammered gold
Rio San Jorge, Córdoba
Width 32.3 cm
MO *2027*

219 Sinú nose ornament
Cast and gilt tumbaga
Ovejas, Sucre
Width 15.7 cm
MO *25.136*

216

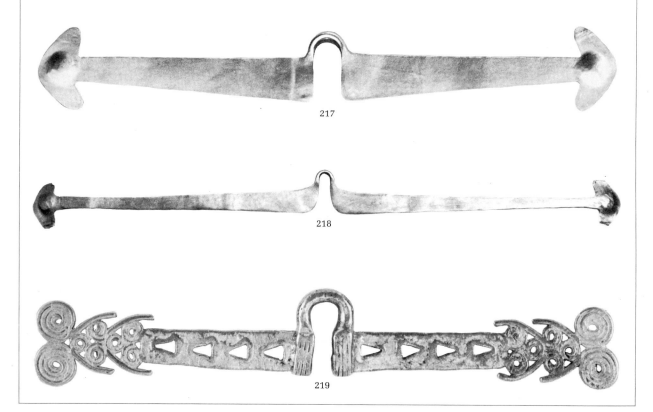

217

218

219

220 Sinú nose ornament
Cast gold; the scar on top of the
hook marks the end of the channel
through which the metal entered
during casting.
Between Ovejas and Carmen de
Bolívar
Width 10.9 cm
MO 24.285

221 Sinú nose ornament, inverted U
Solid gold (Falchetti 1976)
Lorica, Córdoba
Width 4.7 cm
MO 16.109

222 Nose ornament
Gilt tumbaga; hammered.
Hacienda El Japón, San Benito de
Abad, Sucre
Width 11.9 cm
MO 24.219

221

222

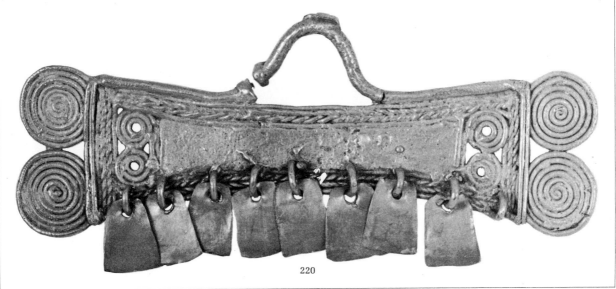

220

223 Pair of bracelets
Hammered gold
Lorica, Córdoba
Heights 8.1 8.3 cm
MO *16.091/2*

224 Disc pendant
Gold, with a suspension loop
soldered to the back.
Hacienda El Japón, San Benito de
Abad, Sucre
Diameter 10 cm
MO *24.050*

**225 Necklace, bells and tubular
beads**
Cast gold
Sinú region, Córdoba
Height of bells 4.2 cm; length of
beads 4.5 cm
MO *6374*

**226 Necklace of claw-shaped
pendants**
Cast gold. Thirty-nine elements.
Sinú region, Córdoba
Average height 2.1 cm
MO *6377*

227 Figure pendant, with head-dress
Cast tumbaga, enriched surface.
Quimbaya region, Department of
Quindío or Antioquia. The form is
more common in the Sinú region
(Falchetti 1976).
Height 3.8 cm
MO *23.282*

**228 Pendant with human head and
the body of a fish**
Cast tumbaga, enriched surface.
Variants on this form are most
common in the Sinú region (Falchetti
1976), but they extend into the
Isthmus of Central America as far as
Panama (Lothrop 1937) and Costa
Rica (Aguilar 1972: 71).
Height 6.2 cm
MO *6025*

**229 Pendant, male figure with
head-dress**
Cast gold
Height 11.6 cm
MO *6417*

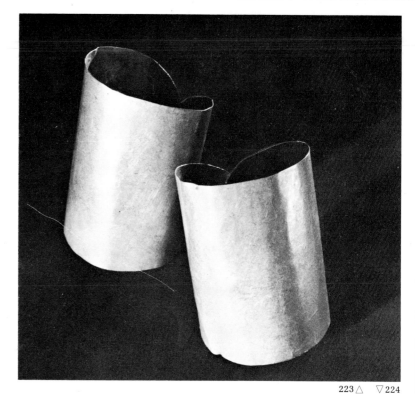

223 △   ▽ 224

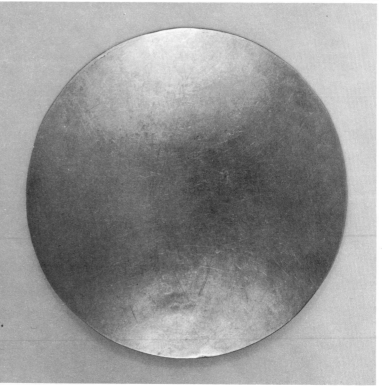

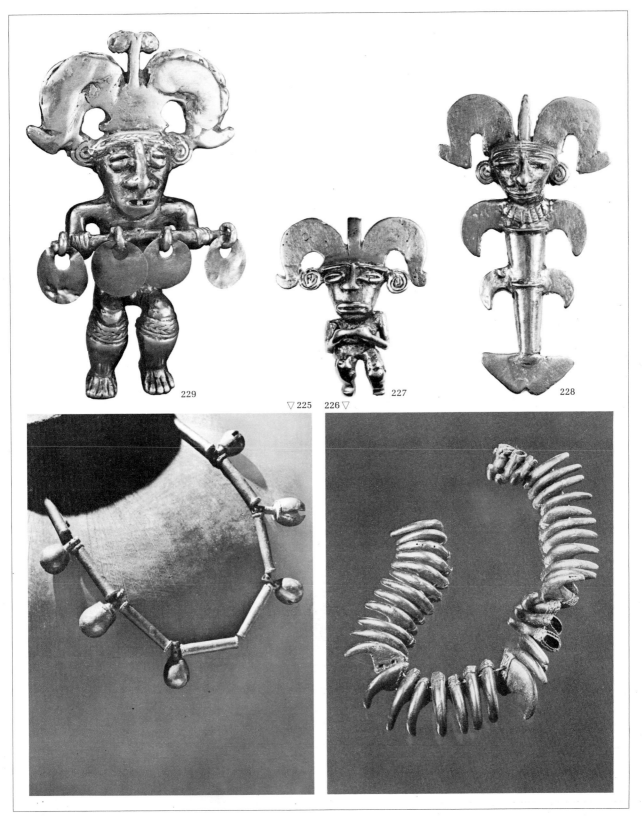

229

▽ 225 226 ▽

227

228

230 Bell, shaped like a human head
Cast gold. The head-dress incorporates two bird heads.
There are two similar bells from San Marcos, Bolívar, in the Sinú zone (Pérez de Barradas 1966, I: 154).
Height 4.7 cm
MO 6513

231 Jaguar pendant
Cast gold
El Banco, Magdalena
Length 12.1 cm
MO 17.170
Colour plate

232 Frog pendant
Gold, open-backed casting.
El Anclar, Montelíbano, Córdoba
Length 2.6 cm
MO 24.392

233 Breastplate
Hammered and repoussé gold, with raised bosses and designs of jaguars attacking snakes.
One of three similar pieces from a funerary mound of Betancí (Sinú) type at Ayapel, Córdoba (Reichel-Dolmatoff 1958: 81). This mound, looted in 1919, yielded one of Colombia's richest treasure hoards: three crescent-shaped breastplates, five circular breastplates, six Sinú staff heads surmounted by birds or animals, eight fan-shaped Sinú ear ornaments, four bells, twenty-six nose ornaments, nine strings of gold beads, a girdle made up of 138 solid gold bars, a helmet, six sheet-gold plaques, twelve discs, eight bracelets, an arm band and a funnel-shaped item (Farabee 1920).
Width 53.5 cm
UMP SA 2703

234 Breastplate
Hammered and repoussé gold, with raised bosses.
Found with no. 233.
Width 55.5 cm
UMP SA 2702

230

232

237

238

235 Sinú staff head, bird
Cast tumbaga with enriched surface. The hooks beneath the beak once held danglers. These objects are conventionally called 'staff heads', though the placement of the sockets makes it clear that most examples were hafted horizontally rather than vertically. They may possibly have served as ceremonial spear-thrower hooks, but this is far from certain. This unusually large and fine specimen was formerly in the collection of the sculptor Sir Jacob Epstein.
Maximum length 16.2 cm
Coll. George Ortiz, Geneva
Colour plate

236 Sinú staff head, human figure
Cast tumbaga with enriched surface. Represents a crouching hunchback, possibly a musician with a flute and a rattle. The hair hangs down behind, and is caught by a diadem. He wears a belt, armbands, a nose ornament and (perhaps) a penis sheath. The chaplet holes, where the inner core was supported during the process of lost-wax casting, can be clearly seen: one on each side of the head, one in each knee, two below the base, and one in the end of the flute or tube.
Barranco de Loba, Bolívar
Height 5 cm
Galería Cano, Bogotá
Colour plate

237 Sinú staff head, bird
Cast tumbaga
Sinú region, Córdoba
Height 6 cm
MO 6379

238 Sinú staff head, two birds
Cast gold
Ovejas, Sucre
Height 3.1 cm
MO 25.131

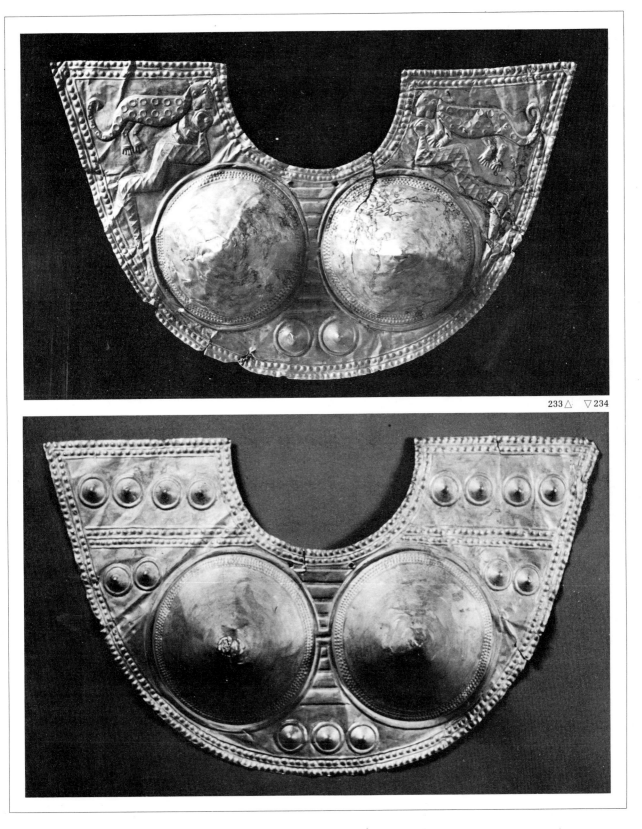

233 △   ▽ 234

239 Sinú staff head, two birds
Cast. Gilded tumbaga.
Colosó, Sucre
Height 2.4 cm
MO 22.628

240 Sinú staff head, bird
Gold; hollow cast.
Sinú river area, Córdoba
Length 7.9 cm
MO 6378

241 Sinú staff head, jaguar attacking alligator
Cast tumbaga
Sucre
Height 5 cm
MO 24.291

242 Sinú staff head, dog
Cast tumbaga with enriched surfaces
Colosó, Sucre
Height 2.4 cm
MO 16.794

243 Sinú staff head, monkey
Cast and gilded tumbaga
Colosó, Sucre
Height 4 cm
MO 17.638

244 Sinú staff head, man with (?)flute
Cast and gilded tumbaga
Sucre
Height 3.2 cm
MO 24.293

245 Sinú staff head, human figure
Cast copper or copper-rich tumbaga. The socket is missing, but the placement of the figure was originally similar to no. 244. Male, wearing a broad-brimmed hat, a pair of crescentic Sinú ear ornaments, necklace, and a belt round the loins.
Height 5.5 cm
MM 1955 Am. 6–7

242

240

243

244

241   239   245

246 Bowl with modelled pedestal
Pottery. The bowl, with a deeply
carved geometric design, stands on a
hollow pedestal foot modelled in the
shape of a woman and child.
Betancí style of the middle Río Sinú,
where it occurs with Sinú gold
objects and is dated to the final
centuries of the pre-Spanish period
(G. and A. Reichel-Dolmatoff 1957).
Height 34 cm
BP S–12566
Colour plate

247 Hollow female figurine
Yellow-grey clay. She wears a nose
ornament.
Betancí, Córdoba. Final centuries
before the Spanish Conquest of the
Sinú region (Falchetti 1976, fig. 88, 1).
Height 11.4 cm
MO CS 3634

248 Hollow female figure
Pottery; rough, yellowish clay.
Kneeling woman wearing a crescentic
pendant and a nose ornament in the
shape of an inverted U. Figures of
this kind were set on round discs
serving as covers or lids for vessels.
During the 1970s this type of pottery
began to appear in burial mounds at
El Japón, in the drainage of the Río
San Jorge (Department of Bolívar),
associated with gold objects in Sinú
style. Glass trade beads (see no. 10c)
date this material to the final
centuries of the pre-Spanish period
and the time of European contact
(Falchetti 1976: 191–209).
Height 14.7 cm
BP S–11449

247

248

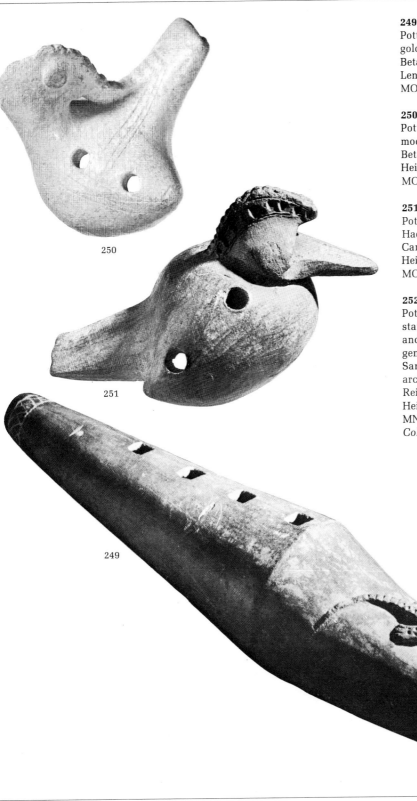

249 Flute, with a modelled alligator
Pottery, Similar alligators occur on
gold ear ornaments (see no. 199)
Betancí, Córdoba
Length 24.7 cm
MO *CS 3891*

250 Whistle in the form of a bird
Pottery. Four holes. The paint is
modern.
Betancí, Córdoba
Height 5.9 cm
MO *CS–4115*

251 Whistle, bird
Pottery
Hacienda El Japón, Ciénaga de
Carate, San Marcos, Sucre
Height 5.3 cm
MO *CS 4252*

252 Lid of a burial urn
Pottery. Seated male figure holding a
staff. He wears a necklace, bracelets
and a woven belt, though the
genitals are bare.
San Jorge River area, Sinú
archaeological region (G. and A.
Reichel-Dolmatoff 1965, pl. 41)
Height 34 cm
MN *No number*
Colour plate

250

251

249

Darien Pectorals

253 Darien pectoral
Cast gold. The so-called 'Darien pectorals' (nos. 253–260) form an easily recognizable group (Falchetti 1976: 133–74). Within the group there is a good deal of variation, from very stylized forms to more naturalistic ones. The basic figure is a human being, sometimes with an alligator-like head. There are spiral, winged devices beside the face, and the head-dress incorporates objects shaped like mushrooms or old-fashioned telephone bells. The figure may or may not wear a mask, but generally holds a pair of cylindrical objects which often end in knobs. Legs are broad and flat, reduced almost to a plaque. These Darien pectorals were at one time thought to constitute a distinct 'Darien *style*' within Colombian goldwork, but it is now clear that they cross cut – and hybridize with – many different regional styles. The distribution of Darien pectorals, or closely related forms, stretches from the Tolima and Calima regions to the Caribbean coast. The greatest concentration of finds is in the Sinú zone, and pectorals of this type are found as exports (or local copies) in Panama, Costa Rica and Yucatan.
Height 11.6 cm
MO *6419*

254 Darien pectoral
Coppery tumbaga with enriched surface. Behind the mask is a human face. Three suspension loops behind.
(*See* no. 253)
San Marcos, Sucre
Height 8.7 cm
MO *24.299*

255 Darien pectoral
Cast gold. (*See* no. 253)
Quindío
Height 8.1 cm
MO *80*

259

254

260

256 Darien pectoral
Cast gold. Alligator-headed variant. The domes on the head-dress have been transformed into shapes resembling double-spouted pots. (*See* nos. 463, 550)
Height 8.2 cm
MO *6031*
Colour plate

257 Darien pectoral
Cast gold-rich tumbaga. (*See* no. 253)
Quimbaya, Quindío
Height 6.5 cm
MO *3065*

258 Darien pectoral
Cast tumbaga. Alligator variant.
(*See* no. 253)
Salento, Quindío
Height 7.2 cm
MO *351*

259 Darien pectoral
Cast gold-rich tumbaga. Snouted figure holding two staffs.
(*See* no. 253)
Height 5.5 cm
MO *4663*

260 Darien pectoral
Cast tumbaga (60.4% gold, 18.8% copper, 18.4% silver). The figure has a human body (with belt and breast ornament), but a snouty, alligator-like face. (*See* no. 253)
Corregimiento La María, Ansermanuevo, Valle del Cauca
Height 7 cm
MO *3492*

253 255
257 258

Tairona Region

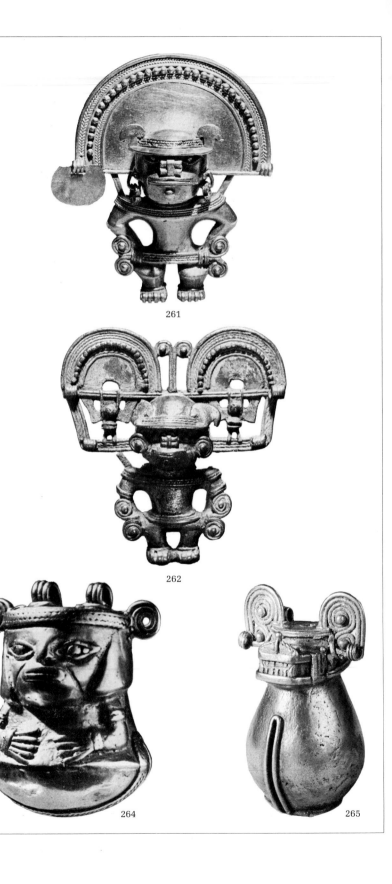

261 Tairona figure pendant
Cast and gilded tumbaga. He wears
the usual Tairona jewellery.
Minca, Santa Marta, Magdalena
Height 5.7 cm
MO *11.415*

262 Tairona figure pendant
Cast and gilded tumbaga. The head-
dress incorporates two bats.
Tairona region, Magdalena
Height 4.2 cm
MO *22.802*

263 Tairona figure pendant
Cast and gilded tumbaga. He wears
a bird head-dress and the full range
of Tairona jewellery: crescentic ear
ornaments, nose bar, lip plug,
necklace and penis cover.
San Pedro de la Sierra, Ciénaga,
Magdalena
Height 10.6 cm
MO *16.300*
Colour plate

264 Tairona bell
Cast and gilded tumbaga. Human
figure.
Canaveral, Santa Marta, Magdalena
Height 3.4 cm
MO *22.640*

265 Tairona bell
Gilt tumbaga; hollow cast. The head
may represent an alligator.
San Pedro de la Sierra, Ciénaga,
Magdalena
Height 4.6 cm
MO *14.855*

266 Pair of Tairona ear ornaments
Cast and gilded tumbaga
Minca, Santa Marta, Magdalena
Width 7.8 cm
MO *22.675/6*

267 Pair of Tairona ear ornaments
Cast and gilded tumbaga
Minca, Santa Marta, Magdalena
Width 6 cm
MO *22.679/80*

268 Pair of Tairona ear ornaments
Cast tumbaga
Canaveral, Santa Marta, Magdalena
Width 7.6 cm
MO *22.637/8*

261

262

264

265

266

267

268

269 Pair of Tairona ear ornaments
Cast tumbaga with enriched surface
Tairona region, Department of
Magdalena
Width 6.8 cm
MO 24.468/9

270 Pair of Tairona ear ornaments
Cast gold
Canaveral, Santa Marta, Magdalena
Widths 7.5, 7.7 cm
MO 22.635/6

271 Tairona nose ornament
Cast gold
Minca, Santa Marta, Magdalena
Width 8.9 cm
MO 11.683

272 Tairona nose ornament
Cast tumbaga with enriched surfaces
Bonda, Santa Marta, Magdalena
Width 6.6 cm
MO 13.787

273 Tairona nose ornament
Cast tumbaga with enriched surface
Minca, Santa Marta, Magdalena
Width 6.8 cm
MO 11.786

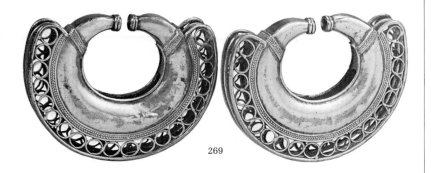

269

270

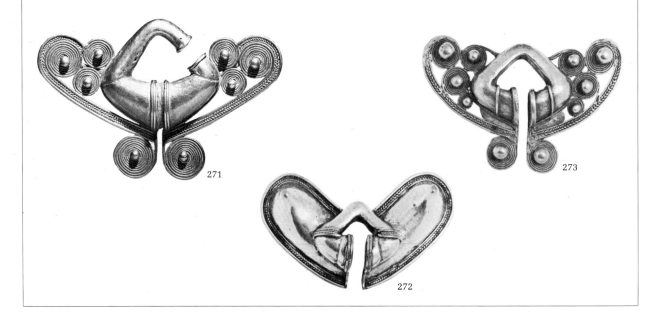

271

273

272

274 Tairona nose ornament
Cast gold
Río Don Diego, Santa Marta,
Magdalena
Width 7.5 cm
MO 24.847

275 Tairona nose ornament
Cast tumbaga with enriched surface
Minca, Santa Marta, Magdalena
Width 4 cm
MO 11.690

276 Tairona nose ornament
Cast gold
Bonda, Santa Marta, Magdalena
Width 7.7 cm
MO 15.842

277 Tairona nose ornament
Cast gold
Río Palomino, Magdalena
Width 11.2 cm
MO 22.650

278 Tairona nose ornament
Cast tumbaga
Río Palomino, Magdalena
Width 8.9 cm
MO 22.651

**279 Tairona nose ornament,
upturned ends**
Cast gold
Bonda, Santa Marta, Magdalena
Width 7.6 cm
MO 13.432

274

275

276

277

278

279

280

281

282

280 Tairona ear ornament, animal head
Cast and hammered gold.
Perhaps an alligator.
Minca, Santa Marta, Magdalena
Length 15.9 cm
MO *13.993*

281 Tairona ear ornament, with animal head
Cast gold
Tairona region, Magdalena
Length 3.6 cm
MO *22.929*

282 Tairona lip plug
Cast and gilt tumbaga
La Secreta, ariba del Rio Aguja, Magdalena
Height 5 cm
MO *24.267*

283 Tairona lip plug
Cast gold. The object fits through a hole in the lower lip, and is held in place by the flange on the inside.
Tairona region, Magdalena
Height 2.7 cm
MO *24.263*

284 Tairona lip plug
Cast gold
Rio Palomino, Guajira, Magdalena
Diameter 2.5 cm
MO *20.779*

285 Tairona lip plug
Cast gold
Las Flores, Guajira
Length 5.6. cm
MO *24.265*

286 Tairona lip plug
Hammered gold
Rio Don Diego, Santa Marta, Magdalena
Diameter 2.3 cm
MO *24.889*

287 Tairona lip plug
Hammered gold
Rio Don Diego, Santa Marta, Magdalena
Diameter 2.3 cm
MO *24.883*

283

284

285

286

287

288 Tairona necklace
Surface-enriched tumbaga. Forty-
three hollow cast elements (some
still containing core material)
separated by stone beads.
Minca, Santa Marta, Magdalena
Average length of metal bead 3.3 cm
MO 13.251

289 Tairona necklace
Cast and gilded tumbaga. Twenty-
two frogs and twenty-six cornelian
beads.
Minca, Santa Marta, Magdalena
Length of largest frog 2.8 cm
MO 12.549

290 Tairona necklace
Cast and gilded tumbaga. The fifty-
one stylized frogs are little bells.
Also fifty-two green stone beads.
Rio Palomino, Guajira, Magdalena
Length of largest frog 2.4 cm
MO 20.791

291 Necklace
Cast gold. Fifty-six stylized animal
pendants.
Rio Palomino, Guajira, Magdalena
Average height 3.3 cm
MO 20.289

292 Tairona necklace
Cast and gilded tumbaga, with
cornelian beads. The arrangement is
a piece of modern conjecture. The
necklace incorporates spacer beads
and anchor-shaped ornaments.
Minca, Santa Marta, Magdalena
Height of bird-headed spacers 6.4 cm
MO 12.302

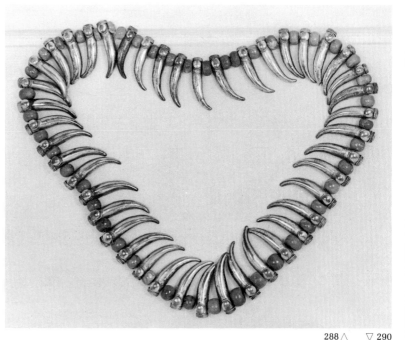

288 △   ▽ 290

291

289
292

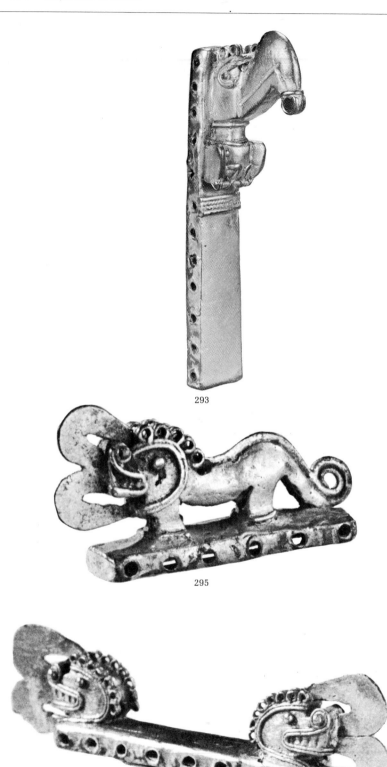

293

295

294

293 Tairona spacer bead, with bird
Cast and gilt tumbaga. These objects
were used to separate and spread
the strings of a multi-strand necklace
or collar (see no. 292). On this
example, the holes indicate a twelve-
strand necklace.
Department of Magdalena
Height 6.3 cm
MO *22.880*

**294 Tairona spacer bead, two
animal heads**
Cast and gilded tumbaga. (See no. 292)
Tairona region, Magdalena
Length 5.6 cm
MO *22.883*

**295 Tairona spacer bead, with
jaguar**
Cast gold. (See no. 292)
San Pedro de la Sierra, Ciénaga,
Magdalena
Length 3.9 cm
MO *12.566*

296 Tairona bird pectoral
Hammered gold
Alto Buriticá, Magdalena
Height 10.4 cm
MO *24.346*

297 Tairona bird pectoral
Cast and gilded tumbaga
Bonda, Santa Marta, Magdalena
Height 12.4 cm
MO *12.984*

298 Tairona pendant, bird
Cast and gilded tumbaga
Bahía de la Traca, Santa Marta,
Magdalena
Height 6 cm
MO *9026*

299 Tairona bird pectoral
Gilt tumbaga; open-backed casting.
Minca, Santa Marta, Magdalena
Height 8.6 cm
MO *13.184*
Colour plate

300 Pendant, big-beaked bird
Gilt tumbaga; cast.
Minca, Santa Marta, Magdalena
Height 6.1 cm
MO *13.831*

297

296

298

300

302

301

303

304   305

301, 302 Pair of pendants, bird heads
Cast and gilded tumbaga
Alto Buriticá, Magdalena
Widths 5.7, 4.5 cm
MO *24.349/50*

303 Tairona pendant, double-headed animal
Cast tumbaga
Bellavista, Magdalena
Length 7.1 cm
MO *24.274*

304 Tairona ornament
Cast and gilt tumbaga
Department of Magdalena
Height 4.8 cm
MO *22.884*

305 Bell, with flange
Cast and gilt tumbaga
Bonda, Santa Marta, Magdalena
(cf. no. 106 from Sinú zone)
Height 4.2 cm
MO *19.834*

306 Set of plaques
Hammered sheet gold. Each plaque has two holes for attachment to a backing.
Tairona region, Magdalena
Average size 1.8 x 2.0 cm
MO *23.841*

307 Tairona pectoral with human figure
Hammered sheet, with repoussé decoration. The central figure wears a nose ornament and pectoral. Two holes above the head, and two more close together at the base.
Bank of the Rio Piedras, Santa Marta, Magdalena
Width 22.5 cm
Galería Cano, Bogotá

308 Tairona pectoral with human figure
Hammered and repoussé gold. Two holes for suspension.
Bonda, Santa Marta, Magdalena
Width 15.4 cm
MO *14.618*
Colour plate

309 Tairona pectoral with three birds

Gilt tumbaga; cast, hammered and folded. The general shape of this piece resembles a common Muisca form (Pérez de Barradas 1958, II, pls. 148, 211, 212) and corroborates 16th-century Spanish accounts of contacts between the two groups. Where a Muisca smith would have made this item as a single-piece lost-wax casting (using stone matrices to produce the birds), his Tairona counterpart has produced the identical effect by entirely different means.

As the rear view (*see* fig. 18) shows, the Tairona ornament is a composite piece, made primarily by hammering and folding. The base plate (including the necks of the birds) is made from a single piece of sheet metal with a band of chased decoration on the front. The bird bodies are embossed from the rear, probably worked over a template. The three heads are separately made, of hammered and folded sheet. The overlap seam is visible beneath each beak. The heads are attached to the base plate by folding and clinching; each head has a flange which goes down behind the corresponding neck, whose sides are folded over to hold it in place. The sides of these folds are also hammered out to form the suspension loops. The join between head and neck is completely concealed by a wire strip, which is simply tied around the neck with the ends tucked in behind. The entire piece is assembled without any use of solder.
Minca, Santa Marta, Magdalena
Height 12.9 cm
MO *13.973*
Colour plate

310 Tairona pendant, human figure
Hammered and repoussé tumbaga
Tairona region, Department of Magdalena
Height 11 cm
MO *22.795*
Colour plate

311 Disc with embossed border
Hammered tumbaga with enriched surfaces. Single central hole.
Rio Palomino, on the frontier between the Departments of Guajira and Magdalena
Diameter 14 cm
MO *16.147*

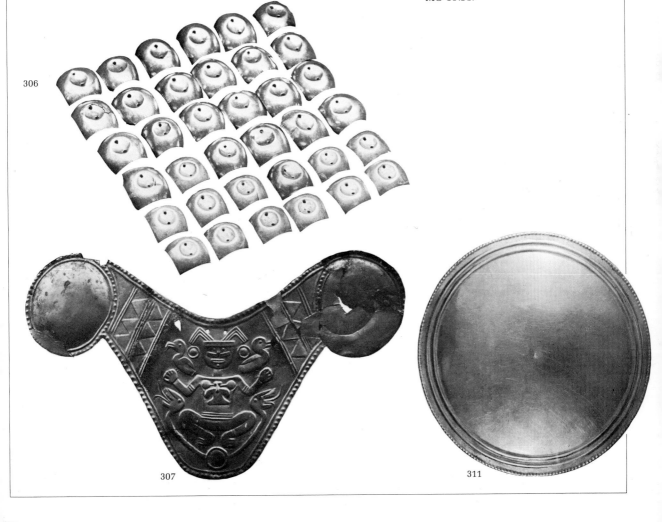

306

307   311

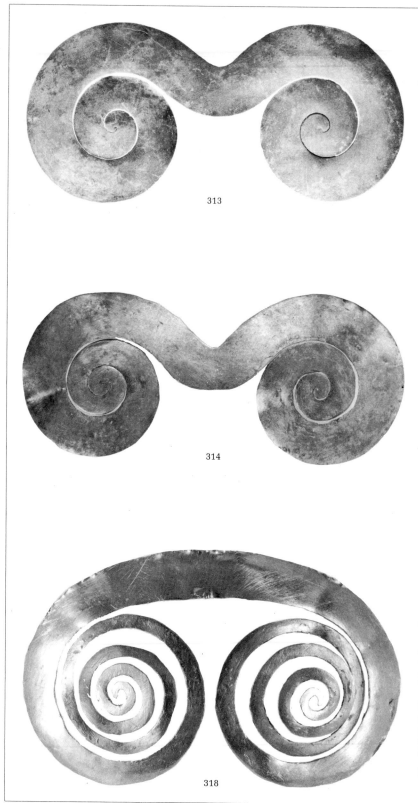

313

314

318

312 Spiral ornament
Hammered gold. Finds of these objects are concentrated in the Tairona zone, but a few examples were exported to the Isthmus. One was discovered (with Quimbaya and Tairona trade pieces) in a cemetery at Guácimo, Costa Rica (Stone and Balser 1965; Baudez and Coe 1966). Another came from a tomb in the Tonosí region of Panama (González Guzman 1971).
Tairona region, Magdalena
Width 18.8 cm
MO *16.896*

313 Spiral ornament
Gold; cut and hammered sheet. (*See* no. 312)
Palmarito, Magdalena
Width 15.5 cm
MO *15.030*

314 Spiral ornament
Gilded tumbaga; cut and hammered sheet. (*See* no. 312)
Minca, Santa Marta, Magdalena
Width 11.2 cm
MO *11.571*

315 Spiral ornament
Hammered gold. (*See* no. 312)
Minca y Bonda, Santa Marta, Magdalena
Width 20.4 cm
MO *16.466*

316 Spiral ornament
Tumbaga with enriched surface; hammered. (*See* no. 312)
Minca, Santa Marta, Magdalena
Width 17.2 cm
MO *13.228*

317 Spiral ornament
Tumbaga with enriched surface; hammered. (*See* no. 312)
Gairaca, Magdalena
Width 18.9 cm
MO *16.897*

318 Spiral ornament
Cut and hammered sheet gold. (*See* no. 312)
Puerto Tejada, Cauca
Width 11 cm
MO *16.806*

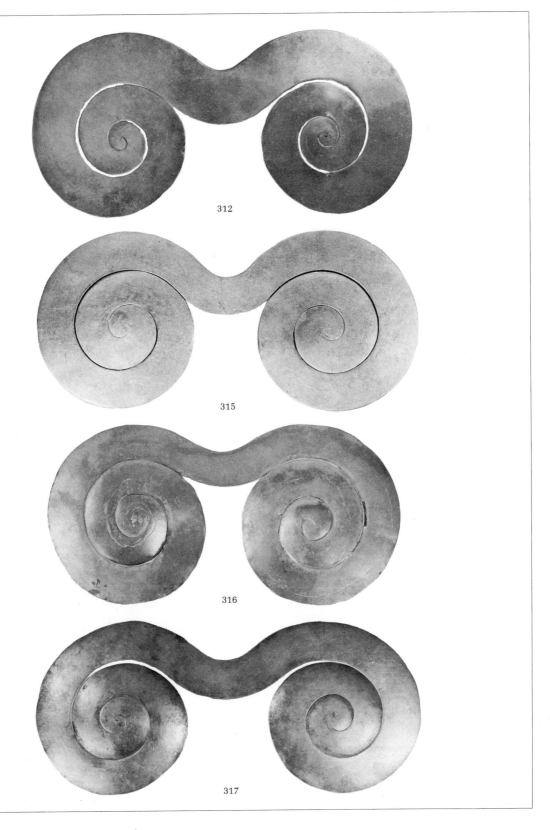

312

315

316

317

319 Ceremonial stone sceptre, with animal heads and monkeys
Archaeologists have found these objects in caches (with other stone items) inside the ceremonial houses of ancient Tairona villages. Among the present-day Kogi and other tribes of the Sierra Nevada de Santa Marta, who descend directly from the Taironas, similar staffs are still carved in wood (no. 319a) and are used in dances and ceremonies – as are prehistoric stone examples, when available (Reichel-Dolmatoff 1953: 43 and pl. 14).
Bonda, Santa Marta, Magdalena
Height 59.4 cm
MO *LT 810*

320 Tairona forked sceptre
Polished stone, greenish grey.
(*See* no. 319)
Bonda, Santa Marta, Magdalena
Length 23.1 cm
MO *LT 671*

321 Tairona stone axe model
Carved from a single piece of dark grey stone. With the other categories of stone object, forms part of the paraphernalia of a Tairona ceremonial house. The present-day Kogi use these axes in solstice ceremonies: green stone to call upon rain, red stone for good weather (Reichel-Dolmatoff 1953: 42).
Minca, Santa Marta, Magdalena
Length 19.4 cm
MO *LT 503*

322 Tairona model stool or milling stone
Polished stone. Used in Tairona rituals, and cached in the ceremonial house. Archaeological examples are still used by Kogi and Ika priests during divination rituals. The priest puts the object on the ground and invites a colleague to sit on the 'stool' and participate in the divination. These objects are also used today as grinding tables on which stone is pulverized for offerings (Reichel-Dolmatoff 1953: 43).
Bonda, Santa Marta, Magdalena
Height 2.3 cm
MO *LT 684*

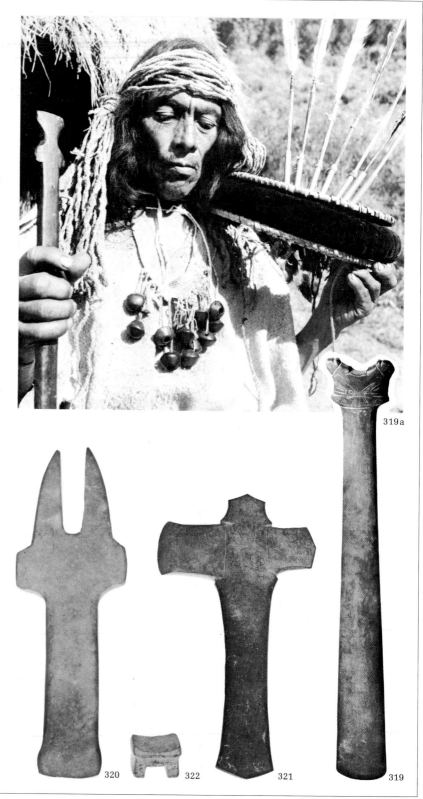

319a

320   322   321   319

323 Tairona winged pendant
Stone. These winged objects were used in Tairona ceremonies and rituals (like the stone sceptres and axes). Among the Kogi today, all priests and men of status possess pendants of this kind, which are said to be inherited, passed on from parents to children, rather than dug up from ancient graves. At present they serve as rattles or tinklers, suspended in pairs from the elbows of dancers (Reichel-Dolmatoff 1953: 42). Given the continuity between the 16th-century Taironas and the present-day Kogi, the pendants may have served the same purpose in the past.
Minca, Santa Marta, Magdalena
Width 40.2 cm
MO *LT 355*

324 Tairona winged pendant
Polished grey-green stone. (*See* no. 323)
Santa Marta, Magdalena
Width 31.7 cm
MO *LT 760*

325 Tairona miniature vessel
Dark coloured clay; incised details picked out with white paste. Coiled serpent with a small bowl on its back.
Minca, Santa Marta, Magdalena
Height 8.7 cm
MO *CT 2295*

325

323

324

326 Tairona miniature jar, seated figure
Pottery; well-polished buff clay. The incised and dotted detail was originally picked out with white material.
Minca, Santa Marta, Magdalena
Height 6.1 cm
MO CT 2304

327 Tairona miniature jar, seated figure
Pottery; yellow-grey. One cheek has a bulge formed by a coca quid. The legs of the stool are conjectural restoration.
San Pedro de la Sierra, Ciénaga, Magdalena
Height 9.5 cm
MO CT 1383

328 Effigy jar, pregnant woman seated on a stool
Grey-black pottery; polished. She wears a necklace, bracelets, arm bands and waist belt.
Minca, Santa Marta, Magdalena
Height 29.1 cm
MO CT 2292

326

327

328

329 Muisca pectoral, with human face
Copper-rich tumbaga; cast. Head made by the matrix technique. All the hooks once held danglers. Territory of the 'Guayaberros' Indians (Empson 1832)
Height 19.6 cm
MM *95–16*
Colour plate

330 Muisca pectoral, human figure
Cast tumbaga with enriched surface; the lower part stretched by hammering. The helmet is in the shape of a bird head (Root 1964).
Height 15 cm
MM *9561*

331 Muisca bird pectoral
Cast tumbaga. The body and arms seem human, though the face is that of a bird.
Height 17.2 cm
MO *6184*

332 Muisca bird pectoral
Gold-rich tumbaga; cast. From the rear, the technique of manufacture can be clearly seen. The base plate, openwork crescent, spiral strip and the bird itself were made as four separate elements at the wax stage (the bird by the matrix technique). These were assembled into a single wax model and cast in one operation (Pérez de Barradas 1958, I: 182).
Neighbourhood of Tunja, Boyacá
Height 14.7 cm
MO *6256*

332

331

330

333 Muisca pendant, with a crested bird
Cast gold. The bird element was made with the aid of a stone matrix.
Gachancipá, Cundinamarca
Height, excluding danglers, 7.8 cm
MO *6783*

334 Muisca pectoral
Gold. Cast and hammered, with embossed decoration.
Vereda de Santo Domingo, Buenavista, Boyacá
Height 14.9 cm
MO *10.091*

335 Pair of circular openwork pendants
Cast gold
Ubaque, Cundinamarca
Height 12.8 cm
MO *7245/6*

336 Circular openwork pendant
Cast and gilded tumbaga
Vereda de Santo Domingo, Buenavista, Boyacá
Diameter 11.4 cm
MO *10.088*

337 Muisca nose ornament
Gilt tumbaga. Lost-wax casting, with the hooks added at the wax stage.
Hacienda San José, Carmen de Carupa, Cundinamarca
Width 8.3 cm
MO *8306*

338 Muisca nose ornament, with two birds
Cast and gilt tumbaga
Cueva de Vélez, Vélez, Santander del Sur
Width 12.1 cm
MO *24.244*

339 Openwork Muisca nose ornament
Cast tumbaga. (See no. 340)
Ferrería, Pacho, Cundinamarca
Width 20.2 cm
MO *252*
Colour plate

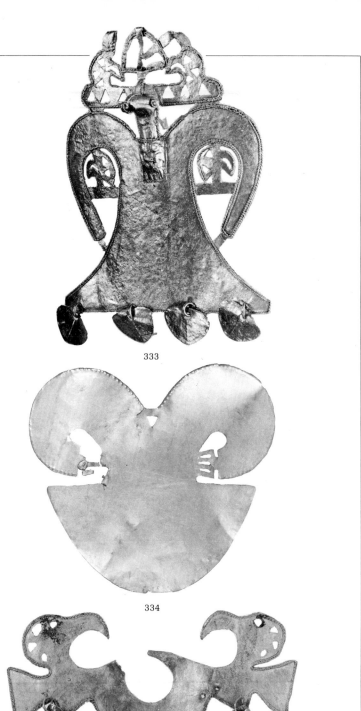

333

334

338

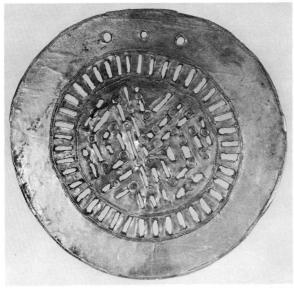

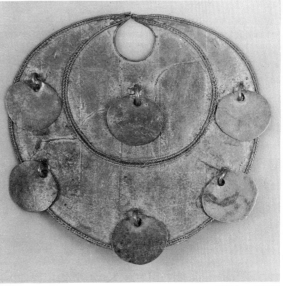

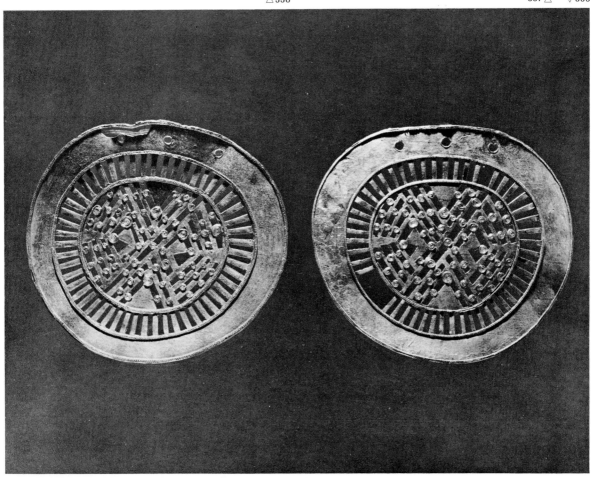

340 Muisca tunjo
Tumbaga; hollow cast, with some
core material remaining within. The
figure wears a nose ornament similar
to no. 339.
Gachancipá, Cundinamarca
Height 12.1 cm
MO *6361*

341 Muisca tunjo, seated man
Cast gold
Height 5 cm
MO *1263*

**342 Muisca snake tunjo, with
human face**
Cast gold
Pasca, Cundinamarca
Length 11.4 cm
MO *24.648*

343 Muisca snake tunjo
Cast gold. The snake has a human
face and animal ears.
Chipaque, Cundinamarca
Length 9.8 cm
MO *24.650*

344 Votive figure, fantastic animal
Cast gold
Muisca style
Length 5 cm
MO *7323*

345 Model of ceremonial staff
Cast tumbaga. Many of the tunjos
depict figures carrying staffs
surmounted by twin birds, or by
forked devices. (*See* no. 346)
Length 16.9 cm
MO *310*

346 Muisca tunjo, masked figure
Cast tumbaga. The figure wears a
necklace and crown. His real face
appears behind the mask, which
is tied on by a cord. In front of him
is a forked staff topped by a pair of
birds (*see* no. 345). The base plate
may represent a mat. The excess
metal below the mat shows the
position of the Y-shaped channel
through which the molten tumbaga
was poured into the mould, and
demonstrates that the tunjo was cast
with the head downwards.
Height 9.4 cm
Coll. Hernán Borrero, Bogotá
Colour plate

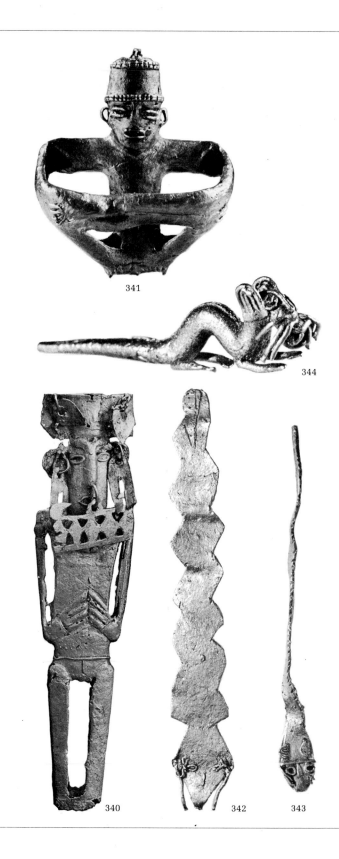

341

344

340

342

343

347 Muisca tunjo, male figure on a bed
Cast tumbaga. The highland Muiscas seem to have slept on beds rather than in hammocks. This figure lies on a framework of seven longitudinal poles, with two crosspieces.
Length 5.7 cm
Coll. Hernán Borrero, Bogotá

348 Muisca tunjo, male figure with crown
Cast tumbaga
El Chocho, Fusagasugá, Cundinamarca
Height 13.4 cm
MO 6307

349 Muisca tunjo, warrior with spear-thrower and lime-container
Cast gold
Vereda del Rincón, Suba, Bogotá D.E.
Height 19.3 cm
MO 22.607

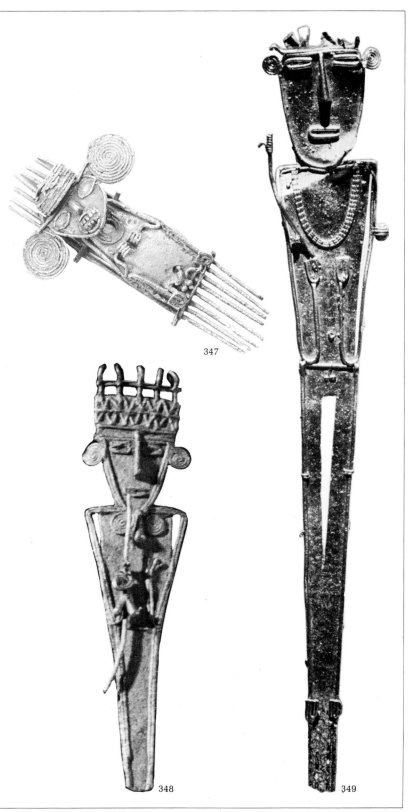

347

345

348

349

350 Muisca tunjo, with spear-thrower
Cast tumbaga
Height 14.4 cm
MO *1860*

351 Muisca tunjo, woman
Cast tumbaga. She wears a fringed skirt and a good deal of jewellery. 'Near the eastern lowlands'. At least one other important find of tunjos has been made along this route to the east (Zerda 1972, I: 68–79).
Height 19.2 cm
MO *1927*

352 Muisca tunjo
Cast tumbaga with enriched surfaces. The figure wears a pendant and carries two spears.
Height 13.4 cm
MO *2050*

353 Muisca tunjo
Cast tumbaga. The smith has not removed the excess metal which filled the flow channels joining the reservoir to the wax model. All tunjos appear to have been cast in the upside-down position. The figure carries a spear-thrower and two javelins.
La Calena, Cundinamarca
Height 11.5 cm
MO *8136*

354 Muisca tunjo, mother with child
Cast gold
Sachica, Boyacá
Height 6 cm
MO *24.686*

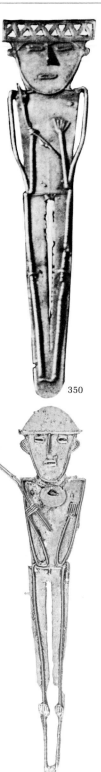

350

351

352

353

354

355 Muisca openwork nose ornament
Cast gold
Vereda Santo Domingo, Buenavista, Boyacá
Width 11.6 cm
MO *10.093*

356 Muisca necklace of pyramid-shaped elements
Cast gold. Each of the thirteen pyramids has a seam down one side, where the original wax sheet was folded and overlapped. The metal pieces are separated by beads of green stone.
Vereda del Toro, Buenavista, Boyacá
Height of pyramids 2.2 cm
MO *9614*

357 Muisca pectoral, human figure
Cast gold
Chiquinquirá, Boyacá
Height 18.1 cm
MO *8576*

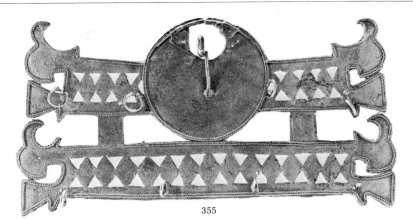

355

356   357

358 Lime-container in the form of a seated man

Cast tumbaga with enriched surfaces. In quality and style, this item (like nos. 359–362, from the same find) is a classic Quimbaya piece. The figure is nude except for jewellery and ligatures round the arms and legs. Suspended from the necklace is a lime-flask similar to no. 359.
Height 12.5 cm
Filandia, Quindío. From the Treasure of the Quimbayas (see p. 51).
MAM 5768

359 Lime-container, with two female figures in relief

Cast tumbaga with enriched surfaces. There are plugged holes for core-supports at the shoulders, base and sides. The general shape is similar to that of the flask worn by no. 358. The feet of the figures project outwards, and give stability when the object is standing vertically. The orifice is closed by a metal stopper.
Height 28 cm
Filandia, Quindío. From the Treasure of the Quimbayas.
MAM 5805

360 Lime-container in the form of a seated, pregnant woman

Cast tumbaga with enriched surfaces. Two suspension loops at the shoulders. Holes for core-supports in the base, buttocks and knees.
Height 18.2 cm
Filandia, Quindío. From the Treasure of the Quimbayas.
MAM 5769

359

358

360

361 Lime-container with decorative lid

Cast tumbaga with enriched surfaces. Seven holes for core-supports. The lid fits tightly and is provided with loops for danglers, and with a central hole to take the lime-dipper. Casting flaws in the neck of the flask and the edge of the lid have been repaired by running in new metal. No. 143 holds a pair of identical containers.
Height 22.3 cm
Filandia, Quindío. From the Treasure of the Quimbayas.
MAM 5795

362 Incense burner(?), in the shape of a human face

Gold-rich tumbaga. Cast in a multi-piece mould. A little metal ran into the join between the two halves of the mould, leaving a raised casting seam which was not completely burnished away. It shows as a vertical line on the forehead and chin, and as a raised seam inside the hollow pedestal foot (see fig. 20). Two suspension loops. The openings in the face are rough and unfinished. This may indicate that they were intended to take an inlay, in which case this item may have served as a flask rather than as an incense burner. The lid fits like a plug, and is in the form of a coiled serpent with crossed fangs.
Height, with lid 13 cm
Filandia, Quindío. From the Treasure of the Quimbayas.
MAM 5770

362

361

363 Pendant, human figure
Cast tumbaga with enriched surface
Quimbaya style
Height 9.6 cm
MM *1928.12–7.1*
Colour plate

364 Necklace pendant, human face
Tumbaga; open-back casting.
Suspension hole in each temple.
Quimbaya style
Collection of R. B. White (a British
mining engineer, who worked and
collected in Antioquia and the
Quimbaya zone). White corresponded
with the botanist Sir Joseph Hooker,
from whom this item was purchased
in 1872.
Height 1.9 cm
MM *8504*

365 Small mask
Cast gold
Calarcá, Quindío
Height 3.1 cm
MO *3083*

**366 Shallow bowl, naked, supine
woman**
Pottery; painted dark red, orange ·
and white. The treatment of the face
suggests possible links with
Quimbaya goldwork.
A few similar vessels come from the
Quimbaya zone of the Cauca Valley,
but the style is still undated.
Length, head to foot 32 cm
BP *Q-8766*
Colour plate

**367 Necklace of forty-six insect
forms**
Cast gold, with crystal beads. A very
similar necklace forms part of the
Treasure of the Quimbayas (Pérez de
Barradas 1966, I, fig. 28).
Quimbaya, Quindío
Length of insects 2.6 cm
MO *2912*

364

365

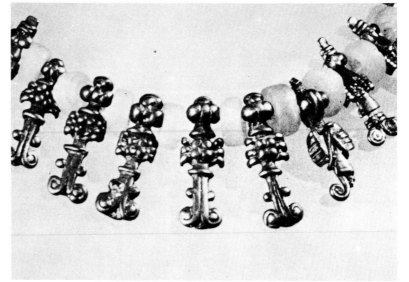

367

368 Embossed helmet

Raised from sheet tumbaga with
enriched surfaces. The helmet is oval
in section, with holes for a strap at
the sides. The outlines of the border
design are traced on the outside, but
the embossed decoration is done
from the inside. Guidelines, to help
the embossing, are still visible on
the outside.

Calarcá, Quindío

   The seventeen objects forming
collection no. 1910.12–2 in the
Museum of Mankind were purchased
as a single lot from Johnson Matthey
& Co of London in 1910. Since this
company specializes in refining
precious metals, it seems likely that
these objects were sent to be melted
down, but were saved when their
quality was realized. The accompany-
ing information says 'these jewels
come from the Quindío region in the
western branch of the Cordillera of
the Andes, where there is a tradition
that the Calarcá Indians used to
live.' This is very close to Filandia,
where the Treasure of the
Quimbayas was discovered in 1891.
In their fine technical quality, and in
the range of forms and stylistic
treatment, the London collection and
the Madrid 'Treasure' have much in
common, and represent the
Quimbaya style in its most classic
form (Pérez de Barradas 1966, I,
figs. 11–45).

Maximum diameter 20.2 cm
MM *1910.12–2.1*

368

369

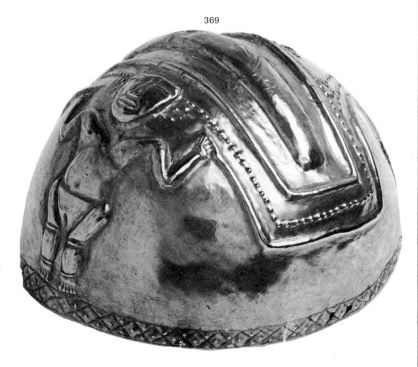

369 Helmet with repoussé figure

Raised from sheet tumbaga with
enriched surface. The circumference
is slightly oval, with paired holes
(for a chin strap) on each side. On the
front is the repoussé figure of a nude
woman in Quimbaya style. The lines
of lozenge pattern are traced on the
front; the embossing is done from the
inside.

Very similar to a helmet in the
Treasure of the Quimbayas, Madrid
(Pérez de Barradas 1966, I, fig. 22).

Diameter (longest axis) 20.4 cm
MM *+342*

370 Mask

Cast gold; open-back. Fragments of the clay casing remain in the hollows of the ears, and there is a casting flaw on the side of the chin. The nose ornament is of typical Quimbaya type, and the mask may depict an individual with filed teeth (Root 1964). Four holes around the edge.
Calarcá region. Quindío. (*See* no. 368)
Height 11.5 cm
MM *1910.12–2.5*

371 Object with two figures

Cast gold. On top of the cylindrical socket are a man and a woman, back to back, represented in pure Quimbaya style, nude except for jewellery: diadems, multiple earrings, necklaces, nose ornaments and leg bands. The top, between the heads, is open.
Calarcá region, Quindío. (*See* no. 368)
Height 3 cm
MM *1910.12–2.14*

372 Finger-grip of spear-thrower (?)

Cast tumbaga with enriched surface. Spiral decoration and a modelled animal with a human head. One end of the cylinder is open, the other closed.
Calarcá region, Quindío. (*See* no. 368)
Length 4.1 cm
MM *1910.12–2.13*

373 Finger-grip of spear-thrower (?), with human head

Cast tumbaga with enriched surface. The large end is open, forming a socket; the small end is closed. Holes (now plugged) for core-supports in the neck and at the closed end (Root 1964). These objects have also been interpreted as musical instruments. There is a similar piece in the Treasure of the Quimbayas (Pérez de Barradas 1966, I, fig. 43).
Calarcá region, Quindío. (*See* no. 368)
Length 12 cm
MM *1910.12–2.10*

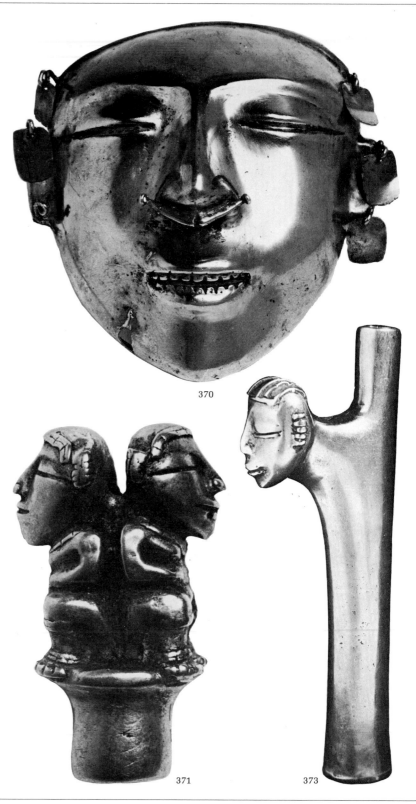

370

371

373

374 Neck of a lime-flask, with six human heads

Cast tumbaga with enriched surface. The top part, with the heads, may have been cast separately, though the traces of solder may also indicate an ancient repair (Root 1964). Round the basal edge are four holes for the attachment of the rest of the flask. (?) Cauca Valley. Quimbaya style. Height 16.2 cm
MM *1940 Am. 11–1*

375 Lime-flask, standing male

Cast tumbaga with enriched surface, still containing some bits of black core. Holes for core-supports (one plugged, one open) in the shoulders. In the base of each foot is a rectangular open hole, one with signs of repair, through which core material could have been extracted after casting. Flaws in the original casting (e.g. behind the right ankle) were repaired by running in new metal. Salento, Quindío (cf. Pérez de Barradas 1966, I, fig. 30)
Height 30 cm
MM *89.10–1.1*

372

374

375

376 Burial urn
Pottery; highly polished and with a chestnut-coloured slip. Two female figures are modelled on the sides in a style identical to that of the finest Quimbaya goldwork (cf. no. 375). Similar vessels, sometimes filled with cremated bones, have come from tombs in Caldas and the Quindío, though none has been found in controlled excavations.
Brownware Incised style (Bruhns 1969–70). Probably about AD 400–800.
Height 25 cm
MN *No number*

377 Lime-container, seated woman
Cast tumbaga with enriched surface. A little core material remains in the legs of the stool, and occasional casting flaws have been repaired by running in new metal. Holes for core-supports at the buttocks and shoulders. The head, stool and lower part of the legs were cast separately from the body and then soldered into place (Root 1964). The head is of noticeably yellower metal than the body. (*See* fig. 26)
(?) Cauca Valley. Quimbaya style. (Cf. Pérez de Barradas 1966, I, figs. 31, 32 for examples in the Treasure of the Quimbayas).
Height 14.5 cm
MM *1940 Am 11–2*
Colour plate

378 Lime-flask
Gold-rich tumbaga; cast. There is a plugged hole for a chaplet (core-support) in the bottom. The handles are soldered on. The upper part may also have been cast separately and soldered into place (Root 1964). (Cf. Pérez de Barradas 1966, I, fig. 40 for an identical example from the Treasure of the Quimbayas.)
Calarcá region, Quindío. (*See* no. 368)
Height 10.8 cm
MM *1910.12–2.6*

378

376

379

379 Receptacle (lime-flask), seated figure

Cast tumbaga with enriched surface. The holes for the core-supports have been plugged, but are still visible (on top of each shoulder, through the upper part of each buttock, and one at the base of the curved sheet). The object was made in several pieces, soldered together. The body and base are a single lost-wax casting, and in the front of the base was left a rectangular hole through which the core material was removed. The upper edge shows as a faint line between the ankles; the other edges are bounded by the beaded lines. The hole was filled by a patch soldered into place. The forearms are of sheet metal, with traces of a joining seam. The feet were cast separately, as were the hands with their spirals (Easby 1956).
Quimbaya style
Height 22.1 cm
UMP *SA 2751*

380 Receptacle (lime-flask), seated woman

Cast tumbaga with enriched surface. There are holes for core-supports at the shoulders and knees. The hands, with their spiral ornaments, were cast separately and then soldered into place (Easby 1956).
Quimbaya style
Height 22.7 cm
UMP *SA 2752*

381 Disc with embossed border

Sheet gold; two holes for suspension.
Municipio of Quimbaya, Quindío
Diameter 18.3 cm
MO *21.789*

382 Pectoral disc, with human figure and birds

Hammered and repoussé tumbaga with enriched surface. Suspension hole at the top.
Diameter 26.8 cm
MM *96.2–3.1*
Colour plate

383 Pectoral disc, with embossed face

Hammered tumbaga
Diameter 12 cm
MO *68*

384 Pectoral disc, with embossed lizard

Hammered tumbaga
Diameter 16.2 cm
MO *66*

381

380

383   384

385 Lizard
Cast tumbaga
Length 13.6 cm
MO *6518*

386 Alligator pendant
Cast gold
Length 7.9 cm
MO *5928*

387 Lizard pendant
Cast and gilt tumbaga. Suspension
loop behind head.
Probably Quimbaya zone
Length 11.6 cm
MO *8138*

388 Pendant with spiral ornaments
Open-backed casting; gilt tumbaga.
Probably Quimbaya zone
Length 14.1 cm
MO *6034*

389 Shell (?)
Cast and surface-enriched tumbaga
Length 13.7 cm
MO *6035*

390 Fish or shell form
Cast gold
Length 8.5 cm
MO *3098*

**391 Necklace, frogs with openwork
tails**
Cast tumbaga, with crystal beads
Quimbaya, Quindío
Length of frogs 3.1 cm
MO *2911*

392 Pendant
Cast and gilt tumbaga, with some
hammer finishing. Ornaments in this
form have been found all over
Colombia from the Sinú and Tairona
zones in the north to Nariño in the
far south.
El Anclar, Montelíbano, Córdoba
Height 9.7 cm
MO *24.394*

393 Pendant
Cast tumbaga. Textile impression on
the base.
Quindío
Height 20 cm
MO *69*

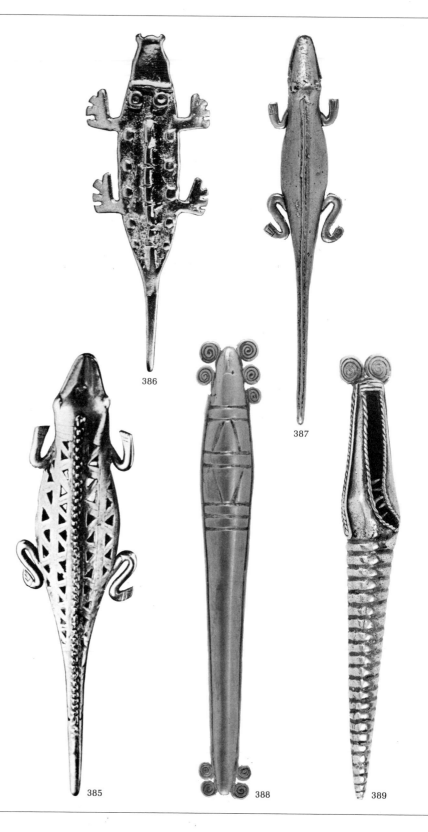

385

386

387

388

389

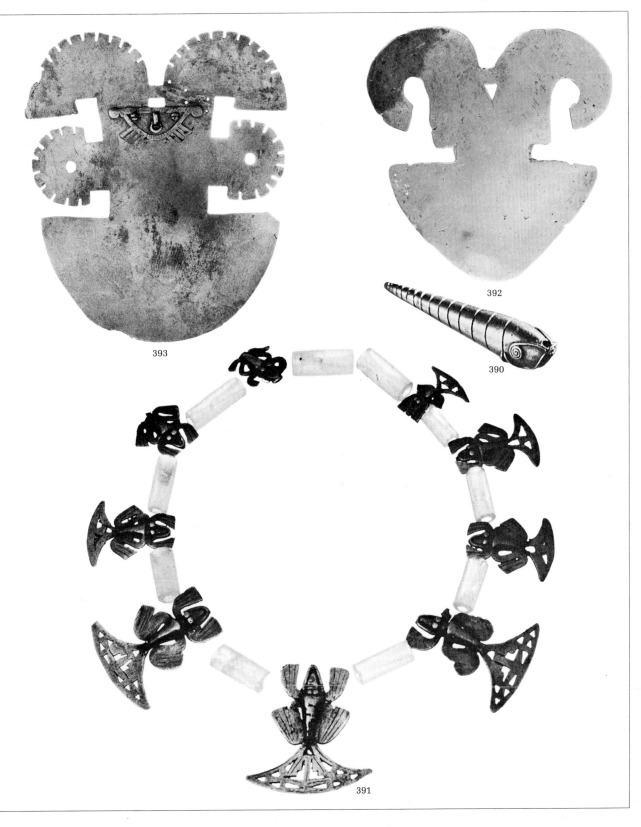

393

392

390

391

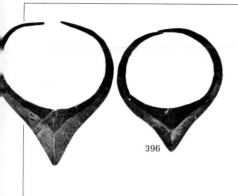

394 Pectoral ornament
Cast and hammered gold. Slightly
curved in section.
Width 19.5 cm
MM *Q. Am. 78 (Christy 1880)*

395 Pair of bracelets
Cast tumbaga sheet, hammered to
shape.
Montenegro, Quindío
Heights 10.5, 11.6 cm
MO *24.455/6*

396 Pair of nose ornaments
Hammered tumbaga. Not a perfectly
matching pair. The smaller one has
zigzag decoration traced on the
triangular projection, and a little
excess metal has been folded over
and hammered down. (*See* fig. 16)
Heights 5.9, 6.9 cm
MM *1836.3–3.1/2*

395

397 Pair of ear ornaments
Cast gold
Unknown provenance. Three similar
rings, but without pendants, were
found at Sitio Conte, Coclé, Panama,
and are considered to be trade pieces
from Colombia (Lothrop 1937: 142).
Height 7.6 cm
MO *6475/6*

396

397

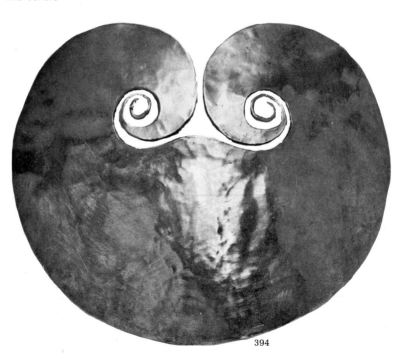

394

395

398

398 Openwork nose ornament
Cast gold
Diameter 3.8 cm
MO 6532

399 Nose ornament
Cast gold
Width 7.4 cm
MO 2443

400 Nose ornament
Hammered and gilt tumbaga.
Slightly curved to fit the contours of
the face. Impression of a woven
textile on parts of the surface.
Montenegro, Quindío
Width 15.8 cm
MO 24.454

401 Nose ornament
Hammered and repoussé gold
Armenia, Quindío
Width 16.1 cm
MO 2346

402 Nose ornament
Hammered gold
Width 11.6 cm
MO 3585

399

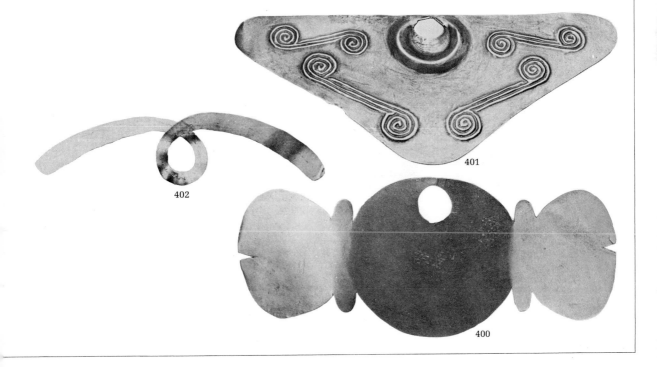

402

401

400

403 Pendant, nude male figure
Solid, cast gold
Height 4 cm
MO *3621*

404 Pendant, human figure
Cast tumbaga with enriched surface.
Fine detail, with clear modelling of
costume and jewellery. On the back
of the head-dress are two standing
human figures, with arms folded.
These figures continue down the
back in the form of two ridges,
perforated for suspension.
Height 3.4 cm
MM *1977 Am. 12.1*

**405 Pectoral, human figure with
danglers**
Cast; gold-rich tumbaga.
Height 12.3 cm
MO *3187*

406 Pectoral, two birds
Cast tumbaga
Montenegro, Quindío. Similar pieces
are found in the Sinú region.
Height 9 cm
MO *24.453*

403

404

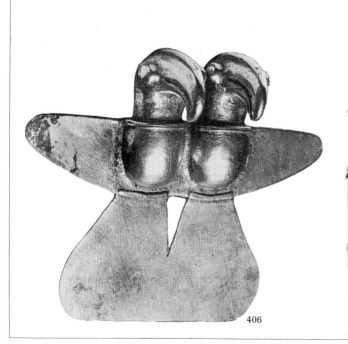

406

405

407 Eagle pendant
Cast and hammered gold
Quindío
Height 7.5 cm
MO *3043*

408 Animal pendant
Gold, open-back casting
Montenegro, Quindío
Length 4.1 cm
MO *24.239*

409 Shell pendant
Gold; hollow cast, with some dark
core material still present inside.
Length 4.1 cm
MO *1159*

410 Shell pendant
Cast gold
Length 5.6 cm
MO *6463*

411 Set of six pendants, fish-like shapes
Cast gold
Quimbaya, Quindío. The form is
found in both Quimbaya and Tolima
zones.
Average length 3.6 cm
MO *2907*

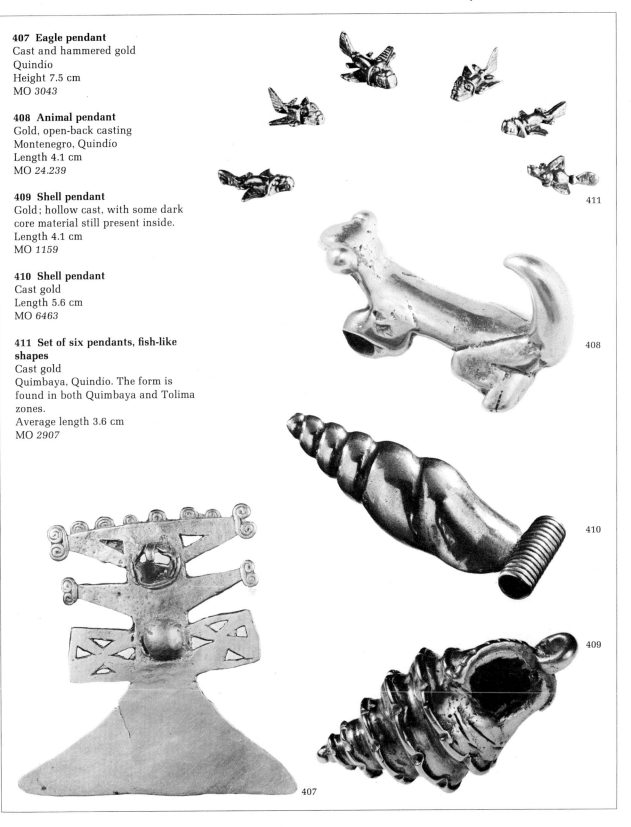

411

408

410

409

407

412 Pendant, female figure
Cast gold
Height 4.9 cm
MO *6424*

413 Chisel
Hammered tumbaga
Length 6.4 cm
MO *4630*

414 Bowl
Burnished brown pottery, with
fluted decoration and deep excisions
separated by rows of dots. The
varnish is modern.
Unknown provenance but almost
certainly from the general area of
Medellín, Antioquia. Age unknown.
Diameter at rim 32 cm
BP *Q-8899*

415 Jar, with two little faces in relief
Pottery; black resist painting over a
red slip.
Calima or Quimbaya zone. AD 1200
to Spanish Conquest (Bray and
Moseley 1969–70; Bruhns 1976).
Height 24.5 cm
BP *Q-3068*

416 Vessel, copying a gourd bottle
Pottery; black resist painting over a
glossy red background.
Unknown provenance. The resist
technique and the 'Yotoco style' of
spiral decoration were employed in
the Quimbaya and Calima zones
from about AD 1000 to 1200 (Bray
and Moseley 1969–70; Sampson *et
al.* 1972; Bruhns 1976).
Height 12.5 cm
BP *Q-8888*

412

413

415

414   416

417 Hollow figure, seated man
Pottery; red slip. Contains a rattle
pellet. Holes beside each ear and in
the base allowed steam to escape
during firing.
Probably middle Cauca Valley
Height 31 cm
BP Q-11080

418–421 Group of four solid figures
Pottery. Each is made from a slab of
clay to which the limbs are added.
These square, solid figures always
consist of nude males (usually
seated), with holes of unknown
function in the heads and bodies.
The noses are perforated for the
insertion of metal ornaments. Most
of these figures come from the
Department of Caldas, within the
Quimbaya zone. AD 1200 to Spanish
Conquest (Bruhns 1976: 150–5).
(418) Rioblanco, El Cairo, Valle del
Cauca
Height 20 cm
MO CQ-2938
(419) Quimbaya, Quindío
Height 20.9 cm
MO CQ-3715
(420) Rioblanco, El Cairo, Valle del
Cauca
Height 18 cm
MO CQ-2942
(421) Rioblanco, El Cairo, Valle del
Cauca
Height 18.6 cm
MO CQ-2937

422 Slab figure
Pottery.
After AD 1200. (See nos. 418–421)
Height 23.7 cm
MO CQ 4548

418–421

417

422

423 Solid slab figure
Pottery. Nude man carrying a child.
Quimbaya zone. AD 1200 to Spanish
Conquest. (*See* nos. 418–421)
BP *Q-1117*

424 Solid slab figure
Pottery
Quimbaya zone. After AD 1200. (*See*
nos. 418–421)
Height 13.9 cm
MO *CQ 38*

425 Solid slab figure
Pottery
Quimbaya, Quindío. After AD 1200.
(*See* nos. 418–421)
Height 21.1 cm
MO *CQ 3718*

426 Solid slab figure
Pottery
Quimbaya, Quindío. After AD 1200.
(*See* nos. 418–421)
Height 20.2 cm
MO *CQ 3717*

427 Solid slab figure
Pottery
Quimbaya, Quindío. After AD 1200.
(*See* nos. 418–421)
Height 18.2 cm
MO *CQ 3772*

428 Hollow slab figure
Pottery. Man, nude except for woven
leg bands, carrying a child. Orange
slip, with reddish-brown face paint.
Quimbaya zone. AD 1200 to Spanish
Conquest (Bruhns 1976).
Height 43 cm
BP *Q-11070*

423

424

425

426

427

428

Tolima Region

429 Tolima pectoral
Cast and hammered gold
Height 19.7 cm
MO *8139*

430 Pectoral
Cast and hammered gold
Restrepo, Valle del Cauca
Stylistically a Tolima piece, though
found in Calima territory.
Height 22.2 cm
MO *6336*
Colour plate

431 Tolima pectoral
Gold-rich tumbaga; cast and
hammered.
Height 10.7 cm
MO *6028*

432 Tolima pectoral
Cast and hammered gold (Farabee
1920, fig. 51)
Height 17.6 cm
UMP *SA 2753*

433 Tolima pectoral
Cast and hammered gold
Height 17.8 cm
UMP *SA 2754*

434 Tolima pectoral
Cast gold; hammer finished.
Height 19 cm
MO *4661*

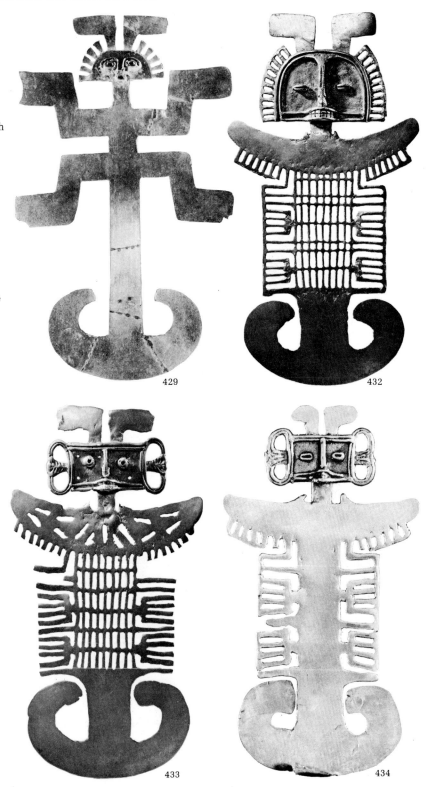

429

432

431

433

434

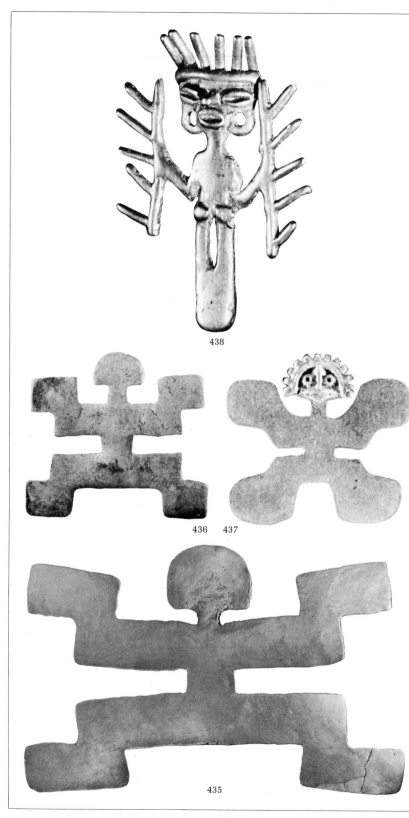

438

436   437

435

435 Tolima pectoral
Cast and hammered gold
Campohermoso, Ataco, Tolima
Height 15 cm
MO *5830*

436 Tolima necklace pendant
Tumbaga
Height 5.4 cm
MO *1963*

437 Tolima pendant
Cast and hammered gold
Height 5.5 cm
MO *6065*

438 Tolima figure pendant
Cast gold
Campohermoso, Ataco, Tolima
Height 5 cm
MO *5880*

439 Necklace of stylized Tolima figures
Cast tumbaga; hammer finished.
Height 3.1 cm
MO *3683*

440 Necklace of Tolima figure pendants
Cast gold
Campohermoso, Ataco, Tolima
Height 3.9 cm
MO *5859*
Colour plate

441 Tolima pendant, fantastic animal
Solid, cast gold.
Campohermoso, Ataco, Tolima
Length 7.5 cm
MO *5869*

442 Tolima pendant, fantastic animal
Solid, cast gold.
Campohermoso, Ataco, Tolimo
Length 6.5 cm
MO *5870*

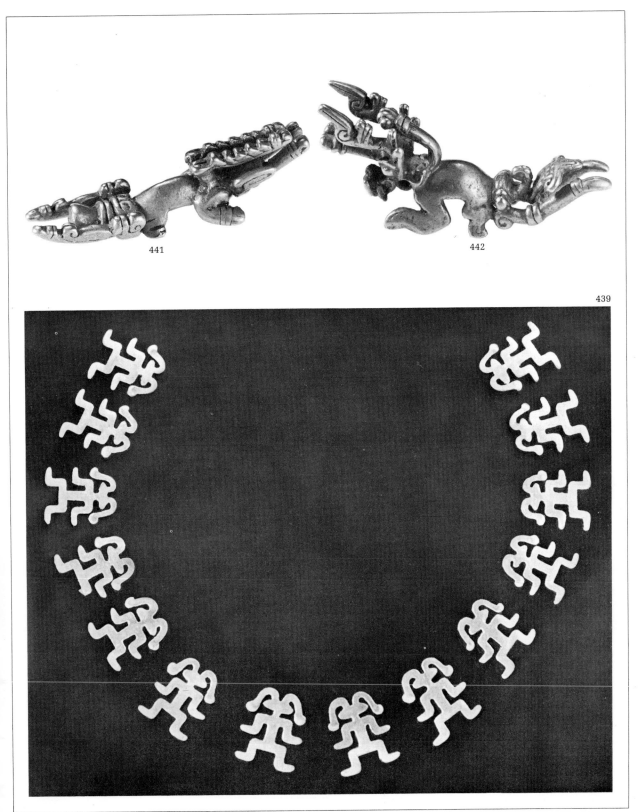

441

442

439

443 Tolima 'batwing' pendant
Cast and hammered gold
Chaparral, Tolima
Width 8.3 cm
MO 5931

444, 445 Pair of Tolima 'batwing' ornaments
Cast gold; hammer finished.
Campohermoso, Ataco, Tolima
Widths 10.7, 10.5 cm
MO 5836/7

446, 447 Pair of Tolima 'batwing' ornaments
Cast gold; hammer finished.
Campohermoso, Ataco, Tolima
Widths 14.5, 12.3 cm
MO 5841, 5838

448 Tweezers, with two birds
Cast and hammered gold
Chaparral, Tolima
Height 6.6 cm
MO 5926
Colour plate

449 Nose ornament
Solid gold; cast.
Rio Blanco, Tolima
Width 2.5 cm
MO 6247

450 Mask, grotesque human face
Pottery; life size. The holes at the sides and upper edge would have allowed the mask to be tied over the face. The nose is pierced for an ornament, and the holes in the chin may have been for the attachment of other decorative objects. Inside the lips are sockets that possibly held teeth.
Rio Blanco, Tolima. Undated.
Height 28.5 cm
MN 46–IX–656

451 Effigy vessel, seated man
Pottery; black painted decoration over a red slip. There are ligatures round the arms and legs, and he wears ear spools, a necklace and a nose ornament.
Most of the similar pieces come from the middle Magdalena Valley in the Department of Tolima.
Height 36 cm
BP Tol-4222

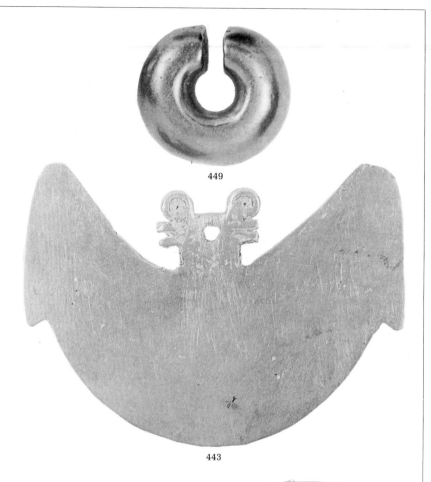

449

443

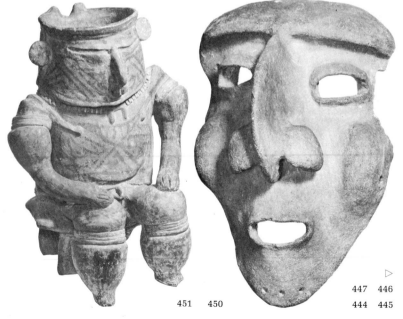

451   450

447   446
444   445

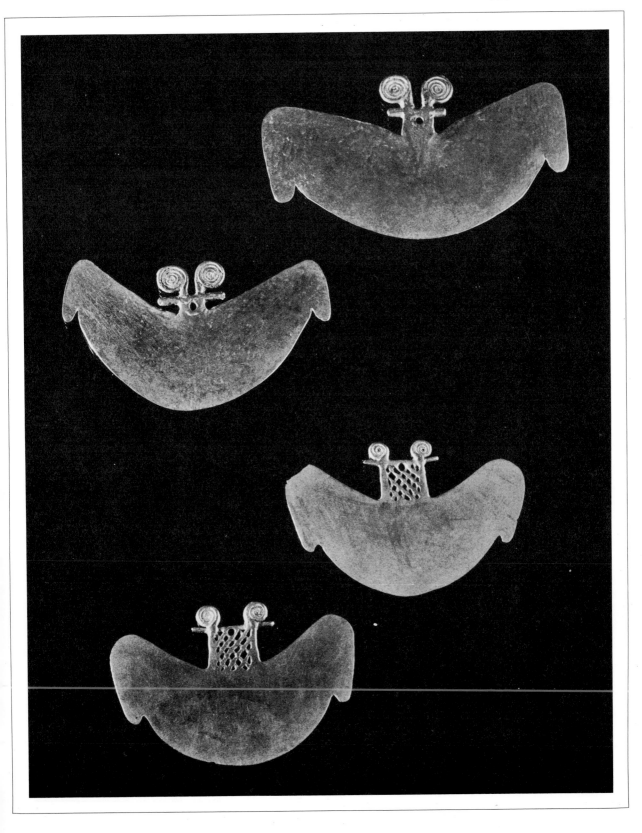

San Agustín Region

452 San Agustín statue
Stone. Human figure (with animal fangs) carrying a shield and a staff or club.
San Agustín style
Height 95 cm
MM Q.78.Am.1

453 Necklace, pendant figures
Gold-rich tumbaga; cast and hammered. Fifteen laminar, stylized human figures with incised detail. The single creature with a forked 'tail' seems to be basically human, with indications of nose, mouth, pubic triangle and necklace. Clear relationship with the Tolima style of goldwork.
Tomb 13, Tourist Hotel, San Agustín, Huila (Duque Gómez 1964: 203–5). Found with no. 454, and with a gold diadem similar to no. 461. The other offerings consisted of stone beads, a stone chisel, and pottery vessels. Mesitas Medio (Isnos) period, early centuries AD.
Height, figure with tail, 3.7 cm
MN 48–V–6624 (with tail); 48–V–6626, 6629–32, 6634–5, 6640, 6642, 6645, 6647, 6649, 6651–3

454 Nose ornament
Hammered gold. Slightly curved to fit the contours of the face.
San Agustín (see no. 453)
Width 13.4 cm
MN 48–V–6621

454

452

453

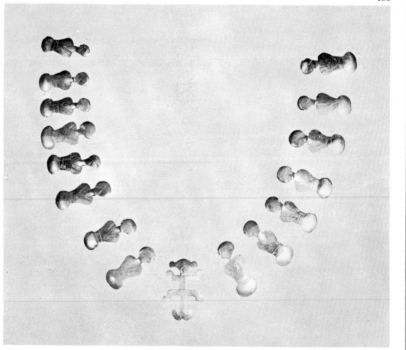

455 Pectoral, figure with head-dress
Cast tumbaga, with enriched surface.
The central figure wears a nose
ornament ending in a disc, similar to
the full-sized gold examples which
have been found in the Upper Cauca
region. The four identical bird-
headed creatures were cast
separately, and soldered to the main
figure. The crescentic blade was
finished by hammering. Stylistically,
this item (and the Popayán group in
general) shows links with other
styles of the Magdalena and Cauca
headwaters. The nose disc and the
crested creatures on the arms can be
matched in the goldwork of San
Agustín (Pérez de Barradas 1966, II,
pl. 186).
Hacienda de la Marquesa, Timbío,
Cauca (Lehmann 1953: 206–12;
Braunholtz 1939). Part of a collection
of objects found by a treasure-
hunter called Leonardo Ramirez in
two adjacent shaft-and-chamber
tombs. According to Ramirez, he
found also a necklace of gold frogs, a
gold bird, two nose ornaments and
some gold sheet. The pottery
included nine crudely modelled
effigy vessels.
(Pérez de Barradas 1966, I, fig. 58).
Height 29.8 cm
MM *1938.7–6.1*
Colour plate

456 Eagle pectoral
Tumbaga with enriched surface;
open-back casting, hammer finished.
The bird has two small human legs
and a phallus. A typical 'Popayán
eagle' (Pérez de Barradas 1966).
Height 9.4 cm
MM *+7827*

457 Pectoral, eagle with human head
Tumbaga with enriched surface;
open-back casting. The body is a
typical 'Popayán eagle' (cf. no. 456),
but the face and crest are in the
Tolima style. An identical nose
ornament appears on no. 455.
Height 7.7 cm
MM *+5803*

456

457

Tierradentro Region

458 Mask
Gold-rich tumbaga, with further surface enrichment. This item is a masterpiece of repoussé metalwork, and must once have covered a hollow-backed wooden mask to which it was attached by pins through the large holes at the sides and top. On the reverse of the face, the metal was folded around the edges of the underlying wooden mask, giving some idea of its profile. The processes used in making the gold mask can be reconstructed:
(1) The tumbaga sheet was prepared, and the surfaces were enriched before being placed over the backing (since both faces have been pickled).
(2) The wooden mask served as a form or template, over which the sheet metal was worked into shape. The metal split at two points (below the chin and beside the left temple). The damage was repaired by over-lapping the edges of the metal and pinning through them into the underlying wood (see fig. 17). At certain points, the metal creased or puckered, and these flaws are still visible on the reverse.
(3) Once the gold was plugged permanently to its backing, the outside face was given a final burnish to remove all blemishes. This process caused a slight ridging of the metal against the heads of the nails (see the hole at the right temple).
Near Páez, Cauca (in the Tierradentro region). Found in 1976 in a tomb with nos. 459–463, with fragments of a second mask, and also a large sheet ornament with an embossed lizard (now in the Museo del Oro). (See notes on no. 463)
Width 12.5 cm
Coll. Hernán Borrero, Bogotá
Colour plate

459 Ear plug
Hammered and repoussé gold. Made from four separate pieces of sheet metal, pinned together with small gold nails (perhaps over a wooden core, which has now disappeared). The inner face of the cylinder, with the end pieces, is a single piece of folded metal. The two strips with raised bosses or cogs were then fitted in place, and their ends overlapped and pinned. Finally, the strip of metal with geometric decoration was wound round the outside and pinned into place, locking the whole construction together. The style and technique of this specimen are so similar to some early Calima pieces (see no. 131) that there must once have been close links between the Tierradentro and Calima zones.
Páez, Cauca (Tierradentro region)
(*See* nos. 458, 463)
Width 5.2 cm
Coll. Hernán Borrero, Bogotá

460 Bird pendant
Cast gold. Danglers attached by wire staples.
Páez, Cauca (Tierradentro region)
(*See* nos. 458, 463)
Width 3.8 cm
Coll. Hernán Borrero, Bogotá

461 Diadem
Hammered sheet gold. A similar piece was found at San Agustín (Duque Gómez 1964, pl. XLV) with a necklace of Tolima pendants (no. 453), and the form also occurs in the early Calima style (e.g. Pérez de Barradas 1954, II, pl. 268).
Páez, Cauca (Tierradentro region).
(*See* nos. 458, 463)
Width 25.6 cm
Coll. Hernán Borrero, Bogotá

462 Set of twenty-eight plaques
Hammered sheet metal. Tumbaga. The colour varies considerably, suggesting either different degrees of surface enrichment or else the use of several pieces of raw material of different compositions. Possibly made over templates, though details touched up by hand. Two varieties are present: a flat-topped form with three holes, and a two-hole form with a spiked head-dress.
Páez, Cauca (Tierradentro region)
(*See* nos. 458, 463)
Height 4.0 cm (rayed form), 3.2 cm (flat-topped)
Coll. Hernán Borrero, Bogotá

463 Four-footed jar
Pottery; coral-red slip, with traces of black resist painting on the feet. At nearby San Agustín, both the form of the vessel and the technique of resist painting are firmly related to the Isnos period, with radiocarbon dates spanning the first four centuries AD and with evidence of goldworking (Reichel-Dolmatoff 1975). Since connections between San Agustín and Tierradentro were always close, the same dating can probably be applied to this pot and the gold objects (nos. 458–463) found in the tomb with it.
Páez, Cauca (Tierradentro region)
Height 22.5 cm
Coll. Hernán Borrero, Bogotá

464 Pendant, human figure
Cast and hammered gold, with incised details.
Páez de Belalcázar, Cauca. The pendant is in the Tolima style, but was found in the Tierradentro region.
Height 6.7 cm
MO *8004*

465 Tweezers
Tumbaga with surface enrichment; hammered.
Tierradentro region
Length 3.6 cm
Coll. Jaime Errazuriz, Bogotá

462

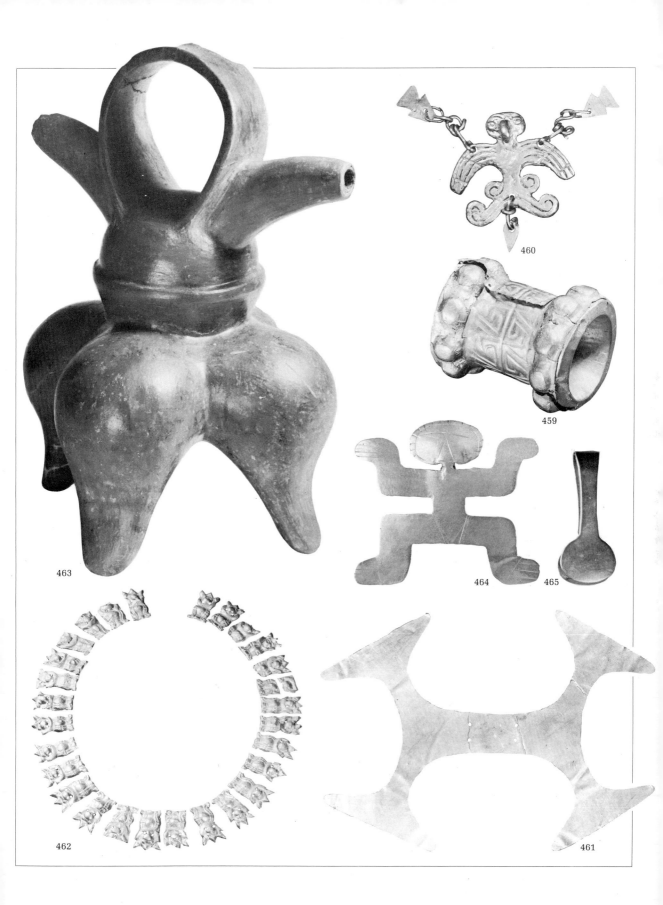

460

459

464　465

463

462　461

466 Pair of ear pendants
Hammered gold
Pupiales, Nariño. Capulí period.
Width 12.6 cm
MO 25.192/3

467 Pair of ear ornaments, spiral design
Hammered and repoussé gold
Puerres, Nariño. Capulí period.
Diameter 8.5 cm
MO 25.216/7

468 Pair of embossed ear danglers
Gilt tumbaga. Loops of hammered wire.
Consacá, Nariño. Capulí period.
Diameter 6.9 cm
MO 25.226/7

469 Pair of ear ornaments
Hammered gold; repoussé bosses.
Consacá, Nariño. Capulí period.
Width 7.8 cm
MO 25.214/5

470 Pair of ear ornaments
Hammered gold; repoussé bosses.
Pupiales, Nariño. Capulí period.
Diameter 8.7 cm
MO 17.753/4

471 Pair of ear ornaments, with human heads
Gold; hammered and repoussé.
Consacá, Nariño. Capulí period.
Width 10.4 cm
MO 25.212/3

472 Pair of ear ornaments, with jaguar faces
Gold; hammered and repoussé.
Pupiales, Nariño. Capulí period.
Diameter 8.5 cm
MO 24.474/5

473 Pair of ear ornaments, with monkeys
Cast and hammered gold
Finca San José, La Victoria, Ipiales, Nariño. Capulí period.
Diameter 6.5 cm
MO 17.179/80

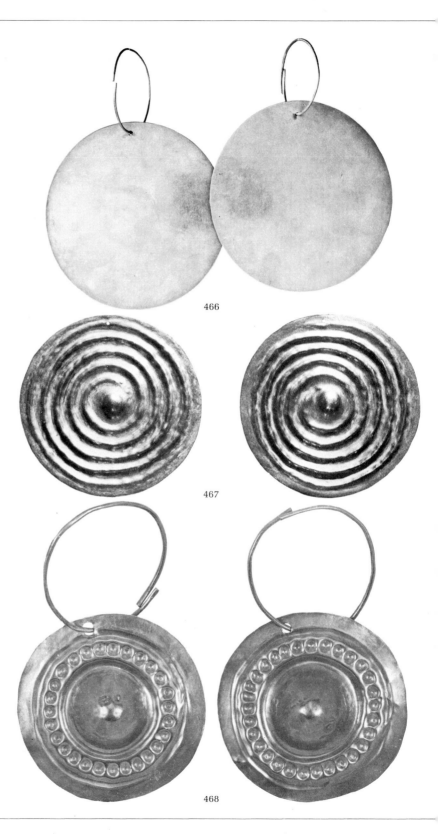

466

467

468

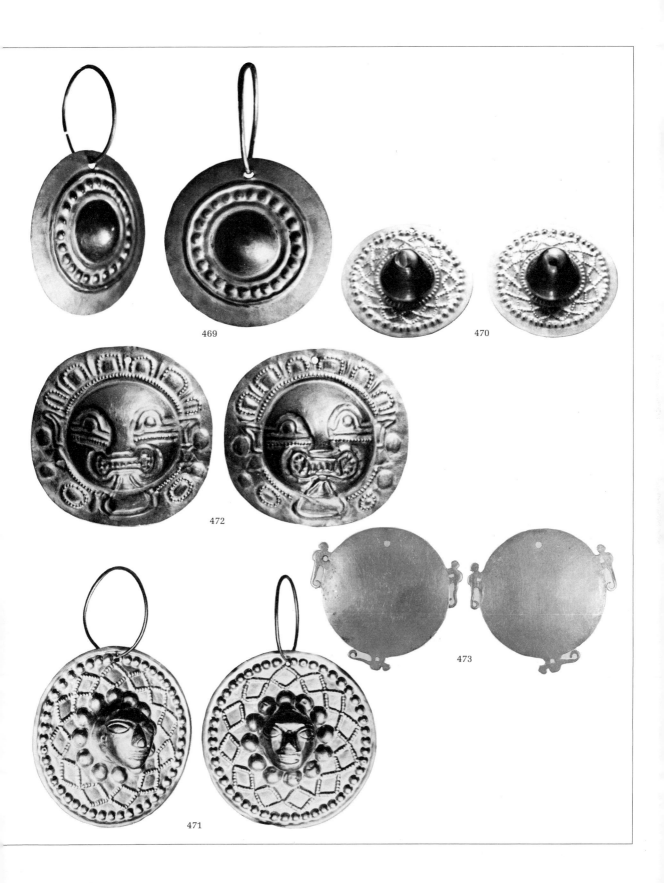

469

470

472

473

471

474 Bowl, with monkeys
Painted pottery. Bowls with low
pedestal feet are one of the
commonest shapes in Nariño. On the
outside of this example is a comb-
like design in black resist painting
over a buff background. Inside is a
series of monkeys executed in the
same technique, with additional
detail in red positive paint. The
same monkeys appear on goldwork
of the Nariño region (nos. 475–476,
478–479). Piartal style of Nariño.
AD 1250–1350 (Uribe 1977).
Rim diameter 20 cm
BP *N-12565*

**475 Pair of circular ear ornaments,
with monkeys**
Cast and hammered gold
Córdoba, Nariño. Capulí period.
Diameters 9.8, 10 cm
MO *25.204/5*

476 Nose ornament, with monkeys
Hammered gold
Vereda de Miraflores, Pupiales,
Nariño. Piartal period.
Width 11.3 cm
MO *16.302*

474

476

475

477 Ocarina, shell surmounted by a monkey
Pottery, brown surface. Similar monkeys occur on Nariño goldwork. Pupiales, Nariño. Possibly Capulí period, AD 800–1250 (M.V. Uribe, personal communication).
Length 12.7 cm
MO CN 4101

478 Pair of ear pendants, with animals
Cast and hammered gold
Consacá, Nariño. Capulí period.
Width 6 cm
MO 25.224/5

479 Pair of crescent ear ornaments
Cast and hammered gold.
Ornamented with human figures and the usual Nariño monkeys.
Consacá, Nariño. Capulí period.
Width 13.7 cm
MO 25.218/9

480 Figure pendant
Hammered and gilt tumbaga
Córdoba, Nariño. Capulí period.
Height 5.5 cm
MO 24.476

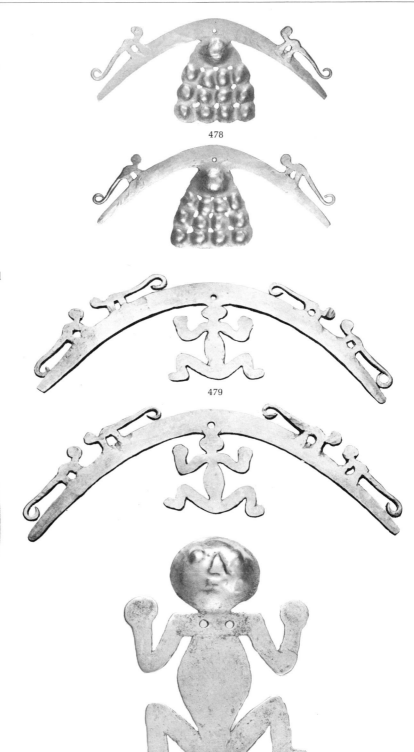

478

479

477

480

481 Necklace of small beads
Gold. Three kinds of beads are
included: (a) cylinders of rolled
strip, (b) cylinders of rolled strip,
welded at the overlap, (c) barrel-
shaped beads with a seam round the
central circumference, made in two
parts and then joined together.
Consacá, Nariño
Length of individual beads 2–4 mm
MO 25.223

482 Necklace, with figure pendant
Cast gold. Sixty-eight tubular beads
(0.7 cm long), seventy-six barrel-
shaped beads (0.5 cm long), and a
human figure (3 cm high).
Consacá, Nariño
MO 25.222

483 Necklace
Hammered and cast gold. Seventeen
tubular beads, sixteen spherical
beads, two conical links.
Pupiales, Nariño
Average length of large tubular
beads 5.5. cm
MO 24.465

484 Pair of conical ornaments
Gilt tumbaga sheet. Sometimes
described as nipple covers.
Sandoná, Nariño
Height 4 cm
MO 25.230/1

485 Two birds
Hammered and welded gold
La Vereda Centro, Guachucal,
Nariño. Capulí period.
Heights 3.2, 3.5 cm
MO 22.027/8

481 (detail)

482 (detail)

483 (detail)

484

485

486 Heavy bell, containing a metal pellet
Cast; gold or gold-rich tumbaga. Very high polish.
Ipiales, Nariño
Height 3.8 cm
MO 22.464

487 Hanging disc, star design
Gilded tumbaga
Pupiales, Nariño. Piartal period.
Diameter 16.5 cm
MO 25.591

488 Ear dangler
Hammered gold alloy, brilliantly polished. On both sides are circles applied in some black material.
Pupiales, Nariño. Piartal period.
Diameter 6.5 cm
MO 22.502

489 Embossed disc pendant
Gilt tumbaga. Embossed from the back and retouched on front. Two suspension holes.
Pupiales, Nariño
Diameter 15.9 cm
MO 21.904
Colour plate

490 Set of seventeen tapered plaques
Hammered tumbaga with enriched surfaces. Each plaque has two holes.
Miraflores, Pupiales, Nariño. Piartal period.
Average height 11.1 cm
MO 20.958

487

486

490

488

491 Nose ornament
Gold; hammered and repoussé.
Pupiales, Nariño. Piartal period.
Width 9.2 cm
MO *16.302*

492 Nose ornament, with spiral terminals
Hammered gold
Vereda de Miraflores, Pupiales, Nariño. Piartal period.
Width 11.3 cm
MO *16.652*

493 Nose ornament
Sheet gold, with pendants attached by hammered wire.
Miraflores, Ipiales, Nariño. Piartal period.
Width 20.4 cm
AMNH *41.2/7209*

494 Nose ornament
Sheet metal; gold alloy with bi-coloured surface. Marks of wrapping material on the central nosepiece.
Miraflores, Ipiales, Nariño. Piartal period.
Width 16 cm
AMNH *41.2/7211*

495 Nose ornament
Hammered gold or tumbaga, with endpieces of spirally-rolled wire.
Miraflores, Ipiales, Nariño. Piartal period.
Width 15.5 cm
AMNH *41.2/7454*

496 Nose ornament
Sheet gold or enriched tumbaga, with danglers attached by hammered wire.
Miraflores, Ipiales, Nariño. Piartal period.
Width 23 cm
AMNH *41.2/7207*
Colour plate

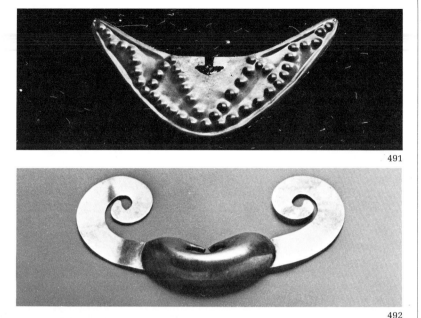

491

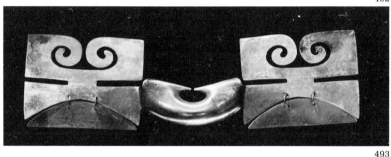

492

493

494 △   ▽495

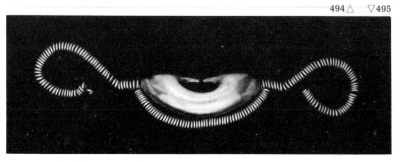

497 Axe head
Polished stone, with a transverse
perforation and representation of a
cord binding. Five similar axes came
from a deep shaft tomb at Las
Cruces, Ipiales, and were found with
a tumbaga plaque, a stone crucible,
a Pacific coast conch shell, and two
clay figurines of Tumaco influence.
This tomb gave a radiocarbon date
of AD 1080 ± 115 years (Uribe 1976;
1977: 74–99). (*See* fig. 43)
Capulí style, Nariño. *c.* AD 800–
1250.
Length 11.8 cm
MO *No number*

498 Hollow vessel, female figure
Painted pottery. Black resist painted
ornament over a red background.
Capulí style of Nariño. AD 800–1250
(Francisco 1969; Uribe 1977).
Height 42.5 cm
BP *N-2016*

499 Hollow vessel, acrobat
Pottery; red slip, with details picked
out in reddish-brown paint. The
figure has a coca quid in one cheek.
Capulí style of Andean Nariño. AD
800–1250 (Francisco 1969; Uribe
1977).
Height 13.5 cm
BP *N-11530*

500 Ocarina, in the form of a shell
Pottery. Chestnut-coloured stripe
over a highly polished buff-cream
slip. The internal structure of the
shell is meticulously modelled.
Finca San José, La Victoria, Ipiales,
Nariño. Piartal or Tuza style. AD
1250 to Spanish Conquest (Uribe
1977).
Length 10.1 cm
MO *CN 3113*

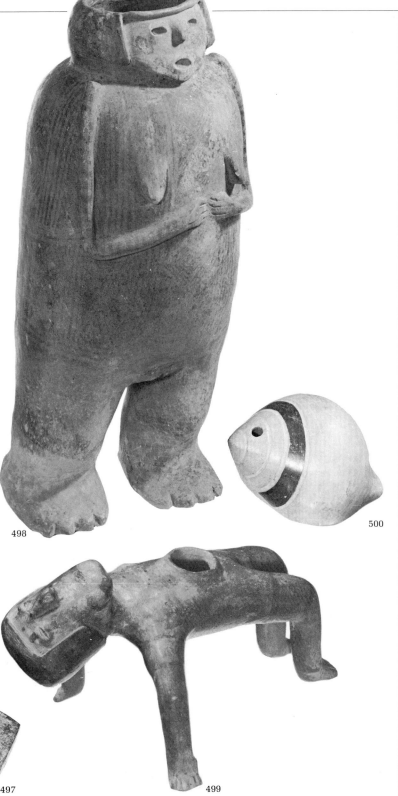

498

500

497

499

501 Pair of human faces
Embossed tumbaga. Perforations on
each edge for attachment to a back-
ing material.
Tumaco region
Heights 3.7, 3.8 cm
Coll. Jaime Errazuriz, Bogotá

**502 Necklace of eighty-eight small
beads**
Tumbaga. The presence of a seam
around the diameter indicates that
each bead was made in two parts,
subsequently joined together.
Barbacoas region, Nariño
Length of individual beads 0.2–
0.3 cm
Coll. Jaime Errazuriz, Bogotá

503 Triangular ornament
Tumbaga, with surface enrichment.
Hammered.
La Tolita region, Esmeraldas,
Ecuador
Length 2.9 cm
Coll. Jaime Errazuriz, Bogotá

504 Small ingot, disc-shaped
Tumbaga. Cast, then hammered into
shape.
La Tolita region, Esmeraldas,
Ecuador
Diameter 0.7 cm
Coll. Jaime Errazuriz, Bogotá

505 Pair of nose or ear studs
Gold. Globular elements forming a
rosette are soldered to a hammered
shank.
La Tolita region, Esmeraldas,
Ecuador
Diameter of rosettes 0.6 cm
Coll. Jaime Errazuriz, Bogotá

**506 Nose ornament, embossed
decoration**
Gold alloy. Hollow; made from a
single, folded sheet.
La Tolita region, Esmeraldas,
Ecuador
Width 2.8 cm
Coll. Jaime Errazuriz, Bogotá

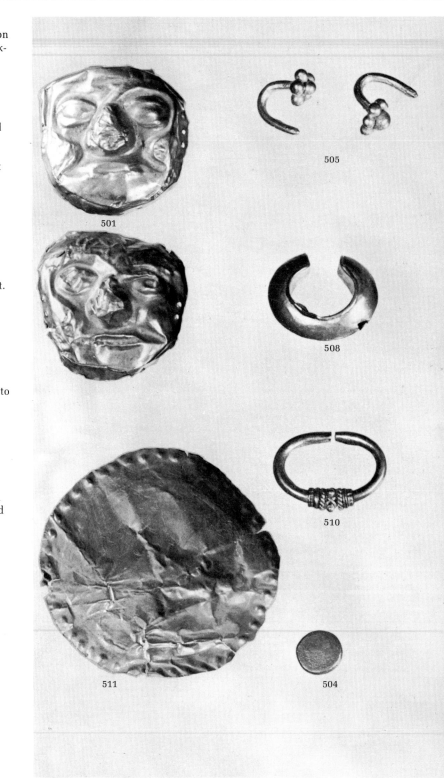

501

505

508

510

511

504

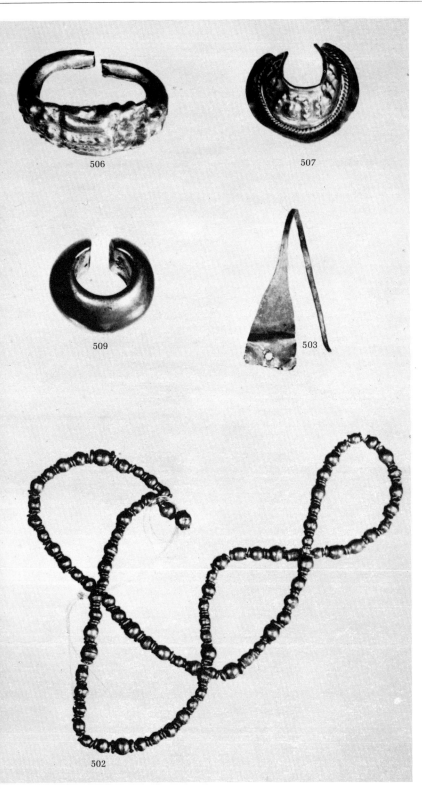

506

507

509

503

502

507 Nose ornament, embossed decoration
Tumbaga with surface enrichment. The base plate and the embossed portion are separate pieces of sheet metal, and the join is masked by a rope-like element.
La Tolita region, Esmeraldas, Ecuador
Width 2.1 cm
Coll. Jaime Errazuriz, Bogotá

508 Nose ornament
Gold. Hollow, formed of two pieces of hammered sheet, joined by clinching.
La Tolita region, Esmeraldas, Ecuador
Width 1.9 cm
Coll. Jaime Errazuriz, Bogotá

509 Nose ornament
Copper-rich tumbaga. Solid and heavy.
La Tolita region, Esmeraldas, Ecuador
Width 1.8 cm
Coll. Jaime Errazuriz, Bogotá

510 Nose ornament
Gold alloy. Cast or granulated decoration.
La Tolita region, Esmeraldas, Ecuador
Width 1.9 cm
Coll. Jaime Errazuriz, Bogotá

511 Disc
Tumbaga with enriched surface. Hammered and embossed.
La Tolita region, Esmeraldas, Ecuador
Diameter 6.5 cm
Coll. Jaime Errazuriz, Bogotá

512 Seated figure
Grey pottery; remains of red paint on the head-dress, and green on the cheeks. The personage was originally seated on a four-legged stool, and wears a wealth of small, fussy ornaments typical of Tumaco jewellery.
Tumaco style
Height 28.8 cm
BP T-7658
Colour plate

513 Large hollow figure
Pottery; traces of orange paint on
the torso. Holes in the bottoms of the
feet allowed the steam to escape,
thus preventing shattering at the
firing stage. The personage wears a
necklace, wrist band, nose stud and
ear plug. Holes around the edges of
the ears may once have held
gold rings. The skull is artificially
deformed.
Tumaco style
Height 67.5 cm
BP T-12384

514 Seated figure
Grey pottery; hollow, with holes in
the top of the head, the feet and at
the base of the spine to allow steam
to escape during firing. The torso
was originally painted orange, and
the necklace and bracelets coloured
reddish-brown. There is a painted
design in orange-red on the cheek.
Tumaco style
Height 38.5 cm
BP T-8846
Colour plate

515 Hollow figure
Grey pottery. Elaborately costumed
and carrying a damaged object
(possibly a jar) on its back. The
figure wears a mouth mask and nose
plug.
Tumaco style
Height 27.5 cm
BP T-0001

516 Pottery head
Grey clay; from a vessel or figure.
The elaborate costume and
ornaments are typical of Tumaco
work.
Tumaco style
Height 11.2 cm
BP T-881

517 Figurine head
Grey pottery; body missing. The
deformation of the cranium does not
follow the usual pattern, and may be
pathological rather than cosmetic in
origin.
Tumaco style
Height 9 cm
BP T-2400

517   516

513   515

518 Mask, human face
Grey pottery. Two suspension holes
in the forehead.
Tumaco style
Height 14 cm
BP T-9929

519 Mask, death's head
Grey pottery. Two suspension holes
in the forehead, one in the chin.
Tumaco style
Height 12.7 cm
BP T-6240

518   519

520 Miniature vessel, parrot
Grey pottery; blue paint on breast
and head.
Tumaco style
Height 8.8 cm
BP T-2500

521 Miniature animal
Grey pottery; traces of red paint on
crest and legs. A fanciful creature,
with human legs and the body, tail
and beak of a bird.
Tumaco style
Height 10.1 cm
BP T-8837

522 Animal-shaped adorno
Grey pottery. Modelled ornament
from some kind of vessel. Dog
holding an object to its mouth.
Tumaco style
Height 8.1 cm
BP T-0121

520   521   522

523 Model of a building
Grey clay. Rectangular structure
with upswept roof. Four holes
around the entrance may have been
for the attachment of a door.
Tumaco style
Height 10.3 cm
BP T-2539

524 Model of a building
Grey clay. Part of a composite
vessel or scene, depicting a single-
room structure with a decorative
roof supported by a pillar.
Tumaco style
Height 20 cm
BP T-2538

523   524

Calima Region

525 Diadem
Cut and embossed sheet gold. Nose ornaments and ear discs stapled with wire. In the centre is a human face.
Early Calima style
Height 28.3 cm
MO 4297

526 Diadem
Cut and hammered gold, with repoussé decoration. Ear discs and nose ornament stapled to the central face.
Early Calima style
Height 27 cm
MO 5202

527 Pectoral, with human face
Sheet gold; hammered. The face seems to have been raised by hammering over a matrix. The border consists of rectangles separated by dots. The outlines of the rectangles were scratched on the front, leaving a slight ridge on the back, and this line served as a guide for the rows of dots, which were embossed from the rear. The curved designs were then traced on the front. On the back and front are signs of a previous attempt to make a pectoral of the same type. The goldsmith scribed the outline and the border onto the metal, then abandoned the design, re-cutting the sheet to a slightly different outline and forming the present pectoral. The necklace may be a later addition, and includes two kinds of beads, one sort made of rolled strip, the other cast (Root 1964).
Early Calima style
Width 36 cm
MM 1906.5–17.1

528 Calima pectoral, with human face
Sheet gold; hammered and embossed.
Ataco, Tolima. Early Calima style.
Height 19 cm
MO 5848

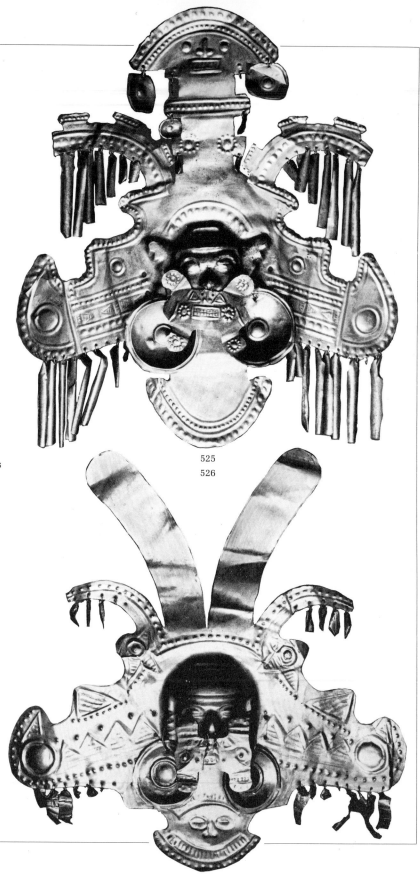

525
526

529 Nose ornament, human face
Tumbaga with enriched surface; cut
and hammered sheet, the various
elements stapled together.
Early Calima style
Maximum width 17.8 cm
MM +5802
Colour plate

530 Nose ornament
Cut and hammered gold. Danglers
attached by wire staples.
Restrepo, Valle del Cauca. Early
Calima style.
Width 15.5 cm
MO 7559

531 Nose ornament
Hammered and repoussé gold
Early Calima style
Width 14 cm
MO 5610

527

530

531

528

532 Nose ornament in the shape of two birds
Hammered gold sheet, cut out and with repoussé decoration. The two parts are stapled together with wire.
Restrepo, Valle del Cauca. Early Calima style.
Height 5 cm
MO 23.207

533 Nose ornament
Sheet gold. The decorative border and the three creatures are worked from the rear and drawn freehand.
Restrepo, Valle del Cauca. Early Calima style.
Width 17.3 cm
MO 5376

534 Nose ornament
Hammered gold
Restrepo, Valle del Cauca
Width 23.7 cm
MO 5382

535 Nose ornament, with embossed monkeys
Hammered gold; decoration executed from the rear.
Width 23.4 cm
MO 3681

536 Sheet metal ornament
Cut and hammered gold, folded double. Designs raised from the inner surface. One side bears a face with nose ornament and ear discs, the other has a stylized human face.
Restrepo, Valle del Cauca. Early Calima style.
Height 26 cm
MO 6282

533

535

534

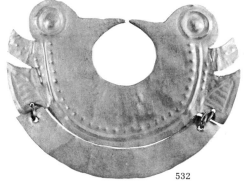

532

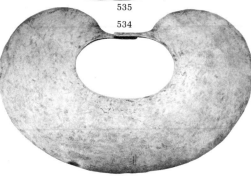

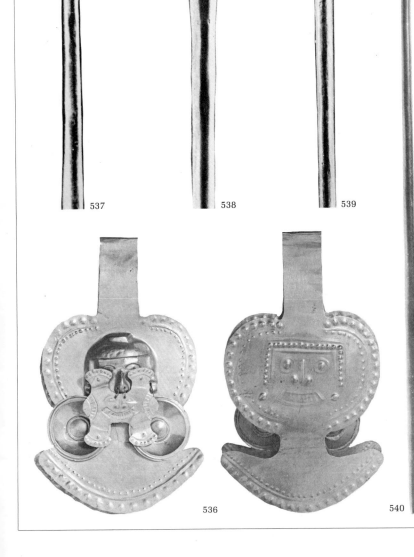

537   538   539

536   540

537 Lime-dipper, with bird
Cast gold
Early Calima style
Length 22 cm
MO *3553*

538 Lime-dipper, masked figure
Cast gold. The figure holds a staff.
Masks and staffs feature in the
ceremonies of several present-day
Indian tribes of the rain forest east
of the Andes.
Early Calima style
Length 32.7 cm
MO *5233*

539 Lime-dipper, masked figure
Cast gold. The mask, hair style and
ear plugs resemble those of certain
San Agustín sculptures (cf. Reichel-
Dolmatoff 1972, pl. 46). There is
another figure on the reverse.
Campohermoso, Ataco, Tolima. Early
Calima style.
Length 31.4 cm
MO *5857*

**540 Lime-dipper surmounted by a
human figure**
Cast gold. Technologically, this item
is a miniature *tour de force*. The
figure is only 2.5 cm high, but the
loin-cloth, crown and pendant are
shown in detail, and there is a
movable ring through the nose. One
hand holds a transverse knife with a
suspension loop; the other grasps a
staff-like object with a dangling
chain. Attached to the back is a
funnel-shaped element with a
perforated stone bead secured by a
loop of twisted wire. Two concave
ear discs, like the full-size examples
from Calima graves, are attached at
the shoulders by wire.
Restrepo, Valle del Cauca. Early
Calima style.
Length 25.8 cm
MO *24.828*
Colour plate

541 Funerary mask
Hammered sheet gold. Face
embossed from behind, with detail
touched up by burnishing and
incision on the front. Five holes
around the edge.
Restrepo, Valle del Cauca
Width 22.3 cm
MO *3308*

542 Pendant, masked figure
Cast gold. He holds a staff (or lance)
and what may be a shield.
Restrepo, Valle del Cauca
Height 5 cm
MO *7469*

543 Pendant, masked figure
Cast tumbaga, with enriched surface.
The face looks out through a large,
plaque-like device, extending from
the chest, round the sides of the
head, and terminating in a spiked
crown. A second, openwork mask
covers the face. In the hands are a
staff (or spear) and a (?)shield,
similar to those depicted on Early
Calima lime-dippers. The treatment
of the legs shows the influence of
'Darien' pendants.
Height 7.3 cm
MM *1902.6–23.1*

544 Nose ornament, pointed ends
Hammered gold
Vereda San Salvador, Restrepo,
Valle del Cauca
Width 23.4 cm
MO *5821*

**545 Hollow nose ornament
containing a rattle pellet**
Hammered sheet gold; made in two
pieces and welded, or soldered,
together.
Restrepo, Valle del Cauca
Width 2.8 cm
MO *6345*

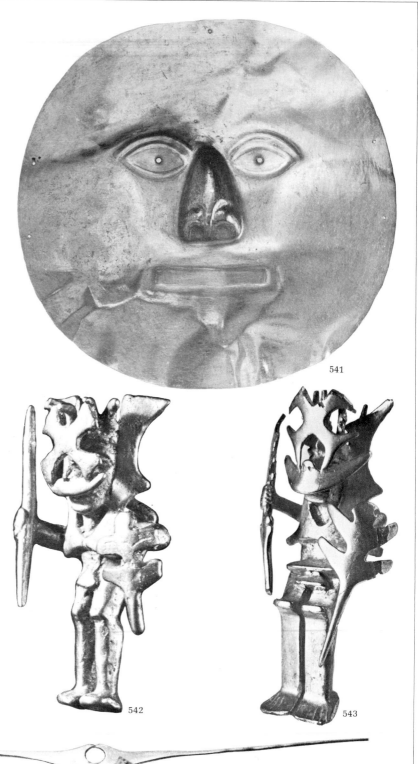

541

542

543

544

546 Ring
Gold
Diameter 2.5 cm
MO 5572

547 Pair of spiral ear ornaments
Hammered gold wire
Late Calima (Sonso style); a pair of
similar ornaments, with a spiral nose
ring like no. 548, were found in
a tomb at the Hacienda Moralba,
Calima Valley, with wooden items
that gave a radiocarbon date of AD
1335 ± thirty years (Bray and
Moseley 1969–70). Cf. description by
Cieza de León on p. 63.
Lengths 4.5, 3.6 cm
MM 96.2–3, 6/7

548 Spiral nose ornament
Hammered tumbaga
The form was used in the Calima
and Quimbaya zones during the final
centuries before the Spanish
Conquest (see no. 547). Cf. descrip-
tion by Cieza de León on p. 63.
Width 1.2 cm
MM 1958 Am. 3.8

549 Necklace of seventy beads
Quartz. Cylindrical and sub-
globular shapes.
Rancho Grande, Restrepo, Valle del
Cauca
Length of largest cylinder 4.3 cm
Galería Cano, Bogotá

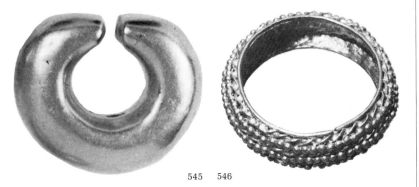

545   546

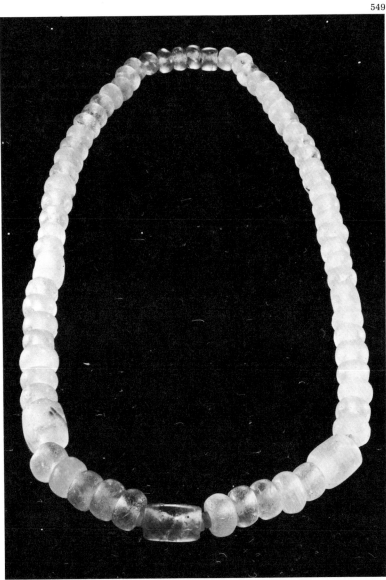

549

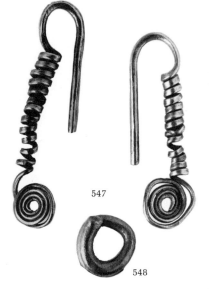

547

548

550 Calima alcarraza
Pottery; red-brown slip. The term *alcarraza* is used for vessels designed to hold liquids, and equipped with two spouts joined by a handle. This pot is modelled in the shape of a group of houses linked by paths. The central, and largest, house stands on a platform, dominating the four smaller huts. Surrounding the scene are objects which may represent trees.
Restrepo, Valle del Cauca. Early Calima style.
Height 21.3 cm
MO *CC 5620*
Colour plate

551 Calima jar, modelled human face
Pottery; chestnut-coloured slip.
Restrepo, Valle del Cauca. Early Calima style.
Height 23 cm
MO *CC 5619*

552 Calima jar, male figure
Pottery; brown slip.
Restrepo, Valle del Cauca. Early Calima style.
Height 10.2 cm
MO *CC 4527*

553 Figure jar
Pottery
Calima Valley. Early Calima style.
Height 14.6 cm
MO *CC 4525*

554 Figure jar
Pottery; brown slip. Some restoration. The limbs are hollow and provided with holes to allow the steam to escape during firing.
Early Calima style
Height 25 cm
MN *46–II–6327*

553

551

552

554

555–567 Full-size reconstruction of a Calima burial chamber, with its contents

The tomb consisted of a deep vertical shaft with a funerary chamber opening from the bottom. The dead person was buried with his gold jewellery, offerings of food and drink, and everything he would need in the afterlife. The vault was then sealed, and the shaft filled with earth.

555 Funerary mask
Hammered gold. Four holes at the sides.
Restrepo, Valle del Cauca. Early Calima style.
Width 20 cm
MO 3950

556 Calima diadem
Embossed gold sheet
Restrepo, Valle del Cauca
Height 21 cm
MO 6570

557 Nose ornament with pendants
Hammered and repoussé gold
Restrepo, Valle del Cauca. Early Calima style.
Width 18 cm
MO 6287

558 Calima pectoral, with human face
Hammered sheet gold, with a typical Calima face embossed from the rear and a border of repoussé decoration. Ear discs attached by wire staples. Rio Blanco, Tolima. Part of a group of objects (a mixture of Calima and Tolima styles) from a single site (Pérez de Barradas 1954, I: 224).
Height 24.8 cm
MO 5907

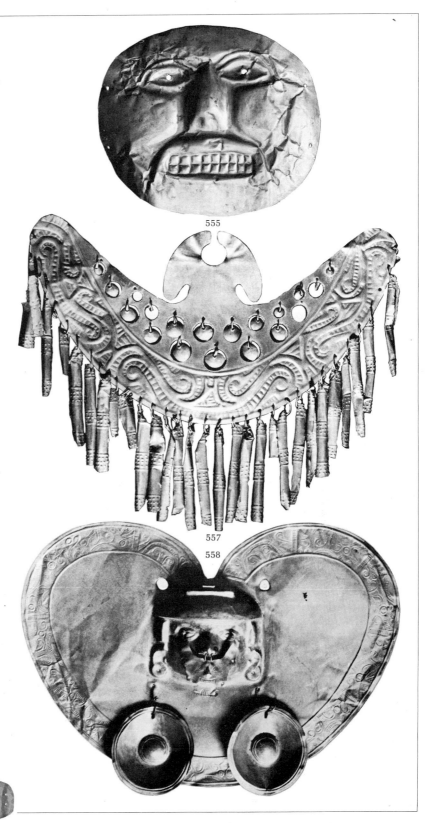

555

557

558

556

559 Axe
Polished stone
Calima Valley, Valle del Cauca
Length 13 cm
Institute of Archaeology, London University

560 Roller stamp
Pottery. Solid cylinder with an incised design, used (with a 'rolling pin' action) to imprint a strip-pattern.
Calima Valley, Valle del Cauca
Length 11.6 cm
Institute of Archaeology, London University

561 Roller stamp
Pottery. A hollow cylinder with a deeply incised design. With a stick through the centre, it was used for imprinting a continuous strip-pattern. Probably for body painting.
Calima Valley, Valle del Cauca
Length 6.8 cm
Institute of Archaeology, London University

562 Wooden stool
Found with a second stool, a tree-trunk coffin and five pots in the burial chamber of a shaft tomb at Finca Varsovia, Darien, Valle del Cauca. Sonso style of the Calima Valley. The coffin gave a radio-carbon date of AD 1235 ± sixty years (Bray and Moseley 1969–70).
Height 17 cm
MN *A-62–VIII–1808*

563 Small jar
Pottery; brown slip. Fine incised decoration.
Calima zone. Before AD 1000.
Height 8.3 cm
Private collection

564 Figure jar
Yellow-brown pottery. Male, nude except for a necklace.
Calima zone. Early Calima style.
Height 10 cm
Private collection

565 Figure jar, fantastic animal
Pottery; red slip with incised and pitted decoration. The creature has a fantastic animal head, human genitals, and limbs modelled as snakes.
Calima zone. Early Calima style.
Height 17 cm
Private collection

566 Figure jar
Pottery; chestnut slip. Male, nude except for necklace. Left forearm restored, and head-dress missing.
Calima zone. Early Calima style.
Height 30.5 cm
Private collection

567 Female figurine
Pottery; brown slip, well polished. Solid. Nude and pregnant woman, with no arms.
Calima zone. Early Calima style.
Height 8.8 cm
Private collection

560

561

559

562

563   566   564

568 Mummy

Adult male, in a seated and contracted position. Covered with a deep red stain, almost black in places, resembling resin. The body cavity is empty, and the internal organs were extracted through an incision in the left flank. As with no. 569, the pubic hair seems to have been removed. The teeth are much worn (Dawson 1928).

'They had various manners of burying the dead. For kings and chiefs they normally took out the internal organs and the intestines at the time of death, and embalmed the corpses with a resin that they called mocoba, made from the sticky sap of certain fig trees and other things with which they mixed this. After mourning in their houses for six days, they interred the bodies in vaults or caves already prepared for the purpose, wrapping them up in fine mantles, and surrounding them with many balls of maize and jars of chicha (maize beer) . . . In the eyes, nostrils, ears, mouth and navel they put emeralds and pieces of gold, according to the wealth of each one, and around the neck they put discs of the same. And with him, in the same vault, they buried the women and slaves who had loved him best.' (Friar Pedro Simón, 1625)

Presented to the British Museum in 1842 by 'R. Bunch Esq., of H.M. Legation'. Found in September 1842 in a cave at 'Gachansipa' (probably Gachantivá), canton of Leiva, Boyacá, with 27 other mummies and textiles including no. 170.
MM Q. 78. Am. 3

569 Mummy

Middle-aged woman, seated, with arms folded over the chest. Impressions of woven cloth still preserved on the skin show that the body had been wrapped for burial. Around the neck was a necklace of animal teeth and carved pendants of sea shell. Traces of red stain on the face and body probably derive from dye in the textile wrapping. The teeth are badly worn, with the pulp cavities exposed, and the mouth is stuffed with fibrous material. The left ear is also plugged. The internal organs seem to have been extracted through an incision in the perineal region, where the anus and vulva are united into a single distended opening. There is no trace of pubic hair. The body was possibly smoke-dried (Dawson 1928).

From a dry cave near Leiva, Boyacá. The mummy was presented to the British Museum in 1838 by W. Turner, Esq., H.M. Envoy to Colombia
MM 38.11–11.1

567

565

568   569

570 Mummy mask

Dome-shaped cap and a frontal flap with eye holes. Made from vegetable fibre (probably *fique*, from Agave species) by a 'looping' or knotless netting technique. On top are attachments for green and yellow feathers and for seeds. More seeds adorn the face of the mask. The crown is separate, and consists of yellow feathers bound with cotton thread.

From the mummy of a child found in a cave at Sibaté, trussed up with cords and wearing a *millefiori* glass trade bead round its neck (Reichel-Dolmatoff 1965, pl. 57).
Muisca
Height of mask (without crown)
16 cm
MN 422–A–422 (mask), 424–A–424 (crown)

571 Burial urn

Pottery; with four little handles and two modelled bird heads. The lid is shaped like a seated male figure, with traces of black paint on the body. Similar urns have been found filled with cremated bones.
Moskito style, lower Rio Magdalena (Reichel-Dolmatoff and Dussan de Reichel 1943)
Height of lid alone 40 cm
BP *No number*
Colour plate

572 Burial urn

Pottery; orange-red, sandy clay, with remains of a reddish-brown slip. The body of the urn forms a female torso, with the lid as the head. Pierced ears are almost concealed by the hair, and the face is covered with an incised design (? a tattoo) formed by rows of dots separated by lines.
Chimila style, frontier region between the Departments of Magdalena and Cesar
Height, with lid, 64.5 cm
BP *CH-12.568*

570

572

573 Painted burial urn
One side has a face in relief (wearing a nose-ring); the other has a modelled lizard. The two handles suggests ears with multiple rings. Made of buff clay, by means of coiling. Painted red, orange, black and white.
Libano, Tolima. Pubenza Polychrome style; after *c*. AD 1000 (Cardale de Schrimpff 1976).
Height 38.8 cm
MO *CTo 1235*
Colour plate

574 Burial urn
Pottery; sandy orange clay with a red-slipped surface. The figure wears a pendant, necklace, and a typical Tairona gold nose ornament.
Tairona style
Height 97 cm
BP *Ta-12569*

575 Tamalameque burial urn
Pottery; with the lid in the form of a human head and bust. These vessels are found in the cemeteries of the Tamalamaque region, on the lower Rio Magdalena, and come from shaft graves with side chambers. The burial ritual is similar to that described by the 16th-century chronicler Oviedo for the Caribbean coast:
'When they have removed the flesh from the bones, and these are clean, they stain them with bixa [Bixa Orellana L.] and put the stained bones and skulls into jars and storage pots, and thus they keep them within the house or just outside.'
Tamalameque style (Reichel-Dolmatoff and Dussan de Reichel 1943)
Height, urn plus lid, 82 cm
BP *RM-6127* (urn), *RM-6085* (lid)

575

574

576 Tamalameque burial urn
Pottery; painted decoration on lid.
(*See* no. 575)
Height 70 cm
MO *C Tam 2035*

577 Tamalameque burial urn
Pottery. (*See* no. 575)
Height 78 cm
MO *C Tam 2034*

578 Tamalameque burial urn
Pottery. (*See* no. 575)
Height 39 cm
MO *C Tam 2443*

579 Tamalameque burial urn
Pottery; painted decoration on lid.
(*See* no. 575)
Height 70 cm
MO *C Tam 2597*

580 Tamalameque burial urn
Pottery; painted decoration on lid.
(*See* no. 575)
Height 72 cm
MO *C Tam 2436*

581 Tamalameque burial urn
Pottery; painted decoration on lid.
(*See* no. 575)
Height 56 cm
MO *C Tam 2037*

582 Tamalameque burial urn
Pottery; painted decoration on lid.
(*See* no. 575)
Height 87 cm
MO *C Tam 1869*

Bibliography

Note: *Revista Colombiana de Antropología* is abbreviated to *RCA*

Aguado, Pedro de, *Historia de Santa Marta y Nuevo Reino de Granada,* (ed. J. Bécker), Real Academia de la Historia, Madrid, 1916

Aguilar, Carlos, H., *Colección de Objetos Indigenas de Oro del Banco Central,* Publicaciones de la Universidad de Costa Rica, Serie Historia e Geografía No. 13, San José, 1972

Ainaud de Lasarte, J., *Ars Hispaniae, X, Cerámica y Vidrio,* Editorial Plus-Ultra, Madrid, 1952

Andagoya, Pascual de, *Narrative of the Proceedings of Pedrarias Davila in the Provinces of Tierra Firme or Castilla del Oro, and of the Discovery of the South Sea and the Coasts of Peru and Nicaragua,* (ed. C. R. Markham), Hakluyt Society, 34, London, 1865

Anderson, R. G. W., *The Mariner's Astrolabe: An Exhibition at the Royal Scottish Museum,* Royal Scottish Museum, Edinburgh, 1972

Arango, C. Luis, *Recuerdos de la Guaquería en el Quindío,* 2 vols, Editorial de Cromos, Luis Tamayo & Co, Bogotá, 1924

Archivo General de Indias, *Averiguaciones en Tamalameque sobre los manyllas que mando hazer Juan de Azpeleta a los yndios de su encomienda de anpihuegas* (Justicia, Legajo 610–12, folios 2520–25), Seville, 1555, quoted in Plazas and Falchetti 1978

Baudez, Claude F. and Coe, Michael D., 'Incised slate discs from the Atlantic watershed of Costa Rica', *American Antiquity 31 (3),* pp. 441–3, 1966

Benzoni, Girolamo, *History of the New World,* (trans. W. H. Smyth), Hakluyt Society, 21, London, 1857

Bergsøe, Paul, *The Metallurgy and Technology of Gold and Platinum among the Pre-Columbian Indians,* Ingeniørvidenskabelige Skrifter No. A.44, Copenhagen, 1937

Bischof, Henning, 'Contribuciones a la cronología de la Cultura Tairona (Sierra Nevada de Santa Marta, Colombia)', *Verhandlungen des XXXVIII Internationalen Amerikanistenkongresses, Stuttgart-München, 1968,* Band I, pp. 259–69, 1969a

Bischof, Henning, 'La Cultura Tairona en el Area Intermedio', *Verhandlungen des XXXVIII Internationalen Amerikanistenkongresses, Stuttgart-München, 1968,* Band I, pp. 271–80, 1969b

Bischof, Henning, *Die Spanisch-Indianische Auseinandersetzung in der Nördlichen Sierra Nevada de Santa Marta (1501–1600),* Bonner Amerikanistische Studien Nr. 1, Rheinische Friedrich-Wilhelms-Universität, Bonn, 1971

Braunholtz, H. J., 'A Gold Pendant from Ancient Colombia', *The British Museum Quarterly,* vol. XIII, pp. 19–21, 1939

Bray, Warwick, 'Ancient American Metal-Smiths', *Proceedings of the Royal Anthropological Institute for 1971,* pp. 25–43, 1972

Bray, Warwick, and Moseley, M. E., 'An archaeological sequence from the vicinity of Buga, Colombia', *Ñawpa Pacha 7–8,* pp. 85–104, 1969–70

Bright, Alec, 'A Goldsmith's blowpipe from Colombia', *Man N.S. 7 (2),* pp. 311–13, 1972

Broadbent, Sylvia M., 'Construcciones megalíticas en el Territorio Chibcha', *RCA XII,* pp. 81–8, 1963

Broadbent, Sylvia M., 'Agricultural Terraces in Chibcha Territory, Colombia', *American Antiquity 29 (4),* pp. 501–4, 1964

Broadbent, Sylvia M., 'Investigaciones Arqueológicas en el Territorio Chibcha', *Antropología 1,* Universidad de los Andes, Bogotá, 1965

Broadbent, Sylvia M., 'The Site of Chibcha Bogotá', *Ñawpa Pacha 4,* pp. 1–13, 1966

Broadbent, Sylvia M., 'La Arqueología del Territorio Chibcha: II. Hallazgos Aislados y Monumentos de Piedra', *Antropología 4,* Universidad de los Andes, Bogotá, 1970

Bruhns, Karen Olsen, 'Stylistic affinities between the Quimbaya gold style and a little-known ceramic style in the middle Cauca Valley, Colombia', *Ñawpa Pacha 7–8,* pp. 65–83, 1969–70

Bruhns, Karen Olsen, 'A Quimbaya Gold Furnace?', *American Antiquity 35 (2),* pp. 202–3, 1970

Bruhns, Karen Olsen, 'The Methods of Guaquería. Illicit Tomb Looting in Colombia', *Archaeology 25 (2),* pp. 140–3, 1972(a)

Bruhns, Karen Olsen, 'Two Prehispanic Cire Perdue Casting Moulds from Colombia', *Man N.S. 7 (2),* pp. 308–11, 1972(b)

Bruhns, Karen Olsen, 'Ancient Pottery of the Middle Cauca Valley', *Cespedesia 5 (17–18),* pp. 101–96, 1976

Caldas, Ana María, Chavez, Alvaro, and Villamizar, Marina, 'Las Tumbas del Valle del Dorado', *Antropologia 5,* Universidad de los Andes, Bogotá, 1972

Cardale de Schrimpff, Marianne, 'Investigaciones Arqueológicas en la Zona de Pubenza, Tocaima, Cundinamarca', *RCA XX,* pp. 335–496, 1976

Castellanos, Juan de, *Elegías de Varones Ilustres de Indias,* Part 4, *Historia del Nuevo Reino de Granada,* Editorial ABC, Bogotá, 1955

Cieza de León, Pedro de, *The Travels of Pedro de Cieza de León, A.D. 1532–50, Contained in the First Part of his Chronicle of Peru,* (trans. and ed. Clements R. Markham), Hakluyt Society, Series I, Vol. 33, London, 1864

Cieza de León, Pedro de, *The Second Part of the Chronicle of Peru,* (trans. and ed. Clements R. Markham), Hakluyt Society, Series I, Vol. 68, London, 1883

Cochrane, Capt. Charles Stuart, *Journal of a Residence and Travels in Colombia during the years 1823 and 1824,* 2 vols, Henry Colburn, London, 1825

Cooke, Richard G., 'Una Nueva Mirada a la Evolución de la cerámica en las Provincias Centrales', *Actas del IV Simposium Nacional de Antropología, Arqueología y Etnohistoria de Panamá, 1973,* pp. 307–65, Universidad de Panamá/ Instituto Nacional de Cultura, 1976

Cortesão, Armando, and Teixeira da Mota, Avelino, *Portugaliae Monumenta Cartographica,* Vol. 1, Lisbon, 1960

Cubillos, Julio César, 'Arqueología de Rioblanco (Chaparral, Tol.), *Boletín de Arqueología I (6),* pp. 519–30, 1945

Cubillos, Julio César, 'Apuntes para el Estudio de la Cultura Pijao', *Boletín de Arqueología II (1),* pp. 47–81, 1946

Cubillos, Julio César, 'Arqueología de las riberas del Río Magdalena, Espinal-Tolima', *RCA II (2),* pp. 128–44, 1954

Cubillos, Julio César, *Tumaco (Notas Arqueológicas),* Editorial Minerva, Bogotá, 1955

Dawson, Warren R., 'Two Mummies from Colombia', *Man,* May 1928, pp. 73–4

Duque Gómez, Luis, 'Notas Históricas sobre la Orfebrería Indígena en Colombia', in *Homenaje al Profesor Paul Rivet,* Academia Colombiana de Historia, Bogotá, pp. 271–335, Editorial ABC, Bogotá, 1958

Duque Gómez, Luis, *San Agustín: Reseña Arqueológica,* Instituto Colombiano de Antropología, Bogotá, 1963

Duque Gómez, Luis, *Exploraciones Arqueológicas en San Agustín,* Instituto Colombiano de Antropología, *RCA,* Suplemento No. 1, Imprenta Nacional, Bogotá, 1964

Duque Gómez, Luis, *Los Quimbayas: Reseña etnohistórica y arqueológica*, Imprenta Nacional, Bogotá, 1970

Dussan de Reichel, Alicia, 'Contribuciones al Estudio de la Cultura Calima en Colombia', *Revista del Museo Nacional, Lima*, Vol. XXXIV, pp. 61–7, 1965–6

Easby, Dudley T., 'Sahagún Reviviscit in the Gold Collection of the University Museum', *The University Museum Bulletin*, University Museum, Philadelphia, Vol. 20, No. 3, September 1956, pp. 3–15

Empson, Charles, 'An Account of some Golden Articles brought from South America by MR. CHARLES EMPSON, and laid before the Society on the 6th February, 1828, with Remarks thereon', *Archaeologia Aeliana*, Vol. II, pp. 252–5, 1832

Enciso, Martín Fernández de, *Summa de Geografía*, Banco Popular, Bogotá, 1974

Falchetti, Ana María, *The Goldwork of the Sinú Region, Northern Colombia*, M. Phil. dissertation, London University Institute of Archaeology, 1976

Falchetti, Ana María, and Plazas de Nieto, Clemencia, 'El Territorio de los Muiscas a la llegada de los Españoles', *Cuadernos de Antropología 1*, Universidad de los Andes, Bogotá, 1973

Farabee, William Curtis, 'Ancient American Gold', *The Museum Journal*, University Museum, Philadelphia, Vol. 11, No. 3, September 1920, pp. 93–129

Federmán, Nicolás, *Historia Indiana*, (ed. J. Friede), Artes Gráficas, Madrid, 1958

Francisco, Alice E., *An archaeological sequence from Carchi, Ecuador*, Ph.D. dissertation, Department of Anthropology, University of California, Berkeley, 1969

Friede, Juan, 'Breves Informaciones sobre la Metalurgia de los Indios de Santa Marta según Documentos Encontrados en el Archivo de Indias, Sevilla', *Journal de la Société des Américanistes*, N.S. Vol. 40, pp. 197–202, 1951

Friede, Juan, *Documentos inéditos para la historia de Colombia*, Vol. 4, (Academia Colombiana de Historia), Artes Gráficas, Madrid, 1956

Friede, Juan, *Los Welser en la Conquista de Venezuela*, Ediciones Edime, Caracas-Madrid, 1961

Friedemann, Nina S. de, *Minería, Descendencia y Orfebrería Artesanal Litoral Pacífico, Colombia*, Universidad Nacional, Bogotá, 1974

Frothingham, A. W., *Talavera Pottery*, Hispanic Society of America, New York, 1944

Goggin, John M., *Spanish Majolica in the New World*, Yale University Publications in Anthropology, No. 72, 1968

González Guzmán, Raúl, 'Informe Preliminar sobre las Investigaciones Arqueológicas Realizadas en El Cafetal, Distrito de Tonosí, Provincia de Los Santos, Panamá', in *Actas del II Simposium Nacional de Antropología, Arqueología y Etnohistoria de Panamá*, Universidad de Panamá, Centro de Investigaciones Antropológicas, pp. 143–74, 1971

Gould, Alice B., 'Nueva lista documentada de los tripulantes de Colón en 1492', *Boletín de la Real Academia de la Historia*, Vols 85–8, 90, 92, 110, 111, 1924–43

Groot, Ana María, Correa, Luz Piedad, and Hooykaas, Eva María, *Estudio etnohistórico y arqueológico de la zona andina nariñense con el fin de establecer los límites de ubicación de los grupos indígenas 'Pastos y Quillacingas' y los alcances geográficos de las incursiones del Imperio Incaico*, MS, Bogotá, 1976

Grossman, Joel W., 'An Ancient Gold Worker's Tool Kit: the earliest metal technology in Peru', *Archaeology*, Vol. 25, No. 4, October 1972, pp. 270–5

Grossman, Joel W., *The Ayllu and Community Self-Sufficiency in Andean Culture History*, unpublished manuscript, 1975

Hagen, Victor W. von, *The Golden Man: the quest for El Dorado*, Saxon House, Farnborough, 1974

Hamilton, Colonel J. P., *Travels through the Interior Provinces of Columbia*, John Murray, London, 1827

Hemming, John, *The Search for El Dorado*, Michael Joseph, London, 1978

Herrera y Tordesillas, Antonio de, *Historia general de los hechos de los Castellanos en los Islas y Tierra Firme del Mar Océano*, 1601–5

Hultgren, Axel, 'The hardness of Colombian tools made from copper-gold-silver alloys', *Comparative Ethnographical Studies*, Vol. IX, pp. 108–12, Gothenburg, 1931

Lechtman, Heather N., 'Ancient Methods of Gilding Silver. Examples from the Old and the New Worlds', in Robert H. Brill (ed.), *Science and Archaeology*, Massachusetts Institute of Technology, pp. 2–30, 1971

Lechtman, Heather N., 'The Gilding of Metals in Pre-Columbian Peru', in William J. Young (ed.), *Application of Science in Examination of Works of Art*, Museum of Fine Arts, Boston, pp. 38–52, 1973

Lehmann, Henri, 'Archéologie du Sud-Ouest colombien', *Journal de la Société des Américanistes*, N.S. XLII, pp. 199–270, 1953

Long, Stanley Vernon, and Yánguez, Juan A., 'Excavaciones en Tierradentro', *RCA* XV, pp. 9–127, 1970–1

López de Gómara, Francisco, *Historia General de las Indias*, Editorial Iberia, Barcelona, 1965

Lothrop, Samuel Kirkland, 'Coclé: An Archaeological Study of Central Panama, Part 1', *Memoirs of the Peabody Museum of Archaeology and Ethnology*, Vol. VII, Cambridge, 1937

Maddison, Francis, *Medieval Scientific Instruments and the Development of Navigational Instruments in the XVth and XVIth Centuries*, Coimbra: Agrupamento de Estudos de Cartografia Antiga, Junta de Investigações do Ultramar, Lisbon, 1969

Martínez Caviro, B., *Cerámica de Talavera*, Instituto Diego Velázquez del Consejo Superior de Investigaciones Científicas, Madrid, 1969

Mason, J. Alden, *Archaeology of Santa Marta, Colombia: The Tairona Culture*, Field Museum of Natural History, Anthropological Series, Vol. XX, Nos 1, 2, 3, Chicago, 1931–9

McDonald, Allen S., and Sistare, George H., 'The Metallurgy of Some Carat Gold Jewellery Alloys; Part 1 – Coloured Gold Alloys', *Gold Bulletin* 11(3), pp. 66–73, 1978

Millar, O., *Silver Jubilee Exhibition: The Queen's Pictures*, Catalogue of an exhibition at the Queen's Gallery, Buckingham Palace, 1977–8

Nachtigall, Horst, *Tierradentro: Archäologie und Ethnographie einer kolumbianischen Landschaft*, Origo, Zurich, 1955

Nisser, Pedro, *Sketch of the Different Mining and Mechanical Operations Employed in Some South American Goldworks, as well ancient as modern*, Stockholm, 1834

Nordenskiöld, E., 'Ancient Colombian Tools of gold alloy (Au-Ag-Cu)', *Comparative Ethnographical Studies* No. 9, Gothenburg, pp. 101–7, 1931

Otero, Jesús M., *Etnología Caucana*, Ediciones Universidad del Cauca, Popayán, 1952

Oviedo y Valdés, Gonzalo Fernández de, *Historia general y natural de las Indias, islas y tierra-firme del mar océano*, Biblioteca de autores españoles, Vols. 117–121, Editorial Atlas, Madrid, 1959

Parry, J. H., *The Age of Reconnaissance*, Sphere Books Ltd (reprint of 1963 edn, Weidenfeld & Nicolson, London), London, 1973

Parsons, James J., *Antioqueño Colonization in Western Colombia*, University of California Press, 2nd edn, Berkeley and Los Angeles, 1968

Parsons, James, and Bowen, William, 'Ancient Ridged Fields in the San Jorge River Floodplain, Colombia', *The Geographical Review 56 (3)*, pp. 317–43, 1966

Perdomo, Lucía R. de, 'Excavaciones arqueológicas en zona Panche, Guaduas-Cundinamarca', *RCA XIX*, pp. 247–89, 1975

Perdomo, Lucía R. de, *Aspectos de la cultura muisca*, Instituto Colombiano de Cultura, Bogotá, 1977

Perdomo, Lucía R. de, *Los Muiscas*, I.B.M. de Colombia, Bogotá, 1977

Perdomo, Lucía R. de, Turbay, Luisa Fernanda de, and Londoño P., Mauricio, 'Estudio Preliminar sobre la Zona Arqueológica de Pupiales (Nariño), *RCA XVII*, pp. 145–83, 1974

Pérez de Barradas, José, *Arqueología y Antropología Precolombinas de Tierra Dentro*, Imprenta Nacional, Ministerio de Educación Nacional, Publicaciones de la Sección de Arqueología, No. 1, Bogotá, 1937a

Pérez de Barradas, José, 'Máscara de oro de Inzá', *Revista de las Indias*, No. 1, pp. 3–7, 1937b

Pérez de Barradas, José, *Los Muiscas antes de la Conquista*, Instituto Bernardino de Sahagún, Consejo Superior de Investigaciones Científicas, Madrid, 1950–1

Pérez de Barradas, José, *Orfebrería Prehispánica de Colombia: Estilo Calima*, Banco de la República, Museo del Oro, Bogotá, Talleres Gráficos 'Jura', Madrid, 1954

Pérez de Barradas, José, *Orfebrería Prehispánica de Colombia: Estilos Tolima y Muisca*, Banco de la República, Museo del Oro, Bogotá, Talleres Gráficos 'Jura', Madrid, 1958

Pérez de Barradas, José, *Orfebrería Prehispánica de Colombia: Estilos Quimbaya y Otros*, Banco de la República, Museo del Oro, Bogotá, Talleres Gráficos 'Jura', Madrid, 1966

Pineda Giraldo, Roberto, 'Material arqueológico de la zona Calima', *Boletín de Arqueología 1 (6)*, pp. 491–518, 1945

Plazas de Nieto, Clemencia, *Nueva Metodología para la Clasificación de Orfebrería Prehispánica*, Jorge Plazas, Bogotá, 1975

Plazas de Nieto, Clemencia, and Falchetti de Sáenz, Ana María, *El Dorado: Colombian Gold*, Australian Art Exhibitions Corporation, 1978

Posada Arango, Andrés, *Ensayo Etnológico sobre los Aborigines del Estado de Antioquia en Colombia*, Imprenta de Rouge Hermanos y Cia., Paris, 1871

Preuss, Konrad Theodor, *Monumentale vorgeschichtliche Kunst, Ausgrabungen im Quellgebiet des Magdalena in Kolumbien, und ihre Ausstrahlungen in Amerika*, Vandenhoeck & Ruprecht, Göttingen, 1929

Ralegh, Sir Walter, *The discoverie of the large, rich, and beautiful Empire of Guiana*, (ed. Sir Robert H. Schomburgk), Hakluyt Society, Series I, Vol. 3, London, 1848

Ramírez, Jesús Emilio, *El Lago de Oro*, Instituto Geofísico de los Andes Colombianos, Serie C, Geología No. 15, Bogotá, 1972

Ramos Pérez, Demetrio, *El mito del Dorado: su génesis y proceso*, Biblioteca de la Academia Nacional de la Historia, Vol. 116, Fuentes para la Historia Colonial de Venezuela, Caracas, 1973

Read, Herbert, *Icon and Idea*, Faber and Faber, London, 1955

Reichel-Dolmatoff, G., 'Los Kogi: Una tribu indígena de la Sierra Nevada de Santa Marta, Colombia, Vol. 1, *Revista del Instituto Etnológico Nacional*, Vol. 4; Vol. 2, Editorial Iqueima, Bogotá, 1950–1

Reichel-Dolmatoff, Gerardo, 'Contactos y cambios culturales en la Sierra Nevada de Santa Marta', *RCA 1 (1)*, pp. 15–122, 1953

Reichel-Dolmatoff, Gerardo, 'Investigaciones Arqueológicas en la Sierra Nevada de Santa Marta', *RCA 2 (2)*, pp. 145–206, 1954

Reichel-Dolmatoff, G., 'Notas sobre la Metalurgia Prehistórica en el Litoral Caribe de Colombia', in *Homenaje al Profesor Paul Rivet*, Academia Colombiana de Historia, Bogotá, pp. 69–94, 1958

Reichel-Dolmatoff, G., *Colombia*, Thames & Hudson, London, 1965

Reichel-Dolmatoff, Gerardo, *San Agustín: A Culture of Colombia*, Praeger, New York, 1972

Reichel-Dolmatoff, G., *Contribuciones al Conocimiento de la Estratigrafía Cerámica de San Agustín, Colombia*, Banco Popular, Bogotá, 1975

Reichel-Dolmatoff, Gerard, and Dussan de Reichel, Alicia, 'Las Urnas Funerarias de la Cuenca del Río Magdalena', *Revista del Instituto Etnológico Nacional*, pp. 209–81, 1943

Reichel-Dolmatoff, Gerardo and Alicia, 'Investigaciones arqueológicas en la Sierra Nevada de Santa Marta', *RCA IV*, pp. 189–245, 1955

Reichel-Dolmatoff, Gerardo and Alicia, 'Reconocimiento Arqueológico de la Hoya del Río Sinú', *RCA VI*, pp. 31–157, 1957

Restrepo, Vicente, *Estudio sobre las minas de oro y plata de Colombia*, Archivo de la Economía Nacional No. 7, Banco de la República, Bogotá, 1952

Restrepo, Vicente, *Los Chibchas antes de la Conquista Española*, Banco Popular, Bogotá, 1972

Rivet, Paul, 'L'Orfèvrerie Colombienne (Technique, Aire de Dispersion, Origine)', *Proceedings of the 21st International Congress of Americanists*, Part 1, pp. 15–28, The Hague, 1924

Rivet, Paul, 'Metalurgia del Platino en la América Precolombina', *Revista del Instituto Etnológico Nacional*, Vol. 1, pp. 39–45, Bogotá, 1943–4

Rivet, P., and Arsandaux, H., *La métallurgie en Amérique précolombienne*, Travaux et Mémoires de l'Institut d'Ethnologie XXXIX, Musée de l'Homme, Paris, 1946

Roberts, P. M., 'Gold Brazing in Antiquity: Technical Achievement in the Earliest Civilizations', *Gold Bulletin 6 (4)*, pp. 112–19, 1973

Roden, Hans, *Treasure Seekers*, Walker & Co., New York, 1963

Rodríguez Freyle, Juan, *El Carnero*, (ed. M. Aguilera), Bedout, Medellín, no date

Root, William C., 'Pre-Columbian Metalwork of Colombia and its Neighbors', in S. K. Lothrop (ed.), *Essays in Pre-Columbian Art and Archaeology*, Harvard University Press, Cambridge, Massachusetts, pp. 242–57, 1964

Sahagún, Bernardino de, *Florentine Codex: General History of the Things of New Spain*, (eds C. E. Dibble and A. J. O. Anderson), Book 9, Monographs of the School of American Research and the Museum of New Mexico, No. 44, Part 10, Santa Fé, 1959

Saloman, Frank Loewen, *The Ethnic Lords of Quito in the Age of the Incas*, Cornell University Latin American Studies Program. Dissertation Series No. 77, 1978

Sampson, E. H., Fleming, S. J., and Bray, W., 'Thermoluminescent Dating of Colombian Pottery in the Yotoco Style', *Archaeometry*, Vol. 14 (1), pp. 119–26, 1972

Sauer, Carl Ortwin, *The Early Spanish Main*, University of California Press, Berkeley and Los Angeles, Cambridge University Press, London, 1966

Schottelius, Justus Wolfram, 'Arqueología de la Mesa de los Santos',

Boletín de Arqueología 2 (3),
pp. 213–25, 1946

Schuler-Schömig, Immina von, 'Patrizen
im Goldschmiedehandwerk der Muisca
Kolumbiens', *Baessler-Archiv, Neue
Folge, XXII*, pp. 1–22, 1974

Schultes, Richard Evans, *Hallucinogenic
Plants*, Golden Press (Western
Publishing Co., Racine, Wisconsin),
New York, 1976

Scott, David Arthur, *The metallurgy of
some prehispanic Colombian
metalwork*, unpublished B.Sc.
dissertation, London University
Institute of Archaeology, 1978

Silva Celis, Eliecer, 'La Arqueología de
Tierradentro', *Revista del Instituto
Etnológico Nacional I (1)*, pp. 117–30,
1943

Silva Celis, Eliecer, 'La Arqueología de
Tierradentro (continuación)', *Revista
del Instituto Etnológico Nacional I (2)*,
pp. 521–89, 1944

Simón, Pedro, *Noticias Historiales de las
Conquistas de Tierra Firme en las
Indias Occidentales*, Bogotá, 1882–92

Stone, Doris, and Balser, Carlos, 'Incised
Slate Disks from the Atlantic
Watershed of Costa Rica', *American
Antiquity*, Vol. 30, No. 3, pp. 310–29,
1965

Suárez, V. (ed.), *Cedulario de las
Provincias de Santa Marta y Cartagena
de Indias (Siglo XVI): Tomo primero,
Años 1529–1535*, (Vol. 14, Colección
de Libros y Documentos Referentes á
la Historia de América), Librería
General de Victoriano Suárez, Madrid,
1913

Sutherland, Donald R., *Preliminary
Investigations into the Prehistory of
Santander, Colombia*, Ph.D. thesis,
Tulane University, 1971

Trimborn, Hermann, 'Tres Estudios para
la Etnografía y Arqueología de
Colombia: Los Reinos de Guaca y
Nore', *Revista de Indias*, Año IV,
No. 11, pp. 43–91; No. 12, pp. 331–47;
No. 13, pp. 441–56; No. 14, pp. 629–81,
1943

Trimborn, Hermann, 'Tres Estudios para
la Etnografía y Arqueología de
Colombia: Las Minas de Buriticá',
Revista de Indias, Año V, No. 15,
pp. 27–39; No. 16, pp. 199–226, 1944

Trimborn, Hermann, *Señorío y Barbarie
en el Valle del Cauca*, Instituto
Gonzalo Fernández de Oviedo,
Consejo Superior de Investigaciones
Científicas, Madrid, 1949

Uribe Alarcón, María Victoria,
'Relaciones Prehispánicas entre la
Costa del Pacífico y el Altiplano
Nariñense, Colombia', *RCA XX*,
pp. 11–20, 1976

Uribe Alarcón, María Victoria,
*Asentamientos Prehispánicos en el
Altiplano de Ipiales, Colombia*,
unpublished Master's thesis, Escuela
Nacional de Antropología e Historia,
Universidad Nacional Autónoma de
México, 1977

Vélez, Manuel, Letter to Dr Liborio
Zerda, *Papel Periódico Ilustrado*,
5 May 1883, pp. 258–60

Wassén, Henry, 'An archaeological study
in the western Colombian cordillera',
Etnologiska Studier 2, pp. 30–67, 1936

White, R. B., 'Notes on the Aboriginal
Races of the North-Western Provinces
of South America', *Journal of the
Anthropological Institute of Great
Britain and Ireland*, Vol. XIII,
pp. 240–58, London, 1884

Wynter, Harriet, and Turner, Anthony,
Scientific Instruments, Studio Vista,
London, 1975

Zerda, Liborio, *El Dorado*, Banco
Popular, Bogotá, 1972

Zevallos Menéndez, C., 'Estudio regional
de la orfebrería precolombina de
Ecuador', *Revista del Museo Nacional*,
Lima, 34, pp. 68–81, 1965–6